Coal and Energy in South Africa

Edinburgh Studies in Urban Political Economy

Series Editor: Franklin Obeng-Odoom

In a world characterised by cities, their disproportionate share of problems as well as prospects, and the limitations of mainstream urban economics as a compass, the *Edinburgh Studies in Urban Political Economy* series strives to publish books that seek to better understand, and to address, such challenges. The Global South is of particular interest, but it is by no means the only focus. As an alternative political economy series, it emphasises social sustainability of urban transformations, encourages the use of transdisciplinary political-economic approaches to urban economics, and welcomes books that are both heterodox and pluralist in their economics. Books in the series strive to both engage and to transcend mainstream urban economics, in methodologies, values, and visions, while placing their insights at the disposal of the wider fields of urban studies and political economy.

Titles in the *Edinburgh Studies in Urban Political Economy* series include:

Published:

Open Access *Coal and Energy in South Africa: Considering a Just Transition*
Lochner Marais, Philippe Burger, Maléne Campbell, Stuart Paul Denoon-Stevens and Deidré van Rooyen

Forthcoming:

Urban Inequality in a Nordic Welfare State
Mika Hyotylainen

Spatial Agency and Occupation: Foreign Domestic Helpers in Hong Kong
Evelyn Kwok

Urban Landed Property: How Land Ownership Shapes the Economies of Cities
Don Munro

Coal and Energy in South Africa

Considering a Just Transition

Edited by Lochner Marais, Philippe Burger,
Maléne Campbell, Stuart Paul Denoon-Stevens
and Deidré van Rooyen

EDINBURGH
University Press

Edinburgh University Press is one of the leading university presses in the UK. We publish academic books and journals in our selected subject areas across the humanities and social sciences, combining cutting-edge scholarship with high editorial and production values to produce academic works of lasting importance. For more information visit our website: edinburghuniversitypress.com

We are committed to making research available to a wide audience and are pleased to be publishing Platinum Open Access ebook editions of titles in this series.

Edinburgh University Press Ltd
The Tun – Holyrood Road, 12(2f) Jackson's Entry, Edinburgh EH8 8PJ

Typeset in 11/15 Adobe Garamond by
IDSUK (DataConnection) Ltd

A CIP record for this book is available from the British Library

ISBN 978 1 4744 8705 4 (hardback)
ISBN 978 1 4744 8707 8 (webready PDF)
ISBN 978 1 4744 8708 5 (epub)

Contents

Figures

Tables

Contributors

Derick Blaauw, School of Economic Sciences, North-West University, Potchefstroom, South Africa.

Philippe Burger, Department of Economics and Finance at the University of the Free State, Bloemfontein, South Africa.

Jesse Burton, Energy Research Centre, University of Cape Town, Cape Town, South Africa.

Falko Buschke, Centre for Environmental Management, University of the Free State, Bloemfontein, South Africa.

Maléne Campbell, Department of Urban and Regional Planning, University of the Free State, Bloemfontein, South Africa.

Jan Cloete, Centre for Development Support, University of the Free State, Bloemfontein, South Africa.

Cornelie Crous, Business School, University of the Free State, Bloemfontein, South Africa.

Stuart Paul Denoon-Stevens, Department of Urban and Regional Planning, University of the Free State, Bloemfontein, South Africa.

Ernst Drewes, Unit for Environmental Sciences and Management, North-West University, Potchefstroom, South Africa.

Katrina du Toit, Independent editor and medical doctor, South Africa.

Surina Esterhuyse, Centre for Environmental Management, University of the Free State, Bloemfontein, South Africa.

Jean-Pierre Geldenhuys, Department of Economics and Finance, University of the Free State, Bloemfontein, South Africa.

Elianor Gerrard, Faculty of Health, School of Public Health and Social Work, Queensland University of Technology, Australia.

Chris Hendriks, Public Administration and Management, University of the Free State, Bloemfontein, South Africa.

Tina Kotzè, Business School, University of the Free State, Bloemfontein, South Africa.

Molefi Lenka, Centre for Development Support, University of the Free State, Bloemfontein, South Africa.

Lochner Marais, Centre for Development Support and Associate to the NRF SARChi Chair on City-Region Economies, University of the Free State, Bloemfontein, South Africa; Adjunct Professor (an honorary position) at the Sustainable Minerals Institute, University of Queensland, Brisbane, Australia.

Sethulego Matebesi, Department of Sociology, University of the Free State, Bloemfontein, South Africa.

Etienne Nel, Department of Geography, University of Otago, Dunedin, New Zealand and Visiting Professor at the Centre for Development Support, University of the Free State, Bloemfontein, South Africa.

Petrus Nel, Department of Industrial Psychology and People Management, University of Johannesburg, Auckland Park, South Africa.

Verna Nel, Department of Urban and Regional Planning, University of the Free State, Bloemfontein, South Africa.

John Ntema, University of Fort Hare, Alice, South Africa.

Mark Oranje, Department of Urban and Regional Planning, University of Pretoria, Tshwane, South Africa.

Rory Pilossof, Department of Economics and Finance, University of the Free State, Bloemfontein, South Africa.

Antonie Pool, Department of Economics and Finance, University of the Free State, Bloemfontein, South Africa.

Anmar Pretorius, School of Economic Sciences, North-West University, Potchefstroom, South Africa.

Rinie Schenck, Department of Science and Innovation/National Research Foundation/Council for Scientific and Industrial Research Chair in Waste and Society, University of the Western Cape, Bellville, South Africa.

Mariske van Aswegen, Unit for Environmental Sciences and Management, North-West University, Potchefstroom, South Africa.

Phia van der Watt, Centre for Development Support, University of the Free State, Bloemfontein, South Africa.

Deidré van Rooyen is currently the Programme Director for Development Studies and a researcher in the Centre for Development Support at the University of the Free State, Bloemfontein, South Africa.

Johan van Zyl, Central University of Technology, Bloemfontein, South Africa.

Peter Westoby, Social Science and Community Development, Queensland University of Technology, Australia; Visiting Professor, Centre for Development Support, University of Free State; and Director Community Praxis Co-operative.

Preface

This book forms part of a larger research project at the University of the Free State (UFS) that is investigating the consequences of mining for local communities and mining towns. We initiated the project in 2015 as a multi-disciplinary project involving a wide range of academic departments at the UFS and building partnerships with local and international universities. This book on Emalahleni follows an edited collection (*Mining and Community in South Africa: From Small Town to Iron Town*) on mining in the small town of Postmasburg (2018). A third book, on Rustenburg, is in progress. The project has also received funding to concentrate on the consequences of mine closure in South Africa. This project on mine closure will take place from 2021 to 2023. In each of these mining towns, our approach has been to carry out a set of 20 to 30 key informant interviews (government, mines and non-governmental organisations), an extensive household survey of approximately 1,000 households and a document analysis of the planning documents at the local level. These pieces of evidence provided a platform for developing the three books.

The project's primary motive was the limited amount of research and data available for mineworkers in South Africa. Neither the census data nor the National Income Dynamics Study provides adequate evidence to understand mineworkers and their communities. We did not understand the inequalities and social stratification that appear to permeate the mining industry and mining towns. Furthermore, we did not understand how changes in the mining environment and government policy affect mineworkers and mining towns. Furthermore, there is the potential effect of mine closure. Sometimes closure is the result of resource depletion or changes in the market. In other cases, such as Emalahleni, it is the result of an economic transition. Whatever the reason, mining seldom results in long-term prosperity. The problem is that virtually nobody plans for closure or economic decline. In many cases, communities and local governments ignore closure. We hope that our book makes a small contribution to addressing the gap in understanding mining towns, their communities and the likely consequences of closure.

How are decisions made when the long-term viability of an area is in doubt? Many of the problems in decision-making about mining areas arise from short-term thinking and a failure to understand the current situation. The transition from coal to renewables, which underlies the notion of a just transition, is one example of how mining affects local communities. The signing of the Paris Agreement (2016) meant that South Africa had to embark on a policy approach that would reduce coal dependence for energy creation. Nobody asked the people of Emalahleni whether the South African government should sign the Paris Agreement. Yet, the closure of coal mines and coal-fired power stations will be detrimental to the economy of Emalahleni. In this context, the book investigates the current situation in Emalahleni and considers the implications of possible mine closure.

This book makes several contributions to the literature. First, the wide variety of focus areas and a multidisciplinary approach emphasise the interrelatedness of factors playing a role in mining communities. For example, the nature of mine work and how mining is a place of work have implications for planning and settlement development. How local institutions respond to this and consider the long-term implications of these decisions are essential. Mine closure needs to take into account changes in minework and mining operations. Second, our evidence shows that mining contributes to inequality and social stratification in mining towns. Third, our focus on explaining the current situation and asking how that will play out when mine closure occurs provides an excellent account of how decisions during mining affect howclosure occurs. Fourth, the South African government has embarked on a process of planning the just transition. This national process has primarily been conceptual. We hope this book and the evidence in this book lays the foundation for thinking about a just transition in Emalahleni. Finally, the book assesses the notion of power in decision-making. The power of capital and its effects on local settlements and communities are crucial to understanding local responses to economic transitions.

The editors
February 2021, Bloemfontein

Acknowledgements

The National Research Foundation of South Africa (Grant number 91054) and the Faculties of Economic and Management Sciences and Natural and Agricultural Sciences at the University of the Free State provided funding for this research.

We would like to thank Dr Di Kilpert for language editing the book.

Abbreviations

CLC	Canadian Labour Congress
COP3	Kyoto Climate Conference of 1997
COP24	2018 UN Annual Conference on Climate Change, Katowice
ESG	environmental, social and governance
EU	European Union
FGT	Foster-Greer-Thorbecke
GDP	gross domestic product
GRI	Global Reporting Initiative
GVA	gross value added
IDP	Integrated Development Plan
ILO	International Labour Organization
IQR	interquartile range
ITF	International Transport Workers Federation
ITUC	International Trade Union Confederation
NGO	non-governmental organisation
OCAW	Oil, Chemical, and Atomic Workers
OECD	Organisation for Economic Co-operation and Development
OHS	occupational health and safety
PCA	principal components analysis
SDF	Spatial Development Framework
SLP	Social and Labour Plan
UN	United Nations
UNFCCC	United Nations Framework Convention on Climate Change

CHAPTER 1

Mining and Mining Towns: A Conceptual Framework

Lochner Marais, Philippe Burger, Rory Pilossof, Molefi Lenka and Antonie Pool

The environmental crises

There is broad agreement among scientists that the earth is becoming warmer (Hughes, 2000). The amount of CO_2 released into the atmosphere through human activities is a leading contributor to global warming (Warner and Jones, 2019). Capitalist-driven economic activity and coal are intertwined (Piketty, 2014). Continuing with these emission levels will increase the nature of the current environmental problems. However, political leaders have been responding slowly. Acknowledging the problem and committing to doing something is a good starting point. The Paris Agreement is one such attempt to slow global warming by reducing CO_2 emissions. A large percentage of these emissions are from using coal to generate energy. Therefore, reducing the role of coal in creating energy would contribute to lowering CO_2 emissions. However, the Paris Agreement only tries to slow the growth rate of global warming. Another response to dealing with the climate crisis prioritises renewable energy sources (Simelane and Abdel-Raman, 2011).

The costs of not attending to the threats of global warming are extensive. The literature points to several concerns, such as increased temperatures, rainfall variation and rising sea levels (Hughes, 2000). These changes are likely to negatively affect animals (including humans), plant life and ecological equilibria. The flooding and erosion of low-lying coastal areas, increased heat-related deaths and health pandemics are likely to have significant economic consequences for humans.

The nature of the problem is clear, but reducing CO_2 emissions is a difficult task loaded with political power plays. For example, most countries in the Global North developed their economies on coal (McGinley, 2011). These countries in the Global North are also the first to move to renewables and there is an expectation that countries from the South should follow. Expecting countries in the developing world to follow suit is not that simple. Brown and Spiegel (2019: 149) highlighted that 'recent struggles around phasing out coal have stimulated renewed critical debates around colonialism, empire, and capitalism more broadly, recognising climate change as an intersectional issue encompassing racial, gender, and economic justice'. For some, the pressure for a transition away from coal to renewables is part of the colonial project. The Global North dictates the terms without paying for the historical pollution. Besides these questions of power and colonialism, there are implications for people in coal production and energy generation areas, where their governments did not ask them for permission to sign the Paris Agreement. The Paris Agreement has specific implications for South Africa, where over 90% of all energy originates from coal. A reduction in coal-generated electricity will have severe implications for places like Emalahleni, where such energy generation takes place. Large numbers of coal miners and people working in coal-generated power stations are likely to lose their jobs. This problem requires sensitive management, taking into account local livelihoods and the need to reduce CO_2 emissions to slow global warming.

Mining and coal in South Africa

Although the South African mining industry's share of the national economy has declined since the 1970s, it still contributes approximately 7% of GDP (gross domestic product) and provides more than 400,000 direct and 1.4 million indirect jobs (Chamber of Mines, 2017). Coal still contributes almost three quarters of South Africa's energy needs, in addition to being a major source of export earnings. The mining industry has moved away from gold and diamonds to include platinum, iron ore and manganese, but its long-standing dependence on coal remains.

The 1980s saw a slump in commodity prices but at the end of the 1990s there was a new boom in the mining industry. South Africa's high economic growth of the 2000s required energy. The abundance of coal meant that the population and economy of coal-mining areas like Emalahleni (formerly Witbank) experienced large-scale growth and new coal-generated energy plants were established.

The mining industry in South Africa benefited from the spike in commodity prices from the late 1990s, but it also had to adjust to the policy changes in the new democracy and the increased global connectedness (after its isolation under apartheid). Historically, low wages, unsafe working conditions and poor living environments (in the case of black mineworkers, mostly men-only compounds) characterised the mining industry (Bezuidenhout and Buhlungu, 2011). The post-apartheid government and the labour unions put pressure on the mining companies to address these historical concerns. Post-apartheid policy produced mixed results. The mining industry still employs large numbers of people and wages have increased, but there is evidence that the industry contributes to new inequalities (Burger and Geldenhuys, 2018) and some reports have highlighted the continuing environmental damage (Munnik, 2010; Sharife and Bond, 2011).

There is increasing consensus that sustainable development cannot be achieved unless people have affordable, reliable and clean energy services (Bhattacharyya, 2012: 260). But South Africa has long been dependent on coal. In their *Political Economy of South Africa* (1996), Fine and Rustomjee (1996) show how heavily the country's economy depends on mining. They show that development in South Africa has been 'path-dependent' on the 'minerals-energy complex' (their term) ever since the mineral discoveries of the 1860s.

Approximately 50% of South Africa's energy comes from the Emalahleni coalfields. However, coal could lose its dominant role in energy provision, with negative consequences for Emalahleni. The collapse or privatisation of Eskom (South Africa's state-owned electricity utility, currently under severe financial stress and largely dependent on government bailouts), could mean that Emalahleni would lose its dominant role in providing electricity to South Africa. Under international pressure to increase the role of renewable energy sources, the South African government could change the energy mix at the expense of coal. And despite current high prices for exports, there are indications that the global demand for coal will decline (see Chapter 2).

At the same time, the possible implication of the COVID-19 pandemic for coal and the transition requires attention. The pandemic has contributed to lower demand (nationally and globally) for coal, which meant lower coal mining levels. Although COVID has reduced global energy use, analysts anticipate that, once governments vaccinate their populations, energy use will soon return to pre-COVID levels. The economic packages designed to re-engineer growth after COVID-19 depend on coal and Obeng-Odoom (2020a) argues it will merely reinforce existing inequalities. However, even if the pandemic translates into an increase in renewables, there are no guarantees that the inequalities we see now will disappear.

It is against this background that we investigated Emalahleni as a mining town. Obeng-Odoom (2014) emphasises the importance of local urban case studies on the extractive industry and Olson-Hazboun (2018) calls for more research and policy focus on the problems facing communities dependent on declining fossil fuels.

Mining towns

Company towns have always been a prominent feature of the mining industry and examples can be found in both the Global North (Amundson, 2004) and the Global South (Littlewood, 2014). The literature on such towns in Africa is increasing (Bryceson and MacKinnon, 2012; Littlewood, 2014; Gough, Yankson and Esson, 2018; Marais, Burger and Van Rooyen, 2018). Company towns are predominantly, though not exclusively, mining towns. Mining towns are not all the same. At one extreme is the kind where the company plays the role of local government: it owns the land, provides housing and services and dominates local culture and thinking. Obeng-Odoom (2018: 447) notes that large transnational companies of this kind tend to 'arrogate to themselves statutory municipal power' while at the same time they 'ignore or manipulate various channels of accountability, and privately appropriate socially created rents'. At the other extreme are 'normalised' or 'open' towns, managed by democratically elected local governments, with the mineworkers mostly housed in either company-owned or privately owned housing.

Normalisation (the opening of company towns) has happened for four reasons. First, since the mid-1980s slump, the mining industry has minimised its role in local management and planning and reduced its long-term expenditure on non-mining elements, to cut costs (Marais, Haslam McKenzie et al., 2018). Second, with the release of *Breaking New Ground: Mining, Minerals and Sustainable Development*, the industry has tried to reduce its dominance in mining settlements, formally announcing normalisation as a policy stance and stating that the mines do not want to play the role of a local government (IIED, 2002; Franks, 2015). Despite this intention, however, many company towns still exist. Third, most governments support efforts to normalise towns and want to see higher local accountability levels (Marais, 2018; Van der Watt and Marais, 2019). And fourth, in some cases, residents and unions, including workers who bring their families to the mining areas, are also in favour of normalised towns.

Most mining towns are small or medium-sized (Marais, Nel and Donaldson, 2016; Marais et al., 2017; Gough, Yankson and Esson, 2018). This means that mining often makes them vulnerable to the volatility of international markets (Marais, 2016). It also means that these towns are underresearched and they reflect forms of neoliberalism and some of the most complex power relationships.

Neoliberalism and changes in the mining industry

How do we understand neoliberalism in this book? We acknowledge that it is not easily definable. Dunn (2017) has questioned the usefulness of the concept. Nevertheless, he does not argue for avoiding its use but suggests that it requires careful definition. A common misunderstanding is to see neoliberalism as a specific economic period. Critics view it as a period of the curtailment of the role of the state and promotion of free-market capitalism, and in the mining sector, specifically as transnationalisation and privatisation of mining and land, a process that started in the 1980s (Bury, 2005). From that point of view, neoliberalism has had significant consequences for the mining industry and mining towns worldwide, playing out in different ways across countries or mine settlements. Often neoliberalism is seen only as free-market fundamentalism or extreme capitalism. This view assumes that all neoliberal theories and policies are the same and that states and firms are distinct entities.

However, these assumptions are debatable. Neoliberalism and markets are embedded in society and cannot be treated as just a phase of development or free-market fundamentalism or a force affecting society from the outside (Polanyi,

2001; Konings, 2015; Dunn, 2017). Cahill (2011) argues that 'neoliberalism is best understood as a historically specific process of state and economic restructuring that is socially embedded through three mechanisms: ideological norms, class relations, and institutional rules'. He notes that neoliberalism is often driven by both states and firms, that neoliberalism does not necessarily lead to a decline in the size of the state, and that neoliberalism is often closely associated with regulatory reform. By simply viewing neoliberalism as an external factor or a specific period of capitalism ignores the reality that in many cases states, unions and societies contribute to neoliberalism.

We do not take a binary view of neoliberalism (the state as good and the market as bad). In this book, we characterise neoliberalism in South Africa as the tendency to favour free-market capitalism over state involvement in the economy. This emphasis on free-market economies in the mining industry relates both to a period in which multinational corporations were powerful and the general social acceptance (social embeddedness) of many of the ideas associated with neoliberalism in the industry (for example, contract work, shift work, a clean wage). We acknowledge that the growth of transnational mining companies is one of the many social manifestations of neoliberalism. The social embeddedness of neoliberalism means that society, the state and the labour unions cannot dissociate themselves from the concept. Consequently, we try to explain this social embeddedness.

This increasingly dominant role has gone hand in hand with changes in the industry's labour regimes (Marais, Burger and Van Rooyen, 2018). Working hours have changed. Daytime work has changed to 24-hour production cycles and 7-day-a-week production process have become the norm. Forty-hour work weeks have changed to shift work and block roster shifts. Full-time mine employment has become contract work. Short-term contracts now dominate production processes and full-time mine employment is less common. Production methods have changed from labour-intensive to capital-intensive approaches, which are mechanised and production oriented. All of the above have also contributed to rapid increases in salaries. Strict labour legislation and labour union dominance have come under threat.

But again we stress that we need to understand the social embeddedness of neoliberalism. In South Africa, for example, some of the above changes in labour practices have been taking place despite strict labour legislation and labour union dominance. Effectively, we shall argue that the unions and the state are content with neoliberalism and directly or indirectly support it. This apparent contradiction that the state and unions are active role players in neoliberalism leads to two conclusions: that seeing new liberalism simply as a phase of development is inappropriate and that one should understand neoliberalism as socially embedded in society. The fact that the unions, the government and the private sector can work together in this process provides evidence for the social embeddedness of the various institutions.

Mining towns have been affected both by the policy changes in favour of normalisation and by the new labour regimes associated with neoliberalism (Marais, Burger and Van Rooyen, 2018). The increased emphasis on contract work, shift work and block roster shifts has reduced the need for permanence in mining towns and given rise to worker camps and fly-in-fly-out policies, especially in Australia. Many mining companies have started transferring the properties they owned to their workforce (a form of individual privatisation). This has also happened in Emalahleni (Cloete and Marais, 2020). The absence of an appropriate housing response has contributed to the development of informal settlements, worker camps, 'hotbedding' and, in some parts of Africa, the re-emergence of the compound. The responsibility for town management, finance and town planning has shifted from the mining companies to democratically elected local governments. In some cases this shift in management, along with the changing labour regime, has led to economic exclusion for the local population and reduced local spending by mineworkers. The local financial risks have shifted from mining companies and national governments to local communities and individual households. The acceptance of normalisation means that local communities themselves now have to manage the long-term risks associated with mining and deal with the powerful transnational companies. Although managing such risks has long been common in Canada (Van Asche et al., 2017), elsewhere it has contributed to underinvestment in mining towns and mines and shifted the mines' responsibilities towards corporate social responsibility programmes. One can easily interpret these changes as a shift in policy at a specific time and in a context where the private sector dominates the direction. Yet governments and unions have been complicit in this process, which shows how these practices are embedded in society.

The storyline is of course somewhat more complex than the above summary would suggest. In parts of Africa, transnational companies continue to play the role of government at the local level. Obeng-Odoom (2018: 447) points out that these companies continue to 'play significant roles in controlling utilities, privately appropriating common resources, and planning urban space'. However, our book looks at how neoliberalism encourages mining companies to withdraw from responsibilities not directly connected with mining. We describe the consequences for mineworkers and other residents of a mining town. Mining companies in South Africa have transferred their liabilities to local governments, workers and local communities and households, and the government and the mining unions have supported this shift in policy.

Changes in the South African mining industry

Some consequences of neoliberalism in the mining industry were peculiar to South Africa. Isolated by apartheid up to the early 1990s, the country felt the main influences of neoliberalism only towards the middle of that decade. Crankshaw (2002) describes four major changes in the South African mining industry in the 1990s: a withdrawal from peripheral activities and a focus on core business; increasingly deep mining; the rise of the unions; and safety concerns. These changes meant that South Africa had to develop new mining legislation. The 1998 White Paper on minerals had to deal with these changes and find a way to improve the management of mining towns and the relationship between the mining companies and the community.

Louw and Marais (2018) note that three principles have guided post-apartheid policy for mining settlements: a preference for open, or 'normalised', rather than company towns; an emphasis on homeownership; and the promotion of collaborative planning. The White Paper encourages open towns by calling for mining communities to be integrated and the benefits of mining to be used to support municipal planning and management (DME, 1998). Integrated communities mean that mining and non-mining communities will not be located separately (i.e. company towns will not be the norm) and mineworkers will be integrated into local economies. The message is clear: mining should play a role in local development and spatial integration. Municipalities are to collaborate with the mining industry to promote local economic development and integrated development. Marais (2018) notes four reasons for this policy: *redress*, by ensuring that black people can access homeownership, as they could not do under apartheid; *local economic development*, by giving mineworkers a stake in their place of work through homeownership; *stability*, by finding ways to upgrade the large-scale informal settlements; and *financial security*, by helping municipalities to develop an appropriate tax base. Local planning now has to link municipal strategic plans (called Integrated Development Plans) with the Social and Labour Plans that the mines have to produce. This has had the effect of enforcing collaborative planning and making the mining industry a local development actor.

Outside this policy framework, the mining industry has actively reorganised the labour regime. Indirectly, this has promoted open towns in three ways. Higher salaries have given mineworkers a wider range of housing choices. The unions have been instrumental in getting the apartheid compound system for black mineworkers shut down and living-out allowances provided. And the mines have closed the company towns and increased the living-out allowances.

The South African government and the unions have played into the hands of the mining companies, who wanted to get rid of their long-term and non-mining liabilities. Both the government and the unions happily transferred these long-term liabilities to local governments and individual households. Furthermore, the new policies link mining and development in naive ways. The government saw mining as a way to create development, but it did not consider the volatility of the mining sector.

The quest for a just transition

Globally, the term 'just transition' is receiving increased attention against a background of mine downscaling and closure in many parts of the world. Chapter 3 of this book discusses the likelihood of mine closure and a reduction in the generation of energy from coal in Emalahleni. Mine closure is likely because of the greater emphasis on renewable energy (including pressure to comply with international treaties on CO_2 emissions), global stagnation in the demand for coal, and the dysfunctionality of the South African electricity utility (Eskom). However, as the coal mining industry still employs about 80,000 workers, and 60% to 70% of them work in Emalahleni, the threat may not be immediate for this town.

Research shows that people in coal-dependent communities often have negative perceptions of renewable energy because of the possible consequences for the local economy and local identity (Olson-Hazboun, 2018). It is in this context that unions, town planners and researchers use the term 'just transition'. Chapter 2 provides a detailed analysis of this concept, so here we give only a brief background.

Oil, Chemical, and Atomic Workers (OCAW) leader Tony Mazzocchi coined the term 'just transition' in the trade union movement in the mid-1980s (Abraham, 2017). For the Canadian Labour Congress (CLC, 2000: 3), a just transition is 'the flip side of Green Job Creation: when we create Green Jobs, there will be an industrial transition'. In the case of Emalahleni, the industrial transition will be from coal to renewables ('green jobs'). To date the government has not located renewable plants in Emalahleni. Unemployment is imminent because of the closure of the coal plants. By 2000, the CLC had tightened up the concept, arguing in favour of a fair sharing of the cost of environmental change. It identified five elements of such a transition: fairness, re-employment or alternative employment, compensation, sustainable production, and programmes. 'Fairness' means 'fair treatment of workers and their communities' when an industry closes and 're-employment' emphasises the importance of continued employment (CLC, 2000: 6). Should continued employment be impossible, 'just compensation is the next alternative' (CLC, 2000: 6). At the same time, the CLC acknowledges that society requires more sustainable production methods and that this will necessitate a deliberate attempt ('programmes') to facilitate the 'sustainable production' and thus the just transition. We use this broad definition of a just transition in our book, but with a particular focus on this transition for the community rather than just the workers – while acknowledging that community and workers constitute to a large extent an integrated whole.

The notion of a 'just transition' brings together ideas from climate, energy and environmental justice (McCauley and Heffron, 2018). Chancel and Piketty (2015) argue that increased CO_2 emissions coincide with an increase in economic inequality. For Heffron and McCauley (2018), society's move towards an economy free of CO_2 emissions should be a just process. But despite some examples where a 'just transition' has been applied successfully (Mayer, 2018), success has been rather limited. And there has been some disagreement over what 'just' implies.

In this book we argue that, besides attending to the plight of workers (for example, for training and relocation), a just transition also requires a focus on local government, business and the original inhabitants of towns occupied by mining communities. In the final chapter of the book, we look at how likely it is that the impending transition in Emalahleni will satisfy the requirements of our definition of a just transition.

Theory, approach, methods and main questions

In the main, we use critical realism as a theoretical lens for this collection. In practice, we blend perspectives from critical theory with critical realism. The literature acknowledges the relationship between critical theory, Marxism and critical realism (Outhwaite, 1987). Critical theory has its roots in the Marxism of the Frankfurt School, which largely emphasises antipositivism and a critical approach to research, questioning the nature and scale of power and interrelationships between agents. Bhaskar's seminal work, *A Realist Theory of Science* (1975), laid the foundation for critical realism. Bhaskar questioned the positivist approach and the deductive nature of social science thinking. Both critical realism and critical theory are critical of the objectivism of positivist social science and emphasise the role of agents and the relationship between agents (Benton, 1998). Furthermore, we ground the book in 'just ecological political economy', which emphasises the importance of justice in the transition from coal to renewable sources (Maathai, 2011; Obeng-Odoom, 2020c.). However, within this framework of a just political economy we also challenge the simplistic assumptions that mining fosters development by emphasising the long-term social and environmental cost of mining.

From a critical theory perspective, transnational and multinational companies are indeed contributing to many of the mining-related social problems globally. Their main concerns – to mine profitably and to benefit their shareholders – often create local conflict. The power of mining companies usually exceeds that of local communities or local governments (Owen and Kemp, 2017). In our approach, we emphasise these power relationships, the inequalities caused by the behaviour of mining companies, and the sustainability concerns. However, we also consider the micro-relationships between actors. Despite being critical about the relationship between coal, energy and development, we are also aware that many people are still directly or indirectly dependent on the coal mining industry. The notion of a just transition developed by the labour movement is central to our approach.

The Emalahleni case study's perspective on this issue differs from that of other Global South literature on neoliberalism and mining. Our book presents a tension between two forces: the developmental state, which pushes for strong state intervention and extensive regulation, and neoliberalism, which essentially argues for the opposite. However, we show that in addition to tensions, the state and the market also work together in this respect.

In our case study we used both qualitative and quantitative methods. We conducted semi-structured interviews with key informants from mining companies, the three spheres of government, the private sector (for example, engineering firms) and civil society. We conducted 49 in-depth interviews in Emalahleni, and also in Mbombela, the seat of the Mpumalanga Provincial Legislator. We initially selected respondents by using snowballing purposive sampling, after which the interviewers engaged with any businessman or -woman, municipal official, mining employee or community leader who agreed to an interview.

We conducted three quantitative surveys. In the first survey, during November and December 2017, we obtained a total of 937 completed questionnaires from households in all areas of Emalahleni. The questionnaires were translated from English into Afrikaans, Zulu and Sepedi, the three languages most commonly spoken in Emalahleni. We used random sampling based on cadastral information (site numbers based on information from the Surveyor General) to obtain the samples for the houses and cluster sampling for the informal settlements sample. In each case a fieldworker administered the questionnaire to the person who self-identified as best able to act as respondent for the household and who therefore answered on behalf of all members of the household. The questionnaire elicited information such as the number of household members, income, assets, migration patterns, employment and municipal services in the house. It consisted of closed-ended multiple choice questions. The fieldworkers were local unemployed youths who underwent intensive training sessions in preparation. We made follow-up telephone calls to 30% of the interviewees to verify that the fieldworkers had presented the questionnaires to them. The questionnaires were completed electronically on tablet computers using CSPro software for CAPI (computer-assisted personal interview) applications. The data were then emailed to a team member for processing.

The second survey, in 2018, was of formal and informal businesses in Emalahleni, using a questionnaire completed by the proprietors themselves. We obtained a random sample of formal businesses from the telephone directory and, as with the informal settlements survey, we sampled the informal businesses using cluster sampling. The questionnaire elicited information about each owner's background, the business's turnover, profits and assets, the municipal services the business received and any problems it was experiencing. The business questionnaires were completed on hard copies.

The third survey (2018) entailed 57 interviews with informal sector workers in Emalahleni. We complemented the survey with 10 in-depth interviews. As this survey built on an initial survey conducted in Emalahleni in 2007, it made comparisons possible.

In addition to the surveys and interviews, we examined the planning documents of the mining companies and the Emalahleni Local Municipality. We studied mining company reports, social and environmental impact assessments and integrated development plans. Other documents we studied were the Strategy on the Revitalisation of Distressed Mining Areas, updates to the Mining Charter, which at the time of writing was undergoing a third revision, and changes to the regulations for the mines' social and labour plans (we were unable to access those plans). We also studied local media reports.

We ask eight main questions in this book:

1. *What will be the implications of mine downscaling or closure in Emalahleni, and how can the mines, the government and the labour unions plan to deal with this?* At the time of writing in early 2019, Emalahleni was still going through a boom period, but decline was imminent. Eskom, South Africa's national electricity utility, has already closed some of the smaller power stations and more closures are pending. The unions are concerned about job losses and have asked for a just transition (Mkhonza, 2018). We describe the current reality and identify possible effects of downscaling on businesses and the community, and the need to diversify the economy of Emalahleni to compensate for the loss of mining employment.

2. *Do outsourcing and contract work create inequalities between contract workers and permanently employed mineworkers in Emalahleni?* Coal mining companies generally pay higher salaries than the rest of the mining industry (Cronje, 2014). Although a recent Appeal Court ruling is set to change the nature of contract employment in mining, at the time of writing approximately 30% of mineworkers in South Africa were contract workers. Contract workers are usually paid lower salaries than full-time mineworkers and receive very few, if any, fringe benefits (Burger and Geldenhuys, 2018). A large proportion of contract workers and lower-paid mineworkers live in informal settlements (Rubin and Harrison, 2016). This employment structure brings to the fore questions about how the neoliberal employment practices of outsourcing and contract work create inequalities between contract workers and permanently employed mineworkers in Emalahleni.

3. *Are there inequalities between mineworkers working in underground mines and those working in open-cast mines in Emalahleni?* Linked to inequalities resulting from mining, consideration should also be given to the social stratification of mining in gender and race (Obeng-Odoom, 2020b). Workers in open-cast mines are usually machine operators who earn higher salaries. Underground mining is

more labour intensive. However, for coal mining this distinction may be less relevant as underground coal mining is usually not deep. The underground coal mines in Emalahleni are mostly about 300 metres deep.

4. *Is the mining industry in Emalahleni responsible for any specific gender inequalities or negative consequences for women?* The mining industry has long been male-dominated. But mineworkers have families and a male-dominated industry may have specific negative consequences for women in Emalahleni (Sesele et al., 2021).

5. *Does the influx of mineworkers to Emalahleni cause social disruption and increase inequalities between mine employees and long-term residents?* Although this influx could create an income gap between mineworkers and other workers in Emalahleni, it could also have benefits for local businesses. The economic multiplier effect of mining creates jobs in formal and informal non-mining sectors, even if those jobs come with salaries that are lower than those paid to mineworkers.

6. *Do the high levels of environmental degradation and poor environmental health create long-term inequalities in Emalahleni?* These inequalities are usually evident in salary scales, working hours, access to medical insurance, and housing conditions. Some of these inequalities are the result of the traditional migrant labour system. Many contract workers and lower-paid mineworkers resort to living in informal settlements as a way to channel their earnings to labour-sending areas instead of investing in the mining area.

7. *Is Emalahleni's coal mining industry sustainable?* We ask what coal mining in Emalahleni does to the physical environment and the inhabitants' health. We also consider how municipal services can be re-engineered sustainably in a period of mine decline. We look at how Emalahleni's mining companies report on the sustainability problems that they encounter.

8. *What would a just transition entail for Emalahleni?* We broaden the scope of the concept to go beyond the needs of unions. A just transition also needs to be just for the local municipality, local communities and non-mining households in Emalahleni.

Addressing these questions is important because it broadens the debate by highlighting the social and environmental consequences and the power relations associated with mining practices. Nevertheless, few research studies have addressed these questions systematically (see, for example, Obeng-Odoom, 2014; Marais et al., 2018). The book's transdisciplinary and multidisciplinary nature also creates a basis for discussing the complexity of an economic transition. Research to date has questioned the sustainability of the coal mining industry in South Africa. Still, it has not investigated these questions within the broader framework of a just transition for a specific locality. This book examines the relationship today between mining and the town of Emalahleni and uses this status quo analysis to assess the likelihood of a just transition for this town.

These questions are addressed in 17 chapters, all of which are linked to two central mainstream concerns: the role of neoliberalism in mining and how neoliberal practices currently affect surrounding communities, and the implications of the current situation for a just transition. Overall, our book provides evidence of how neoliberal practices at the mines place extraordinary pressure on local government and create long-term burdens, which will hamper a just transition.

The case study area

The town of Witbank was named for the ridge of white quartz near the present railway station. The area is now the Emalahleni Local Municipality. It is situated in the Mpumalanga province of South Africa, to the east of Gauteng, South Africa's economic heartland (see Figures 1.1 and 1.2). The Ndebele word *eMalahleni* means 'place of coal'. For convenience in this book we use the anglicised spelling 'Emalahleni', and we use four terms to make it clear which areas we mean. We refer to our study area, the urban area originally known as Witbank, as 'Emalahleni'; the city centre, the original Witbank CBD, as 'Emalahleni CBD'; the municipality, which includes the towns of Emalahleni, Kwa-Guqa, Ga-Nala and Ogies, as 'Emalahleni Local Municipality'; and the coalfields as 'Emalahleni-Witbank'.

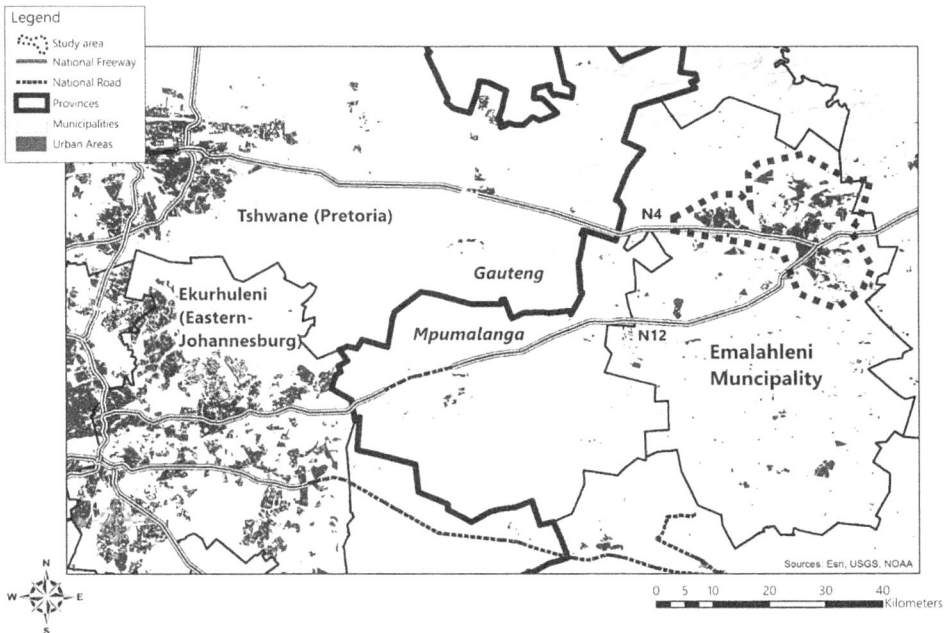

Figure 1.1 Location of Emalahleni in relation to municipality in the wider region.
Source: Authors.

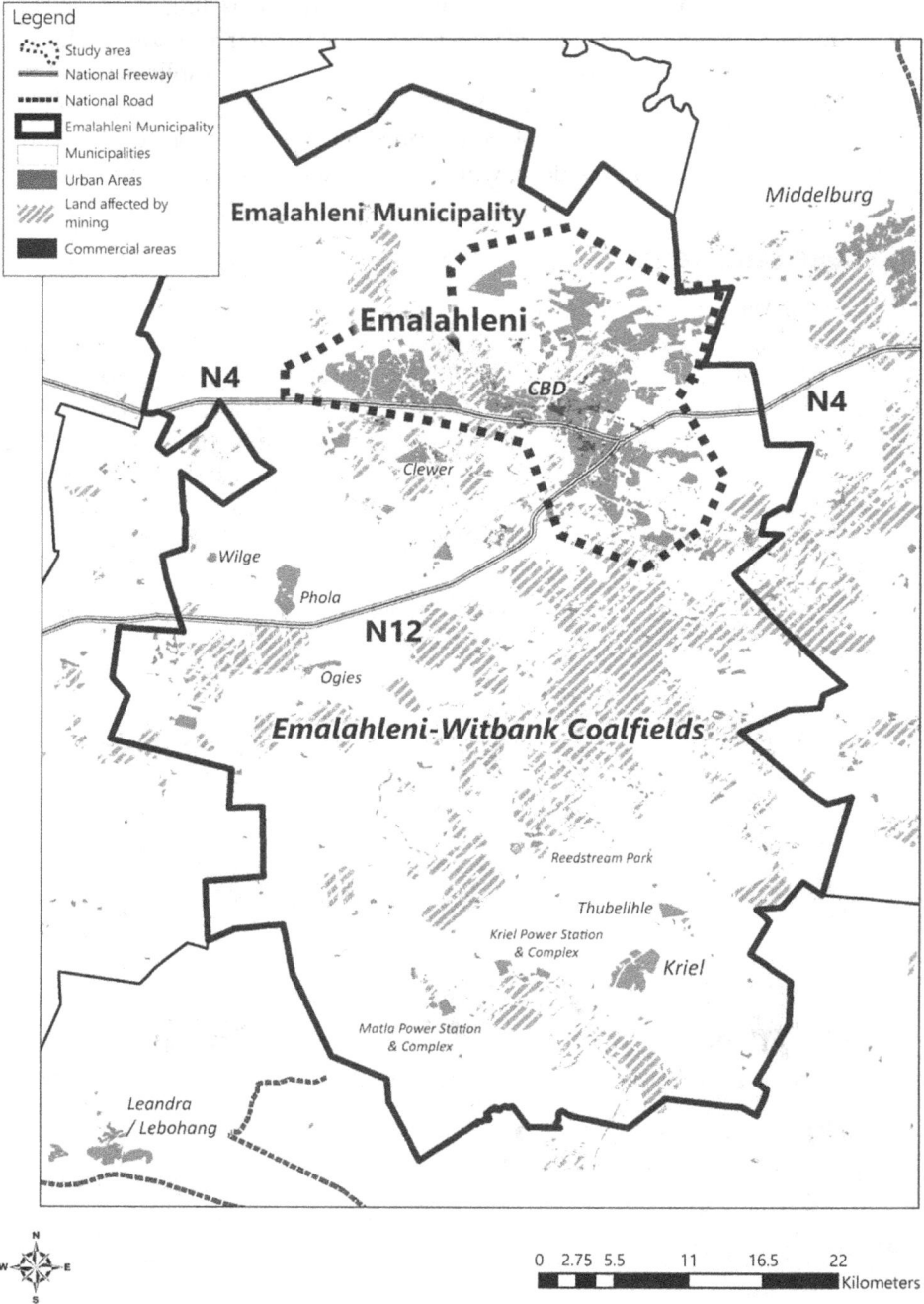

Figure 1.2 Location of the study area, Emalahleni urban area, in Emalahleni Municipality. Source: Authors.

The first buildings in Witbank were a shop and a hotel erected by a Samuel Stanford, who in 1903, together with the Neumann Group, sank the first shaft and established the Witbank Colliery. The town grew slowly, reaching a population of just under 2,000 by 1920. A local newspaper, the *Witbank News*, created awareness of the area and attracted residents. By 1938 Witbank's population had grown to nearly 9,500 and the town had a power station and was home to several large industries, such as Rand Carbide Corporation, Witbank Engineering and SA Cyanamid. With its underground and open-cast coal mines, it looked like many similar towns during the Industrial Revolution in England.

Emalahleni today owes its existence and fortunes largely to its abundant coal reserves. The town and its economy are growing rapidly on the basis of coal mining, energy generation and the steel industry and attracting an inflow of migrants to the town. As with the towns of the Industrial Revolution, its growth has far outpaced its ability to absorb the additional population and provide basic services and housing. In addition, the town suffers from severe water and air pollution, and these problems are compounded by the municipality's internal governance problems. It appears that although the town is booming, it is doing so largely in the absence of municipal management and guidance.

The abundance of coal (Emalahleni has more than 20 collieries) and good transport routes also attracted the steel industry. Until recently, one prominent iron and steel plant was Highveld Steel, established in 1957 and by 1996 the world leader in the production of vanadium. In 1978 Highveld acquired Rand Carbide and moved the production of ferrosilicon and char to Emalahleni from Johannesburg. The company Evraz later acquired shares in Rand Carbide and in 2010 the amalgamated company became Evraz Highveld Steel and Vanadium, one of the world's biggest vertically integrated steel and mining companies. However, the steel company ran into a financial crisis and stopped production in 2015 and in early 2016 it was announced that Evraz Highveld Steel and Vanadium was shutting down, putting 1,753 employees out of work (Witbank News, 2016).

A large proportion of the coal mined in Emalahleni is used by the Duvha Power Station, operated by Eskom. Activities generated from this have attracted foreign investment and many international companies have a presence in the area, among them Anglo American, BHP Billiton, Exxaro, Joy, Komatsu, the Renova Group, SABMiller, Samancor Chrome, Shanduka Beverages, Xstrata and Zenith.

Chapter overview

The chapters in this book are grouped into four themes: *inequalities caused by mining*, *sustainability and the mining industry*, *mine decline and business*, and *consequences of mining for local government*. There are three introductory chapters: on mining and mining towns, on the concept of a just transition in the context of mine closure, and a review of the literature. The concluding chapter highlights the main findings.

The first of the four theme groups consists of three chapters, on the new inequalities created in society, in the workplace and in housing conditions. The second group consists of four chapters, on long-term environmental consequences, environmental health problems, how the collieries report on sustainability annually, and people's current perceptions of coal and alternative sources of energy. The third group consists of two chapters, on the current formal business sector, and the status quo in the informal business sector. The fourth group consists of four chapters, on the consequences of mining for local government viability and planning against the background of the mining industry, and shifting responsibilities towards the public sector. The chapters in this fourth group analyse the current situation and ask how it will influence the possibility of a just transition.

Chapter 1 (this chapter) explains how mining towns have been influenced by neoliberal practices in the mining industry – globally and in South Africa. The future of coal mining depends on the use of renewable sources, the global demand for coal and Eskom's ability to remain a going concern. The shift from coal to renewables is highly likely. It is in this context that the notion of a just transition becomes prominent in the debates. Chapter 2 by Elianor Gerrard and Peter Westoby ('What Is a Just Transition?') looks at what constitutes a just transition and how mineworkers have challenged a transition that is likely to cause job losses. Chapter 3 by Lochner Marais, Jesse Burton, Maléne Campbell and Etienne Nel ('Mine closure in the Coal Industry: Global and National Perspectives') reviews the global and African literature on mine downscaling and closure and discusses the implications for South Africa and Emalahleni.

Inequalities created by mining: The changing labour regime has created new inequalities since the late 1980s. This group of chapters looks at the current inequalities between mineworkers, non-mineworkers and contract workers, and between open-cast and underground workers. They investigate inequalities in income, assets, housing, gender and working conditions. Jean-Pierre Geldenhuys and Philippe Burger ('Household Welfare in Emalahleni') investigate the income and asset inequalities between mineworkers, non-mineworkers and contract workers, providing evidence that outsourcing increases inequalities in the mining environment. This chapter challenges the notion that economic development through mining brings equal financial benefit to all. The authors argue that these new inequalities, mainly created by practices in mine management, complicate a just transition. For example, contract workers will find the transition more difficult as their wages are lower and they do not have pensions or medical benefits. Petrus Nel and Tina Kotzè ('Work and Life Satisfaction of Mining Employees') describe the consequences of the current mining in Emalahleni for the family and women, showing that the male-dominated mining environment is often not conducive to gender equality. They show how unequal job satisfaction is related to mine management practices, which support outsourcing and contract work. Understanding these current issues should be considered in planning a just transition. The spouses and families of mineworkers should not be excluded when planning such a transition in a male-dominated industry. Finally, Lochner Marais, John Ntema, Maléne Campbell, Jan Cloete and Molefi Lenka ('Informal Settlements in the Mining Context') show how mining leads to informal settlement development. They argue that informal settlements are a complex adaptive system established by people for whom mobility is crucial. Modernisation often views informal settlements as undesirable or as a by-product of the economy, but the authors argue that informal settlements are the consequence of the mining boom and mining companies relinquishing their historical role in housing, shifting their responsibilities onto the local government and thousands of mining households. They show how structural problems associated with mining underlie the housing profiles they describe and speculate about what this means for a just transition.

Sustainability and the mining industry: These chapters discuss the negative environmental and health consequences of the coal industry, which are often described in South Africa in the context of the minerals-energy complex. Surina Esterhuyse and Falko Buschke ('Coal and Water: Exploiting One Precious Natural Resource at the Expense of Another?') build on this concept and provide a concise overview of the effects of mining on the physical environment. They describe some of the immediate or direct effects but argue that the real risk is in long-term cumulative damage. While communities already experience some of the negative effects of mining, future generations will have to live with the long-term consequences. They conclude that the problem is compounded by private ownership of mines, which results in damage to public spaces, water quality and air quality. Research on the minerals-energy complex also emphasises the health consequences of mining. Stuart Paul Denoon-Stevens and Katrina du Toit ('The Health Impacts of Coal Mining and Coal-based Energy') take on this topic. They investigate the health problems caused by mining and energy generation, which offset the benefits of a growing economy and large-scale employment. They deviate from mainstream economic thinking, which holds that only the direct cost of mining is essential. They argue that the calculation of the real cost of mining should include the health cost. Cornelie Crous ('Sustainability Reporting by Collieries') investigates sustainability reporting by the four multinational mining companies operating in Emalahleni and finds the quality of the reports poor even though all four companies are in the top 30 on the Johannesburg Stock Exchange. The reports tend to manage external impressions for possible investors rather than relate to the reality on the ground, and they reflect the neoliberal mining ethos which prioritises profits and shareholders above sustainability. Anmar Pretorius and Derick Blaauw ('Residents' Perceptions of Coal Mining and Energy Generation') look at how Emalahleni residents perceive different energy sources. They show that the more closely people are connected with coal mining, the less likely they are to support renewables. But they also find that residents, particularly the women, are seriously concerned about the pollution of the environment and damage to health, rating the risks associated with coal mining higher than the benefits. Their chapter suggests that the more invested one is in the coal industry, the harder the transition will be.

Mine decline and business: Deidré van Rooyen and Johan van Zyl ('Boom or Bust for Emalahleni Businesses?') discuss the current boom in the business environment. They note that the current mining boom makes it difficult for businesses to imagine decline or closure or to plan for it. The illusion of continued growth in the coal mining industry persists among business people in Emalahleni. A just transition will require a longer-term perspective, taking into account the risk of decline and closure. In a longitudinal study, Derick Blaauw, Anmar Pretorius and Rinie Schenck ('Socio-economic Dynamics of the Informal Sector') describe the historical and current patterns of the informal sector. According to their findings, Emalahleni's informal sector is most at risk in the event of downscaling. Some of the effects are already visible; for example, informal sector workers are earning less than they did 10 years ago. Both these chapters make the point that a just transition also requires a just response to the local economy and those working outside the mining industry.

Consequences of mining for local government: This section starts with two chapters that show different approaches to spatial planning. The first assumes continued growth and provides an adequate spatial planning framework. Mariske van Aswegen and Ernst Drewes ('A More Resilient Policy Approach to Spatial Fragmentation') explain how spatial planning is done in Emalahleni and identify the planners' main problem as the spatial fragmentation caused by mining. They recommend that the municipality use the latest thinking on spatial planning to improve densities and minimise fragmentation. In contrast, Verna Nel and Mark Oranje ('Planning in the Dark') argue that the main problem is uncertainty, because of the lack of open communication between the mines and local government. Uncertainty also means that planners should think carefully about how to manage the economic boom and possible decline. Unlike Van Aswegen and Drewes, they argue that it will be difficult to plan for a just transition and that spatial planning should consider the broader problem of mine closure. In the third chapter, Phia van der Watt and Sethulego Matebesi ('"The mines must fix the potholes": A Desperate Community') evaluate the municipality's struggle to provide adequate services, largely the result of mines attempting to relinquish their historical local government role. They observe a desire to return to the past. The mines are expected to perform some of the local government functions, which they did up to the early 2000s. Effectively, the mines have been responsible for the current problems at the local government level. Asking them to solve these and provide public services creates problems. But the privatisation of public services to the mines is not an option. While critical of the mines for shifting their responsibilities to local government, Van der Watt and Matebesi also argue that reverting to past practices has serious shortcomings, particularly in the case of mine closure, which would leave Emalahleni with a much bigger problem. Chris Hendriks ('Municipal Finances') investigates the state of municipal finance in Emalahleni. In theory, Emalahleni has a revenue base; in practice, the municipal finances are a shambles – something often seen in mining municipalities. Hendriks explains this contradiction and looks at how mining creates the illusion of wealth and prosperity while in reality causing substantial disruption. Mine closure and a just transition will need to take into account the poor state of municipal finance.

In the concluding chapter, Lochner Marais and his fellow editors ('Is a Just Transition Possible?') revisit the definition of 'just transition', evaluate the evidence from the case studies, and consider the likelihood of such a transition being achieved in Emalahleni.

References

Abraham, J. 2017. Just transitions for the miners: Labor environmentalism in the Ruhr and Appalachian coalfields. *New Political Science*, 39(2), 218–40.

Amundson, M. 2004. *Yellowcake Towns: Uranium Mining Communities in the American West.* Boulder, CO: University Press of Colorado.

Benton, T. 1998. Realism and social science: Some comments on Roy Bhaskar's *The Possibility of Naturalism*. In M. Archer, R. Bhaskar, A. Collier, T. Lawson and A. Norrie (eds), *Critical Realism: Essential Readings*. London: Routledge, 297–312.

Bezuidenhout, A. and Buhlungu, S. 2011. From compounded to fragmented labour: Mineworkers and the demise of compounds in South Africa. *Antipode*, 43(2), 237–63.

Bhaskar, R. 1975. *A Realist Theory of Science*. Leeds: Leeds Books.

Bhattacharyya, S. 2012. Energy access programmes and sustainable development: A critical review. *Energy for Sustainable Development*, 16, 260–71.

Brown, B. and Spiegel, S. 2019. Coal, climate justice, and the cultural politics of energy transition. *Global Environmental Politics*, 19(2), 149–70.

Bryceson, D. and MacKinnon, D. 2012. Eureka and beyond: Mining's impact on African urbanisation. *Journal of Contemporary African Studies*, 30(4), 513–37.

Burger, P. and Geldenhuys, J. 2018. Work, wages and welfare in Postmasburg. In L. Marais, P. Burger and D. van Rooyen (eds), *Mining and Community in South Africa: From Small Town to Iron Town*. London: Routledge, 173–98.

Bury, J. 2005. Mining mountains: Neoliberalism, land tenure, livelihoods, and the new Peruvian mining industry in Cajamarca. *Environment and Planning A*, 37, 221–39.

Cahill, D. 2011. Beyond neoliberalism? Crisis and the prospects for progressive alternatives. *New Political Science*, 33(4), 479.

Chamber of Mines. 2017. *Mine SA 2017 Facts and Figures Pocketbook*. www.chamberofmines.org. za/industry-news/publications/facts-and-figures/send/17-facts-and-figures/532-facts-and-figures-2018 (last accessed 20 April 2021).

Chancel, L. and Piketty, T. 2015. *Carbon and Inequality: From Kyoto to Paris*. Paris: Paris School of Economics.

CLC (Canadian Labour Congress). 2000. *Just Transition for Workers during Environmental Change*. Ottawa: Canadian Labour Congress.

Cloete, J. and Marais, L. 2020. Mine housing in the South African coalfields: The unforeseen consequences of post-apartheid policy. *Housing Studies*. doi: 10.1080/02673037.2020.1769038.

Crankshaw, P. 2002. Mining and minerals. In A. Lemon and C. Rogerson (eds), *Geography and Economy in South Africa and its Neighbours*. Burlington, VT: Ashgate, 63–80.

Cronje, F. 2014. *Digging for Development: The Mining Industry in South Africa and Its Role in Socio-economic Development*. Johannesburg: South African Institute for Race Relations.

Dunn, B. 2017. Against neoliberalism as a concept. *Capital and Class*, 41(3), 435–54.

DME (Department of Minerals and Energy). 1998. *White Paper: A Minerals and Mining Policy for South Africa*. Pretoria: Government Printer.

Fine, B. and Rustomjee, Z. 1996. *The Political Economy of South Africa: From Minerals-Energy Complex to Industrialisation*. Boulder, CO: Westview.

Franks, O. 2015. *Mountain Movers: Mining, Sustainability and the Agents of Change*. London: Routledge.

Gough, K., Yankson, P. and Esson, J. 2018. Migration, housing and attachment in urban gold mining settlements. *Urban Studies*, 56(4). https://doi.org/10.1177%2F0042098018798536

Heffron, R. and McCauley, D. 2018. What is the 'just transition'? *Geoforum*, 88, 74–7.

Hughes, L. 2000. Biological consequences of global warming: Is the signal already apparent? *Trends in Ecology & Evolution*, 15(2), 56–61.

IIED (International Institute for Environment and Development). 2002. *Breaking New Ground: Mining, Minerals and Sustainable Development*. London: Earthscan.

Konings, M. 2015. *The Emotional Logic of Capitalism: What Progressives Have Missed*. Stanford, CA: Stanford University Press.

Littlewood, D. 2014. 'Cursed' communities? Corporate social responsibility (CSR), company towns and the mining industry in Namibia. *Journal of Business Ethics*, 120(1), 39–63.

Louw, H. and Marais, L. 2018. Mining and municipal finance in Kathu, an open mining town in South Africa. *The Extractive Industries and Society*, 5(3), 278–83.

Maathai, W. 2011. Challenge for Africa. *Sustainability Science*, 1, 1–2.

Marais, L. 2016. Local economic development beyond the centre. *Local Economy*, 31(1–2), 68–82.

Marais, L. 2018. Housing policy in mining towns: Issues of race and risk in South Africa. *International Journal of Housing Policy*, 18(2), 335–45.

Marais, L., Burger, P. and Van Rooyen, D. 2018. *Mining and Community in South Africa: From Small Town to Iron Town*. London: Routledge.

Marais, L., Haslam McKenzie, F., Deacon, L., Nel, E., Van Rooyen, D. and Cloete, J. 2018. The changing nature of mining towns: Reflections from Australia, Canada and South Africa. *Land Use Policy*, 76, 779–88.

Marais, L., Nel, E. and Donaldson, R. 2016. *Secondary Cities and Development*. London: Routledge.

Marais, L., Van Rooyen, D., Nel, E. and Lenka, M. 2017. Responses to mine downscaling: Evidence from secondary cities in the South African Goldfields. *The Extractive Industries and Society*, 4, 163–71.

Mayer, A. 2018. A just transition for coal miners? Community identity and support from local policy actors. *Environmental Innovation and Societal Transitions*, 28, 1–13.

McCauley, D. and Heffron, R. 2018. Just transition: Integrating climate, energy and environmental justice. *Energy Policy*, 119, 1–7.

McGinley, P. 2011. Climate change and the war on coal: Exploring the dark side. *Vermont Journal of Environmental Law*, 13(1).

Mkhonza, T. 2018. NUM to march against Eskom privatisation retrenchments. *IOL Business Report*, 14 November.

Munnik, V. 2010. *The Social and Environmental Consequences of Coal Mining in South Africa: A Case Study*. Cape Town: Environmental Monitoring Group, and Amsterdam, Both ENDS.

Obeng-Odoom, F. 2014. *Oiling the Urban Economy: Land, Labour, Capital and the State in Sekondi-Takoradi, Ghana*. London: Routledge.

Obeng-Odoom, F. 2018. Transnational corporations and urban development. *The American Journal of Economics and Sociology*, 77(2), 447–510.

Obeng-Odoom, F. 2020a. COVID-19, Inequality, and Social Stratification in Africa. *African Review of Economics and Finance*, 12(1), 3–37.

Obeng-Odoom, F. 2020b. *Property, Institutions and Social Stratification in Africa*. Cambridge: Cambridge University Press.

Obeng-Odoom, F., 2020c. *The Commons in the Age of Uncertainty. Decolonising Nature, Economy and Society*. Toronto: University of Toronto Press.

Olson-Hazboun, S. 2018. 'Why are we being punished and they are being rewarded?' Views on renewable energy in fossil fuels-based communities of the U.S. west. *The Extractive Industries and Society*, 5, 366–74.

Outhwaite, W. 1987. *New Philosophies of Social Science: Realism, Hermeneutics and Critical Theory*. New York: St. Martins.

Owen, J. and Kemp, D. 2017. *Extractive Relations: Countervailing Power and the Global Mining Industry*. New York: Routledge.

Piketty, T. 2014. *Capital in the Twenty-First Century*. Cambridge, MA: The Belknap Press of Harvard University Press.

Polanyi, K. 2001. *The Great Transformation: The Political and Economic Origins of Our Time*. Boston, MA: Beacon Press.

Rubin, M. and Harrison, P. 2016. An uneasy symbiosis: Mining and informal settlement in South Africa with particular reference to the Platinum Belt in North West Province. In L. Cirolia, T. Görgens, M. van Donk, M. Smit and S. Drimie (eds), *Upgrading Informal Settlements in South Africa: A Partnership-based Approach*. Cape Town: University of Cape Town Press, 145–74.

Sesele, K., Marais, L., Van Rooyen, D. and Cloete, J. 2021. Mine decline and women: Reflections from the Free State Goldfields. *The Extractive Industries and Society*, 8(1), 211–19. doi: 10.1016/j.exis.2020.11.006.

Sharife, K. and Bond, P. 2011. Above and beyond South Africa's mineral-energy complex. In S. Pillay, J. Daniel, P. Naidoo and R. Southhall (eds), *New South African Review 2*. Johannesburg: Wits University Press, 279–99.

Simelane, T. and Abdel-Rahman, M. (eds) 2011. *Energy Transition in Africa*. Pretoria: HSRC Press.

Van Asche, K., Deacon, L., Gruezmacher, M., Summers, R., Lavoie, S., Jones, K., Ganzow, M., Hallstrom, L. and Parkins, J. 2017. *Boom and Bust: Local Strategies for Big Events*. Groningen: Coöperatie In Planning.

Van der Watt, P. and Marais, L. 2019. Normalising mining company towns in Emalahleni, South Africa. *The Extractive Industries and Society*, 6(4), 1205–14.

Warner, K. and Jones, G. 2019. The 21st century coal question: China, India, development, and climate change. *Atmosphere*, 10, 476.

Witbank News, 2016. Highveld closed. *Witbank News*, 17 February. https://witbanknews.co.za/61365/highveld-closed/ (last accessed 5 May 2021).

CHAPTER 2

What Is a Just Transition?

Elianor Gerrard and Peter Westoby

A just transition and climate change

'There are no jobs on a dead planet.' This campaign slogan adopted by the International Trade Union Confederation (ITUC) goes to the heart of what 'a just transition' means, particularly for Emalahleni.

Transition to a low-carbon economy is a necessity if the global community wants to avoid the dangerous effects of climate change. Such a transition, predominantly from the fossil fuel industry to renewable or clean technologies, implies not only technological but also social, economic and political change. At the same time, if responding to climate change is the impetus to transition, *climate change policy* is the medium. Climate change policy, like setting emission reduction targets, ending fossil fuel subsidies, and so on, is helping along this process of transformation. And while climate change affects humanity in unequal ways (Bambrick, 2018), so do mitigation and adaptation policies. In shaping such policy that shifts away from a fossil fuel economy, the ethics of the procedural and distributional impacts must be assessed (Healy and Barry, 2017).

The term 'just transition' is becoming widely known. It refers to the social justice issues that need to be considered in developing climate change policy and protecting the environment. Broadly speaking, just transition advances the idea that the burdens of decarbonisation – such as job losses from the closing of fossil fuel industry or high costs of clean technologies – should not unfairly impact any one group. Just transition can therefore be understood as a framework for navigating the political, practical, policy and ethical complexities of inequality in a carbon-constrained future. This chapter presents a synopsis and critical appraisal of the concept. The narrow focus on labour issues in just transition debates should be expanded to include a broader range of issues.

Historical and contemporary overview

What is a just transition?

A 'just transition' is a concept that assumes various meanings contingent on context. In academic debates it gathers threads of environmental, energy and climate justice, socio-technical transitions and sustainable development debates and works them into a theoretical framework that insists the process of decarbonising the global economy is socially just. (See Swilling and Annecke, 2012; Newell and Mulvaney, 2013; Stevis and Felli, 2016; Healy and Barry, 2017; Heffron and McCauley, 2018; Swilling, 2020.)

The ITUC and the International Labour Organization (ILO) see a just transition as a tool to help workers in fossil fuel industries find viable employment in the move towards green technologies (ITUC, 2018; ILO, 2015, 2018). Politicians tend to use it as reassuring rhetoric, but in some cases as meaningful policy (IndustriALL, 2018). Grassroots movements see it as a means to equitable ecological and social transformation, beyond the dominant imagery of capitalism (Newell and Mulvaney, 2013; Patterson and Smith, 2017). Stevis and Felli (2016: 35) note that 'there are varieties of Just Transition, reflecting the politics of its various advocates'.

Indicative of a near-global consensus to reduce global warming, many institutions and influential organisations are calling for just transitions (WBGU, 2011; UNFCCC, 2015; ITUC, 2017; ILO, 2015, 2018), but measures to support such transitions vary from conservative to radically reformative (Felli, 2014; Stevis and Felli, 2015).

History

While there are competing accounts of the genesis of the term 'just transition', most versions attribute it to trade union movements in the United States and Canada during the 1970s and 1980s, with developments occurring through to the 1990s (Newell and Mulvaney, 2013; Morena, 2018; Pollin and Callaci, 2018). Largely, observers concede that Oil, Chemical, and Atomic Workers (OCAW) leader Tony Mazzocchi developed the concept through his work in the trade union movement in the mid-1970s (Abraham, 2017; Robinson and Palmer, 2018; Morena, Krause and Stevis, 2020). Just transition, as an idea, emerged from Mazzocchi's sustained efforts to 'reconcile environmental and social concerns' (Morena, Krause and Stevis, 2020: 9). Alternative accounts, such as that of Anabella Rosemberg (former policy officer with the ITUC), note that the term first entered these movements' parlance in the 1990s (Rosemberg, 2010). Brian Kohler, a Canadian union activist, is said to have coined the term as he sought to reconcile the union prerogative of decent work with the pressing need to protect the environment. Rosemberg (2010: 141) cites Kohler saying in 1996: 'The real choice is not jobs or environment. It is both or neither.' Irrespective of these various views, just transition clearly originated as a trade union term concerned with the 'intersection' of labour and environment (Morena, Krause and Stevis, 2020: 10).

Burrows (2001) notes that an early objective of the labour unions' just transition policy was to encourage support within their constituencies for environmental concerns. Programmes designed to protect workers' livelihoods would make workers feel less threatened by environmental action and sustainability directives. Burrows (2001: 30) notes that in the late 1990s the Canadian Labour Congress (CLC) created a just transition policy that reflected this:

> The just transition policy [of the CLC] calls on governments to establish fair and positive arrangements that help workers who are displaced by environmentally desirable initiatives to shift to alternative, environmentally desirable jobs. The idea is to ensure that workers are willing participants rather than victims of environmental improvement.

In the early use of the term, 'just transition' referred to the needs of a workforce tied to a polluting industry that was forced to close because of environmental policy or legislation. It called attention to the need for adequate protection of workers as environmental protection policy became prominent. Burrows (2001: 29–30) notes that environmental policy in the 1980s to 2000 was framed as seeking to 'eliminate certain toxic chemicals' and advance 'environmental improvements'. She cites the ban by several nations in 2000 on asbestos production as a notable example of just transition policy being adopted by unions in response to the enforced closure of a toxic industry.

Over the past 20 years, the term has evolved considerably, drawing from sustainable development debates, human rights agendas (Morena, 2018) and climate change concerns. It has come to represent much more than a fair transition for workers in a specific location or industry. Rosemberg (2010: 141) notes that the evolution of the term is indicative of contemporary complexities:

> Today, 'Just Transition' can be understood as the conceptual framework in which the labour movement captures the complexities of the transition towards a low-carbon and climate-resilient economy, highlighting public policy needs and aiming to maximise benefits and minimise hardships for workers and their communities in this transformation.

The term 'just transition' thus encapsulates the merging of two socio-economic priorities: the protection of workers, and thereby the communities they live in, and the pressing urgency of decarbonisation.

Policy for affected workers

To organised labour, a just transition is a conceptual tool but also a policy for ensuring that shifts to new low-carbon technologies do not come at the expense of workers. The policy is also intended to include broader social justice issues, under the banner of 'decent work for all' (ILO, 2015, 2018; ITUC, 2018). A just transition is therefore a strategy for achieving sustainable development goals (Abraham, 2017). Morena (2018: 293) cites the ITUC as saying that just transition is a 'conceptual tool that the trade union movement shares with the international community aiming to ensure a soft passage towards a more sustainable society'. Labour and trade say there are clear policy components that a just transition must contain.

Rosemberg (2010: 142–5) identifies the following six components which inform and constitute effective just transition policy and programmes:

1. Sound investments in low-emission and labour-intensive technologies and sectors.
2. Research and early assessment of social and employment impacts.
3. Social dialogue and democratic consultation of social partners and stakeholders.
4. Training and skills development.
5. Social protection.
6. Local analysis and economic diversification plans.

Component 1 means government investment must prioritise industry and infrastructure that will achieve lower carbon emission *and* stimulate job growth. This can be effected through quotas or requirements for 'procurement, infrastructure projects and public regulations' (Rosemberg, 2010: 142). Component 3 calls for all stakeholders to be involved in decisions about industry closure and phase-out. The ITUC (2017: 11) defines social dialogue as 'institutional discussions between trade unions, employers and governments, as well as other community groups'. This makes it an apparatus for democratic agreement-reaching. Component 4 refers primarily to concerns about organised labour: workers must be trained and equipped with the skills necessary to move into the 'green economy'. Component 5 refers to the income security measures needed to minimise social damage incurred by sudden mass unemployment. One of the aims is to reduce backlash from trade unions and encourage them to support responsive and preventative policy for dealing with climate change. Component 6 speaks to the need for *regionally relevant* economic diversification plans as climate and environment policies are implemented (Rosemberg, 2010).

Although there has been strong leadership within the trade union movement to devise and promote just transition programmes, to date real-world applications of such programmes have been limited (Snell, 2018). However, to the credit of the trade union movement, the notion of a just transition has been taken up in the policy of leading global institutions, such as the United Nations Framework Convention on Climate Change (UNFCCC, 2016).

Global policy discourse
In recent years, the term 'just transition' has become prominent in global policy discourse, particularly in relation to climate change and environmental protection policy, mostly because of the ITUC's lobbying efforts. As a vocal institutional advocate, the ITUC has been working to ensure that the term is included in discussions and policy documents across numerous global platforms (Morena, 2018). These efforts started with an official statement at COP3 (the Kyoto Climate Conference of 1997) by the then International Confederation of Free

Trade Unions (which later merged with the World Confederation of Labour to become the ITUC). However, it was over a decade later that the term began to be mainstreamed within the trade union community and lobbied for in the United Nations' (UN) processes and agreements (Morena, 2018). A testament to the tenacity of trade movement advocates is the inclusion of the term in the global community's signature climate change policy, the Paris Agreement, which speaks of 'taking into account the imperatives of a just transition of the workforce and the creation of decent work and quality jobs by nationally defined development priorities' (UNFCCC, 2015: 2). Recent developments include the 'Solidarity and Just Transition Silesia Declaration' presented at the 2018 UN Annual Conference on Climate Change (COP24), where concerns about the impact on workers' lives, livelihoods, communities and families were a central theme (ITUC, 2018). Just transition's shift from predominantly a union movement objective to an acknowledged element of a global framework for addressing climate change indicates the term's gravitas and mobilising potential.

National just transition agendas
Some nations are proactively considering the implications of decarbonisation policy for their economies and, consequently, their populations. Scotland, New Zealand and Canada have all formed just transition assemblies to begin developing relevant strategies for an effective transition away from fossil fuels (Government of Canada, 2018; Scottish Government, 2019; MBIE, 2019). A requirement of these assemblies is a representation of – or at minimum, engagement with – a diverse range of actors and interest groups, from universities and researchers to local governments, since enacting transitions in just ways entails collective decision-making (Abraham, 2017).

While it is too early to discern or evaluate the effectiveness of these assemblies, they indicate intention and progress towards just national decarbonisation plans. Further examples of ways to achieve a just transition, though the term may not be used explicitly, are evident in some countries' emissions reduction schemes and policies. Spain and Germany, for example, have schemes (which include ending government subsidies for the coal industry) that are having the effect of restructuring their coal industries. Their just transition policies, including social dialogue, training and skills development, have made them exemplars of just industry reform for workforces and their communities (Abraham, 2017; IndustriALL, 2018; Sheldon, Junankar and De Rosa Pontello, 2018).

Beyond union prerogatives and global and national policy debates, the notion of just transition has become prominent in academic research on how to achieve a socially and ecologically sustainable global future.

Academic discourse
The notion of 'just transition' has aroused the interest of many academics who are researching the at times competing, yet connected, issues of ecological and

social injustice. A large transdisciplinary field, known as 'sustainability transitions' or 'transformations towards sustainability', is investigating transition to more sustainable ends in, for example, the energy, agriculture and transport sectors. While some scholars in the field are interested in the complex interconnections between society and the diffusion of new 'clean' technologies, others are looking at the justice aspect of system transformation. (For further information, see Schot and Geels, 2008; Meadowcroft, 2011, Swilling and Annecke, 2012; Swilling, Musango and Wakeford, 2016; Patterson et al., 2017; Mayer, 2018.)

Heffron and McCauley (2018) note that just transition surfaces as a recurrent theme in the fields of energy, environmental and climate justice. They note that these fields have conflicting ideas of what justice entails. Rapid decarbonisation requires a unified policy, rather than siloed efforts to achieve similar social and sustainability objectives. A common understanding of just transition could unite them (Heffron and McCauley, 2018).

Mayer (2018: 2) notes that a focus on sustainability is not sufficient and questions 'who benefits and who is harmed' by the transition. Shapiro and Verchick (2018) see just transition as a conceptual merging of environmental regulations with social protection policies. Energy justice scholars Healy and Barry (2017) and Vachon and Sweeney (2018) see just transition as a way to achieve energy democracy. A central concern is to address three interrelated 'root causes': 'economic, social and climate injustice', using the mechanisms of 'social action and public policy' (Vachon and Sweeney, 2018: 62, 64).

Climate justice proponents note that the burdens of climate change are unevenly distributed between nations (Newell and Mulvaney, 2013). Consequently, a just transition will need to deal with inequities between the Global North and South. Swilling and Annecke (2012: xix) emphasise that a shift to renewable and green technology is a simplistic approach that will inevitably exacerbate global inequality, leading ultimately to a 'divided, poverty-stricken, conflictual and socially unsustainable low carbon world' torn apart by resource wars. There is a spectrum of ways to understand justice in the process of transition and it can depend on a country's political economy (Newell and Mulvaney, 2013). Some see a just transition as the way to achieve 'a post-capitalist eco-socialist state' (Satgar, 2018: 64). Swilling, Musango and Wakeford (2016: 651) see just transition in South Africa as 'structural transformation that results in the achievement of two linked goals: developmental welfarism and a sustainable transition'. The diversity of political, social, economic and environmental contexts in which a just transition is being discussed inevitably means there will be disagreements over ideological viewpoints and practical applications.

Finally, Agyeman (2013) argues that the term 'just sustainabilities' broadens the concept of sustainability to refer to sustainable communities. For Agyeman (2013), sustainable communities include food, hunger and space, while Obeng-Odoom (2020) adds the notion of 'just land'.

Viewpoints on a just transition

Just transition beyond workers

In the trade unions' just transition policy, it is not just the workers but also their communities who must benefit. Abraham (2017: 222) states that just transitions will guarantee 'economic security' for affected workers and 'reinvestment and development plans' for affected communities. However, it is not always clear who constitute the 'community'. Industry reform or transition has effects far beyond the workers. In some cases, local governments lose income through industry contraction or closure, resulting in reduced budgets for necessities like schools and hospitals (Pollin and Callaci, 2018). Whole regions invariably feel the impacts of transition. Scholars have also pointed out the gendered and ethnic lines that carve through just transition policy, noting that the fossil fuel industry has a male-dominated workforce and, in countries like the United States, a largely white male workforce (Stevis and Felli, 2016; Pollin and Callaci, 2018). In South Africa's fossil fuel industry, ownership and control are still in the hands of whites more than blacks (Bischof-Niemz and Creamer, 2018). What governments or civil society formulate as a just transition may turn out to be formulated along unjust lines. As Stevis and Felli (2016: 38) explain:

> Compensation or retraining may alleviate the distress of laid-off workers, but they often do not extend to the community in which these workers are embedded or do not address the gendered nature of their jobs. For both political and ethical reasons, just transitions have to take into account all the affected parties, as well as the unequal power relations amongst them.

Just transitions are thus profoundly political processes (Newell and Mulvaney, 2013; Healy and Barry, 2017). Rather than redress injustices between genders or ethnicities, they can further harm social dynamics if not attentive to inequities from the outset. This prompts questions about the social and geographical parameters of just transitions: to whom and where does justice extend? Invariably, the ideology behind the driving group – such as academics or trade unions – will determine the scope of procedural and distributional justice in the just transition process.

Bridging the divide

Organised labour has traditionally been associated with an ethos of protection and justice for workers, placing it at times in direct ideological opposition to environment and climate justice movements (Räthzel and Uzzell, 2011, 2012). These ideological differences are responsible for the polarised view of 'jobs versus the environment' (Evans and Phelan, 2016). However, the school of thought known as labour environmentalism, often associated with just transition, advances the alternative view that sustainable development is a fundamental objective of the trade union movement and that 'just transition' is the 'strategy' that combines 'the needs of workers with the imperative of environmental reform' (Abraham, 2017: 222). Indeed, as mentioned earlier, bridging the divide between labour and environment was an intention of the trade unions' early use of the term 'just transition' (Burrows, 2001). Morena (2018) observes that the value of a just transition lies in its capacity to mend the perceived ideological rift between climate action and trade union imperatives. As a result, the term has been adopted widely by diverse fields and stakeholder groups. Conversely, it is this same widespread popularity that threatens to undermine its mobilising potential within the labour movement, which is historically resistant to climate and environment policy. Morena (2018: 296) warns that as soon as just transition 'goes from being a trade union concept to an "unbranded" one' there is a risk that its 'awareness-raising role within the trade union movement' may be undermined. In this way, the trade unions' objective of garnering support within their constituencies for proactive climate change policy may be compromised. The term 'just transition' thus becomes diluted and ambiguous through adaptation, co-option or reinterpretation.

Conceptual ambiguity

The term 'just transition' has broad appeal for its capacity to instigate dialogue between two seemingly dissonant concerns – labour and social justice, and climate and the environment. This has added to its growing popularity. But details of the concept remain 'hotly debated' by labour unions and environmentalists alike (Stevis and Felli, 2015: 29). Furthermore, the practice of a just transition remains elusive: as a fairly new concept, it lacks clarity in its real-world application. Snell (2018: 561) argues that conceptual academic debates are 'subordinate' to the ground-level dynamics of transition. He (2018: 550) also posits that the term 'lacks both conceptual clarity and empirical evidence of its practical applications'. Similarly, Felli (2014: 379) notes that the term 'just transition', like other terms used in environmental politics, 'owes its success to the fact that it has somehow become an empty signifier through which conflicting visions can be expressed without, however, having to expose their disagreements'.

As an 'empty signifier' the term is open for interpretation by various groups who bring to it details and meanings appropriate to their contexts (Felli, 2014). Some scholars argue that this ambiguity helps to make the concept flexible, allowing for novel approaches when implementing just transitions in real-world settings like coal power communities (Snell, 2018). Others speculate about the need for agreed-upon details in a just transition policy to expedite appropriate climate change policy (Heffron and McCauley, 2018). While discussions about just transition's meaning and details are ongoing, so are debates about the broader paradigm in which just transitions will take place.

Questioning the paradigm

Felli (2014) notes that, in approaching the pressures of climate change, organised labour will take a variety of ideological stances. Most unions emphasise moving to 'green jobs' in a 'green economy', but others, such as the International Transport Workers Federation (ITF), favour more radical socialist measures to ensure just transitions. Nevertheless, the prevailing inclination is towards a green capitalist or 'ecological modernisation' approach, in which economic growth remains the dominant aim (as growth equates to more jobs) and 'technological fixes' are favoured as solutions to the climate crisis (Felli, 2014). According to the ILO (2015: 4), a 'greening' of the current capitalist system through the use of 'environmentally friendly technology' will improve global ability 'to manage natural resources sustainably, increase energy efficiency and reduce waste, while addressing inequalities and enhancing resilience'. Paradoxically, while trade union policies call for social justice and 'decent work for all', criticism of the economic paradigm, which causes and perpetuates the inequalities a just transition seeks to cure, is seldom heard (see Swilling and Annecke, 2012; Klein, 2014; Escobar, 2015; Heffron and McCauley, 2018). The trade union movement has a propensity to assume technology will enable climate-friendly development. However, more radical understandings of just transition, beyond the trade unions, see it as a way to challenge 'the various forms of green capitalism and green growth competing for hegemony' (Stevis and Felli, 2016: 38). Many scholars, especially from the Global South, are questioning the sustainable development and growth paradigm, giving rise to 'degrowth' and post-development debates in which views of labour, trade, production and consumption differ radically from the status quo. Enacting just transitions of this nature would be radically transformative. (For detailed discussion of these arguments, see Latouche, 2010; Swilling and Annecke, 2012; Felli, 2014; Klein, 2014; Escobar, 2015; Stevis and Felli, 2016, Heffron and McCauley, 2018; Morena, 2018.)

Conclusion

The notion of a just transition, for workers and communities, has attracted widespread attention. From global policy to energy justice scholarship, the term 'just transition' has sparked critical debate on the ethical dimensions of decarbonisation strategies. But where debate can be productive it can also cause inertia, and facing the effects of climate change demands action. Further work needs to be done to develop a collaborative understanding of, and policy for, just transition. In particular, the gendered and ethnic dimensions of just transition programmes need to be better understood. A just transition for Emalahleni will entail broadening the parameters of current labour and trade union policy. Broadening the concept should include reflections on public space, land and alternative economic options to coal.

References

Abraham, J. 2017. Just transitions for the miners: Labor environmentalism in the Ruhr and Appalachian Coalfields. *New Political Science*, 39(2), 218–40.

Agyeman, J. 2013. *Introducing Just Sustainabilities: Policy, Planning, and Practice*. London: ZED Books.

Bambrick, H. 2018. Three hundred thousand children: The public health verdict on new coal. In D. Ritter (ed.), *The Coal Truth: The Fight to Stop Adani, Defeat the Big Polluters and Reclaim Our Democracy*. Perth: UWA Publishing, 113–21.

Bischof-Niemz, T. and Creamer, T. 2018. *South Africa's Energy Transition*. London: Routledge.

Burrows, M. 2001. Just transition. *Alternatives Journal: Canada's Environmental Voice*, 27(1), 29–32.

Escobar, A. 2015. Degrowth, post-development, and transitions: A preliminary conversation. *Sustainability Science*, 10(3), 451–62.

Evans, G. and Phelan, L. 2016. Transition to a post-carbon society: Linking environmental justice and just transition discourses. *Energy Policy*, 99, 329–39.

Felli, R. 2014. An alternative socio-ecological strategy? International trade unions' engagement with climate change. *Review of International Political Economy*, 21(2), 372–98.

Government of Canada. 2018. Just transition task force. www.canada.ca/en/environment-climate-change/news/2018/02/just_transition_taskforce.html (last accessed 20 April 2021).

Healy, N. and Barry, J. 2017. Politicizing energy justice and energy system transitions: Fossil fuel divestment and a 'just transition'. *Energy Policy*, 108, 451–9.

Heffron, R. J. and McCauley, D. 2018. What is the 'just transition'? *Geoforum*, 88, 74–7.

ILO (International Labour Organization). 2015. *Guidelines for a Just Transition towards Environmentally Sustainable Economies and Societies for All*. www.ilo.org/wcmsp5/groups/public/---ed_emp/---emp_ent/documents/publication/wcms_432859.pdf (last accessed 20 April 2021).

ILO (International Labour Organization). 2018. *World Employment and Social Outlook: Trends 2018*. www.ilo.org/global/research/global-reports/weso/2018/WCMS_615594/lang-en/index.htm (last accessed 20 April 2021).

IndustriALL. 2018. Spanish coal unions win landmark Just Transition deal. www.industriall-union.org/spanish-coal-unions-win-landmark-just-transition-deal (last accessed 20 April 2021).

ITUC (International Trade Union Confederation). 2017. *Just Transition – Where Are We Now and What's Next? A Guide to National Policies and International Climate Governance*. www.ituc-csi.org/just-transition-where-are-we-now (last accessed 20 April 2021).

ITUC (International Trade Union Confederation). 2018. Unions support Solidarity and Just Transition Silesia Declaration. www.ituc-csi.org/unions-support-solidarity-and-just (last accessed 20 April 2021).

Klein, N. 2014. *This Changes Everything: Capitalism vs. the Climate*. London: Penguin.

Latouche, S. 2010. Degrowth. *Journal of Cleaner Production*, 18(6), 519–22. doi: 10.1016/j.jclepro.2010.02.003.

Mayer, A. 2018. A just transition for coal miners? Community identity and support from local policy actors. *Environmental Innovation and Societal Transitions*, 28, 1–13. doi: 10.1016/j.eist.2018.03.006.

MBIE (Ministry of Business, Innovation and Employment, New Zealand). 2019. About the Just Transition Summit. https://www.mbie.govt.nz/business-and-employment/economic-development/just-transition/ (last accessed 17 May 2021).

Meadowcroft, J. 2011. Engaging with the politics of sustainability transitions. *Environmental Innovation and Societal Transitions*, 1(1), 70–5. doi: 10.1016/j.eist.2011.02.003.

Morena, E. 2018. Securing workers' rights in the transition to a low-carbon world: The just transition concept and its evolution. In S. Duyck, S. Jodoin and A. Johl (eds), *Routledge Handbook of Human Rights and Climate Governance*. Abingdon: Taylor & Francis, 292–8.

Morena, E., Krause, D. and Stevis, D. (eds) 2020. *Just Transitions: Social Justice in the Shift Towards a Low-carbon World*. London: Pluto Press.

Newell, P. and Mulvaney, D. 2013. The political economy of the 'just transition'. *Geographical Journal*, 179, 132–40. doi: 10.1111/geoj.12008.

Obeng-Odoom, F. 2020. *Property, Institutions and Social Stratification in Africa*. Cambridge: Cambridge University Press.

Patterson, J. Schulz, K., Vervoort, J., van der Hel, S. C., Widerberg, O., Adler, C., Hurlbert, M., Anderton, K., Sethi, M. and Barau, A. 2017. Exploring the governance and politics of transformations towards sustainability. *Environmental Innovation and Societal Transitions*, 24, 1–16. doi: 10.1016/j.eist.2016.09.001.

Patterson, J. and Smith, J. 2017. Environmental justice initiatives for community resilience: Ecovillages, just transitions, and human rights cities. In B. S. Caniglia, M. Vallee and B. Frank (eds), *Resilience, Environmental Justice and the City*. London: Routledge, 216–33.

Pollin, R. and Callaci, B. 2018. The economics of just transition: A framework for supporting fossil fuel-dependent workers and communities in the United States. *Labor Studies Journal*, 44(2), 93–138. doi: 10.1177/0160449X18787051.

Räthzel, N. and Uzzell, D. 2011. Trade unions and climate change: The jobs versus environment dilemma. *Global Environmental Change*, 21(4), 1215–23. doi: 10.1016/j.gloenvcha.2011.07.010.

Räthzel, N. and Uzzell, D. (eds) 2012. *Trade Unions in the Green Economy Working for the Environment*. London: Routledge.

Robinson, M. and Palmer, C. 2018. *Climate Justice: Hope, Resilience, and the Fight for a Sustainable Future*. New York: Bloomsbury.

Rosemberg, A. 2010. Building a just transition: The linkages between climate change and employment. *International Journal of Labour Research*, 2(2), 125–61.

Satgar, V. (ed.) 2018. *The Climate Crisis: South African and Global Democratic Eco-Socialist Alternatives*. Johannesburg: Wits University Press.

Schot, J. and Geels, F. W. 2008. Strategic niche management and sustainable innovation journeys: Theory, findings, research agenda, and policy. *Technology Analysis and Strategic Management*, 20(5), 537–54. doi: 10.1080/09537320802292651.

Scottish Government. 2019. Just Transition Commission: Overview. www.gov.scot/groups/just-transition-commission/ (last accessed 20 April 2021).

Shapiro, S. A. and Verchick, R. R. M. 2018. Inequality, social resilience, and the green economy. *UMKC Law Review*, 86(4), 963–95.

Sheldon, P., Junankar, R. and De Rosa Pontello, A. 2018. *The Ruhr or Appalachia? Deciding the Future of Australia's Coal Power Communities*: IRRC Report for CFMMEU Mining and Energy. https://me.cfmeu.org.au/news/download-report-deciding-future-australias-coal-power-workers-and-communities (last accessed 20 April 2021).

Snell, D. 2018. 'Just transition'? Conceptual challenges meet stark reality in a 'transitioning' coal region in Australia. *Globalizations*, 15(4), 550–64. doi: 10.1080/14747731.2018.1454679.

Stevis, D. and Felli, R. 2015. Global labour unions and just transition to a green economy. *International Environmental Agreements: Politics, Law and Economics*, 15 (1), 29–43.

Stevis, D. and Felli, R., 2016. Green transitions, just transitions? Broadening and deepening justice. *Kurswechsel*, 3, 35–45.

Swilling, M. 2020. *The Age of Sustainability: Just Transitions in a Complex World.* Abingdon: Routledge.

Swilling, M. and Annecke, E. 2012. *Just Transitions: Explorations of Sustainability in an Unfair World.* New York: United Nations University Press.

Swilling, M., Musango, J. and Wakeford, J. 2016. Developmental states and sustainability transitions: Prospects of a just transition in South Africa. *Journal of Environmental Policy and Planning*, 18(5), 650–72. doi: 10.1080/1523908X.2015.1107716.

UNFCCC (United Nations Framework Convention on Climate Change). 2015. *The Paris Agreement.* https://unfccc.int/process/conferences/pastconferences/paris-climate-change-conference-november-2015/paris-agreement (last accessed 20 April 2021).

UNFCCC (United Nations Framework Convention on Climate Change). 2016. Just transition of the workforce, and the creation of decent work and quality jobs. Technical paper by the Secretariat. https://unfccc.int/resource/docs/2016/tp/07.pdf (last accessed 20 April 2021).

Vachon, T. and Sweeney, S. 2018. Energy democracy: A just transition for social, economic, and climate justice. In G. Muschert, K. Budd, M. Christian, B. Klocke, J. Shefner and R. Perrucci (eds), *Global Agenda for Social Justice*, vol. 1. Bristol: Bristol University Press, 61–70.

WBGU (German Advisory Council on Global Change). 2011. *World in Transition: A Social Contract for Sustainability.* https://www.wbgu.de/en/publications/publication/world-in-transition-a-social-contract-for-sustainability (last accessed 17 May 2021).

CHAPTER 3

Mine Closure in the Coal Industry: Global and National Perspectives

Lochner Marais, Jesse Burton, Maléne Campbell and Etienne Nel

Introduction

For over a century, coal has provided much of the energy for development worldwide. The literature has documented the adverse environmental and social aspects of coal mining (Obeng-Odoom, 2020a). However, the threat of global warming means that the world is now looking for cleaner forms of energy. The EU (European Union), for example, has a transition policy that will help to make Europe carbon neutral by 2050. In May 2019 the United Kingdom had its first week without using coal-generated energy. By 2030, more than half of India's electricity capacity will be renewable. The pressure for cleaner forms of energy comes from the Paris Agreement, which compels signatories to limit greenhouse gases, and from banks, which are increasingly wary of financing coal for reputational reasons particularly as it grows increasingly uncompetitive. Coal-powered energy provision will inevitably decline and large numbers of coal mines will close.

South Africa's economy is still heavily dependent on coal, the source of over 90% of its electricity and 20% of its liquid fuels (Department of Energy, 2015). This dependency is bound to change. New coal plants are now more expensive than renewable energy across most of the world, and in many major markets, new renewable energy is cheaper than the running costs of coal plants. South Africa has also signed the Paris Agreement to reduce greenhouse gas emissions. In practice, this means the country must close all its coal-fired plants (Simelane and Abdel-Rahman, 2011; McCall et al., 2019), which will cause a huge reduction in production and employment in the coal mining industry (Burton, Marquard and McCall, 2019). South Africa has embarked on a renewable-energy programme, but the programme has not received universal support. Workers and unions in the coal industry are actively campaigning against the renewable programme, while some analysts also argue that the apparent costs/benefits are more complex than anticipated. For Emalahleni, these debates are real, as the economy is built on coal.

This expected decline in local demand for coal is likely to coincide with a decline in the demand for exported coal. Countries to which South Africa has been exporting coal are also actively looking for cleaner sources of energy. Asian demand for coal is likely to fall given the growing uncompetitiveness of coal versus wind and solar, and energy, climate change, industrial, and air pollution policies that drive shifts away from coal (Fei, 2018; Sartor 2018). India, for example, has downscaled its construction of new coal-generated power plants substantially over the past few years (Strambo, Burton and Atteridge, 2019).

In the previous chapter we discussed the call for a 'just transition'. We now switch from that idealistic perspective to consider the practical consequences of mine decline and closure. We highlight the need to address the social aspects of mine closure and we look at international perspectives on the topic. We argue that normative approaches such as those advocated in the just transition literature are essential but must be careful not to overlook the socio-economic realities and complexities that mine closure brings.

Social aspects of mine closure: the literature and policy

Mine closure is a worldwide phenomenon. Apart from the World Bank's forecasts on mine closure about 20 years ago, predicting closures has not received much attention. Arguably this is because they are so tricky to predict. But it is also because many governments and mining companies do not take mine closure seriously. Historically, mining companies simply abandoned mines. State regulation has increased over the past three decades in an attempt to prevent this. The mining industry's response has been to place mines under care and maintenance to avoid the full costs of closure. How the industry closes mines has huge implications for its commitment to sustainable development.

Defining 'closure' – something which the just transition literature does not do – is central to the issue of a just transition. In practice, mine closure means extended care and maintenance (Vivoda, Kemp and Owen, 2019). It means that a mine will usually stop producing a resource but does not rehabilitate the land. Stopping production has severe socio-economic consequences. Communities have to live with the risks of unrehabilitated land for much longer. Some large mines avoid the care and maintenance option and sell their assets to smaller companies that cannot carry out closure effectively and in accordance with the regulations. In most cases, mine closure is a process of downscaling. The downscaling could mean a decline in production or an end to production, but often without land rehabilitation. These international trends are also seen in South Africa (Cornelissen et al., 2019).

The literature points to several policy voids, despite the mining industry asking for a more appropriate response to closure (MMSD, 2002). We can identify three possible reasons for this. First, there is little global or country-level information about possible closures. Back in 2002, the World Bank estimated that 25 large mines would close in the developing world in the next decade. Extensive analysis has been done of resource availability and the number of new mines that may open, but we see few projections of mineral resources becoming exhausted and mines closing (Bainton and Holcombe, 2018). The lack of adequate information makes planning for a just transition difficult and the industry's practice of avoiding full closure compounds the difficulty further.

Second, policies focus mostly on the environmental aspects of mine closure and simply assume that the social aspects will be included. Where regulations for the social aspects do exist, they are often not as strict as the environmental regulations and the guidance is less developed and prescriptive. There is a danger that the industry will manage the social aspects of mine closure in the same linear way as the environmental aspects. This means that once a company has completed the land rehabilitation process it could abrogate its other responsibilities. South African policy and practice, as is the case globally, pay limited attention to mine downscaling and closure outside the provisions for environmental rehabilitation.

Third, the social aspects of mine policies focus on 'front-end approaches' (i.e. large investments to obtain a social licence to operate) and guidelines are not set up for when the mine closes. Mining companies' cash flows usually begin to dry up as the mine reaches the end of its life, resulting in financial constraints before closure. Effectively, the company's interest in managing closure dwindles as the economic resource nears exhaustion. Consequently, the research advocates a shift in focus from a front-end to a back-end approach, to accommodate the social aspects of mine closure. But a back-end approach should go beyond merely adding social projects or dealing with social impact: responsible social closure should be part of the planning when a mine opens. (For more detailed discussions of this issue, see Andrews-Speed et al., 2005; Bainton and Holcombe, 2018; Cornelissen et al., 2019; Vivoda, Kemp and Owen, 2019.)

In addition to the policy voids, the body of research on the social aspects of mine closure is small and limited in scope (Matebesi, 2020). It looks mainly at the behaviour of the mine during closure and not at the behaviour of the state or the community. It lacks critical assessment of policies, local case studies and raw data. Nevertheless, it does draw attention to a wide range of impacts under the heading of 'social aspects of mine closure', underlining the need for a broad practical basis to support the aim of achieving a just transition.

Bainton and Holcombe (2018: 468) define the social aspects of mine closure as 'the socioeconomic, political, cultural and institutional impacts that arise at the end of the project life-cycle; the planning and management processes that are required to mitigate these impacts; and the post-mining future'. Vivoda, Kemp and Owen (2019) list 14 aspects and 30 elements associated with the social aspects of mine closure: the economy, business, employment, security, education and training infrastructure, amenity, livelihoods, land, housing, health, environment, demography, participation, inclusion and general social aspects. This is probably not an exhaustive list and can be expanded. It does, however, explicitly show that arguments for a just transition must not be focused on employment and environmental aspects alone. A critical issue is how the front-end approach of the mining industry and mining policy creates liabilities at closure.

We outline here four of the many aspects of closure and discuss the implications for a just transition. First, mine closure damages the market. The just transition literature is correct in assuming that closure creates unemployment and that many mineworkers are ill equipped for other work. But the social aspects of mine closure go beyond this direct impact on workers. The collapse of housing markets affects both mineworker and non-mineworker families. Another example of market-based liabilities is the closure of businesses and especially local enterprises in the mining value chain as they are usually the less diverse businesses.

Second, mining towns and communities need to deal with the environmental consequences of mine closures, such as land damaged by mining, acid drainage polluting water sources, and disasters associated with tailings dams. A just transition must include measures that will help communities deal with these consequences. The notions of repurposing infrastructure and the mining landscape, establishing alternative economic opportunities and addressing environmental problems created by mines are high on the agenda in many areas that experience mine closure. Although closure may have some positive environmental implications, such as less pollution, the long-term problems are sure to affect the level of environmental justice for communities who remain in the area.

Third, mines and communities both depend on infrastructure created for mining, from basic infrastructure to social infrastructure such as schools, clinics and hospitals, in many cases created and maintained partly by mining companies. Continuing to service town and social infrastructure after mine closure remains a problem for many mining towns and their communities. In many cases, this infrastructure creates assets that provide local tax incomes that might be lost by mine closure (Andrews-Speed et al., 2005; Owen and Kemp, 2018). Just transitions must take a long-term perspective on these infrastructure concerns and make sure that the existing infrastructure can be maintained.

Fourth, initial research on mining communities, using social disruption theory, focused on explaining boom town conditions. However, mine closure also brings social disruption and communities have to deal with this problem at the back end. At mine closure, most communities do not have a firm footing from which to negotiate. Complex social relationships and competing agendas are common. Agreements reached at the start of mining are no longer relevant at mine closure. There are concerns about the local economy, employment, gender implications and human rights (Andrews-Speed et al., 2005; Bainton and Holcombe, 2018). Sesele (2020) and Sesele et al. (2021) have highlighted the effect of mine closure on women in the Free State Goldfields, particularly the way it reinforces their household role.

A growing body of work is documenting local responses to mine closure. An idea that has gained prominence over the past few years is that mine closure is an economic transition that can be planned for. Among the issues considered are redeployment and reskilling of workers and the funding of early retirement.

Strategies for economic diversification and building resilience are common. In some cases, the government has set up institutions to manage just transitions. Creating jobs through mine rehabilitation is gaining momentum. However, successful examples of economic diversification strategies are limited in South Africa. One of the main reasons is the remote location of many mines. Linking these remote areas with the value chains in the mainstream economy is difficult, and impractical in some cases. The strand of this literature that deals with shrinking cities even sees a positive side to decline of which a town can take advantage (Pallagst, Wiechmann and Martinez-Fernandez, 2014).

Mine closure is particularly problematic in Africa for several reasons: the regulations are often not well developed, governments cannot enforce them, dependencies between mines and communities are profound, closure worsens existing social conflict created by mining and the scale of artisanal mining hugely complicates closure plans (Morrison-Saunders et al., 2016; Besa, Kabwe and Banda, 2019). The large-scale dependencies are often the result of mining companies still performing public functions in urban management in many mining areas of Africa. These dependencies, combined with problems of institutional capacity, are a recipe for conflict.

The complexity of the issues discussed above shows that a just transition is much more than a matter of dealing with the problems of redundant labour. A just transition will depend on the nature and scale of environmental degradation that the remaining communities will have to live with, which in turn depends on whether rehabilitation takes place or whether the mines land up in care and maintenance indefinitely. When existing dependencies are broken by mine closure, mineworkers, other residents and institutions struggle to function without them.

The future of coal in South Africa

Coal mining contributed 2.3% of GDP in South Africa in 2012 and currently employs 78,000 people (down from 140,000 in 1984). In our opinion, five factors identified in the literature will determine the future of coal in South Africa (Burton and Winkler, 2014; Burton, Caetano and McCall, 2018; Strambo, Burton and Atteridge, 2019).

First, the Paris Agreement is a multilateral commitment to prevent global temperature rising more than 2 °C above pre-industrial levels, with the aim of limiting warming to below 1.5 °C (globally we have already reached an increase of around 1.1 °C). Globally, this means an 80% reduction in coal use by 2030. This target is a challenge for a country whose power supply depends largely on coal. Cutting back on coal will force mines to close or resources to be left in the ground. Should South Africa meet its Paris Agreement commitments, estimates show that employment in the coal mines will drop to just over 20,000 by 2045 (Burton, Caetano and McCall, 2018).

Second, most of the countries South Africa exports coal to have also signed the Paris Agreement. Many South African coal mines are profitable only because they export a portion of their coal. And although they are probably benefiting from the weaker rand in 2020, they face competition from other coal exporters and limited growth opportunities.

Third, the restructuring of Eskom is likely to have an impact on coal. Currently, the Eskom board is planning to restructure Eskom into three units: generation, transmission and distribution. Despite the government's assurances that the restructuring is not privatisation, it is unlikely that job losses at Eskom and in the mining industry can be avoided. This clinical business restructuring model for Eskom may be hampered by the fact that a large number of existing power stations are old, inefficient and not competitive. Eskom has already, in the past, announced closures of plants but then retracted its intentions. While Eskom's access to finance will depend on improvements in its financial performance, it will also depend on its ability to manoeuvre through the transition from coal in the midst of a debt crisis. Eskom's financial woes will in turn impact financing for new coal mining.

Fourth, the global financial system has become reluctant to finance new coal mining investments and this has spilt over to South Africa. In May 2020, there were over 120 banks, insurers and asset managers with coal exclusion policies worldwide. In South Africa, all major commercial banks – ABSA, Investec, Standard Bank, RMB and Nedbank – have pulled back from financing coal, with degrees of exclusion applied to their lending rules. The banks' unwillingness to finance new coal comes partly because of pressure from shareholders and civil society, but also partly because of increased transparency in the global reporting of listed companies. Financial institutions do not want investors to view them as fuelling an industry that creates greenhouse emissions.

Fifth, coal is facing competition from renewables. The Department of Energy is appointing independent power producers to provide renewable energy to Eskom. The costs of the initial programme were high, but have fallen over successive auction rounds, and by 2015 new renewables were 40% cheaper than new coal. Since then, costs have continued to come down in the rest of the world. One problem with renewables is their variability (for example, solar and wind energy depend on time of day and weather conditions), which requires complementary resources to be dispatched by grid operators. In South Africa, these resources, combined with new renewables, still offer the lowest cost electricity in the future. There is also competition from outside the formal government system. Renewables allow for decentralised energy production, which means that households, manufacturing firms and shopping malls can generate their own electricity. The mines can do the same, as the government has in principle given the mining industry permission to generate its own energy. These decentralised systems will reduce the country's dependence on coal.

The regional and local consequences of coal mine closure in South Africa

Figures from Global Insight (2019) show the extent to which Emalahleni and the Mpumalanga province depend on coal. In 2018, mining contributed 50% of Emalahleni's GVA (gross value added) and electricity generation a further 9%. From 1996 to 2018, the Tress Index increased from 51 to 60, showing that the area has become more dependent on mining over the past two decades. In 2018, approximately 35,000 people in Emalahleni worked in the mining industry (up from about 19,000 in 1996). Electricity generation accounts for about 8,000 jobs. Estimates are that every mineworker supports three more people. Mine closure and the subsequent job losses in Emalahleni will be devastating.

At a South African Cities Network workshop in 2019, the Deputy Minister of Cooperative Governance and Traditional Affairs, Mr Parks Tau, pointed out that 'nobody asked the people of Emalahleni whether they should sign the Paris Agreement'. Effectively, the government did not conduct a referendum among the residents of Emalahleni. So what are the possible consequences for Emalahleni? Burton and colleagues (2018) noted four in particular.

First, the number and timing of job losses will depend on the closure time-tables of specific plants and mines, and the age profile of the workforce. Large-scale job losses are likely, and offering early retirement may be challenging as mineworkers are relatively young. This issue is critical to the debates on a 'just transition' and the government and the mining companies cannot ignore it. Closure and decline are likely to affect black mineworkers and electricity workers more than the white workers. Black mineworkers generally have lower skills levels and perform more elementary work than white workers (Nkosi, 2017). This racial bias is likely to increase racial inequalities and reinforce social stratification in Emalahleni (Obeng Odoom, 2020b).

Second, job losses will take place elsewhere in the value chain. Eskom has become dependent on the transport sector to truck the coal from the mines to the power stations. The shift to trucking coal (as opposed to constructing conveyor belts) has created an opportunity for new black business to be incorporated into the mining value chain. A rapid decline in coal mining and coal power stations is likely to reduce the value in the transport sector and the growing black business sector associated with it. Other sectors that may be affected are businesses providing and repairing mine machinery, and financial and business services. Finding redundant mineworkers jobs in other economic sectors will not be easy. One distinct possibility is replacing coal plants with renewable energy plants. The government has prioritised the area for new renewable projects. There are also job creation possibilities in mining rehabilitation. Job losses will make it hard for people to service their debt (most notably mortgages) and pay for their municipal services.

Third, mine closure and job losses will have consequences for local government. Dependencies remain, despite a concerted attempt by the mining companies to close their company towns and shift housing responsibilities to the municipality and individual households. The mines have played a crucial role in purifying water, and their employees pay for services and property tax. The centralised way in which mine development and environmental regulations are managed means that many municipalities are not included in discussions about mine closure. There is a need for more transparency and coordination, inclusion of provincial and local governance structures, and careful thought about the long-term implications of strategies while mines are active. Planning a just transition is not something that can be done at the last minute. Early planning is essential. Currently, coal mining companies say in their social and labour plans that their primary response is the establishment of a mine closure committee. This is not helpful, and only confirms that mines manage closure at the back end of the process.

Fourth, the long-term environmental consequences of mining will remain. The two worst problems are acid mine water pollution and land that is too damaged to use for agriculture. One point on the bright side is that a decline in mining and coal-powered plants will reduce the current levels of air pollution. South African mines are required by law to follow a stringent process when they close. There are legitimate concerns about whether this is possible. However, two other options are more likely to play out. As mentioned earlier, large mines may sell off their mines to smaller firms that may not have the capacity to manage mine closure, or they may place the mines in care and maintenance, delaying attempts to rehabilitate the land.

The government and the mining industry must take serious measures to manage the risk of downscaling and closure, so as to gain social acceptance and reduce resistance to transformation and ensure that poverty and inequality are not made worse by an unplanned transition (Strambo, Burton and Atteridge, 2019; Marais and De Lange, 2021).

Conclusion: Mine closure and a just transition

Too often, the just transition literature emphasises only the plight of mineworkers. The previous chapter argued for a broader framework and this chapter helps to provide it. The focus on the workers is indeed required, but the problems of mine decline and closure are more complex than that. Like concerns about a just transition, closure concerns emerge only towards the back end of the mining process. The social aspects of mine closure require a front-end approach, where mines and communities agree on how to manage closure at the start of the mining process. Such an approach must, however, avoid creating long-term liabilities that mines, institutions or households cannot manage at the end. The quest for a just transition should start early.

This chapter argues that the just transition literature should consider a wide range of impacts of mine closure. These must include the long-term environmental impacts, the economic liabilities of unrehabilitated mine land, the inability to use the land for other economic purposes, the institutional dependencies associated with mine closure, increased inequality and social stratification and the direct social consequences.

The chapter also offers some lessons for policy development. Policy should pay more attention to the social aspects of mine closure. The current drive in South Africa for a just transition started because current policy does not pay enough attention to closure, and ignores the social issues or is often not explicit about them.

The likelihood of mine closure and decline in the coal industry is high. Emalahleni will be very hard hit. The challenge to the just transition literature is to consider all the complexities. These should go beyond worker issues and include the institutional, inequalities, spatial planning, environmental and economic implications. In some cases it may be advantageous to focus on the potential value of decline rather than only trying to find alternative economic options. Dealing with mine closure will not be easy and power play will be prominent.

References

Andrews-Speed, P., Ma, G., Shao, B. and Liao, C. 2005. Economic responses to the closure of small-scale coal mines in Chongqing, China. *Resources Policy*, 30, 39–54.

Bainton, N. and Holcombe, S. 2018. A critical review of the social aspects of mine closure. *Resources Policy*, 59, 368–478.

Besa, B., Kabwe, J. M. J. and Banda, W. 2019. Socio-economic impact of mine closure and development of exit strategy for rural mining areas in Zambia: A case study of Kalumbila District. Proceedings of the 28th International Symposium on Mine Planning and Equipment Selection (MPES).

Burton, J., Caetano, T. and McCall, B. 2018. *Coal Transitions in South Africa. Understanding the Implications of a 2oC-Compatible Coal Phase-out Plan for South Africa*. Cape Town: Energy Research Centre (ERC), University of Cape Town. www.iddri.org/sites/default/files/PDF/Publications/Catalogue%20Iddri/Rapport/20180609_ReportCoal_SouthAfrica.pdf (last accessed 20 April 2021).

Burton, M., Marquard, A. and McCall, B. 2019. *Socio-economic Considerations for a Paris Agreement-Compatible Coal Transition in South Africa*. Cape Town: Energy Research Centre (ERC), University of Cape Town.

Burton, J. and Winkler, H. 2014. *South Africa's Planned Coal Infrastructure Expansion: Drivers, Dynamics and Impacts on Greenhouse Gas Emissions*. Cape Town: Energy Research Centre (ERC), University of Cape Town.

Cornelissen, H., Watson, I., Adam, E. and Malefetsea, T. 2019. Challenges and strategies of abandoned mine rehabilitation in South Africa: The case of asbestos mine rehabilitation. *Journal of Geochemical Exploration*, 205, 105354.

Department of Energy, 2015. *Strategic Plan 2015–2020*. Pretoria: Department of Energy.

Fei, T. 2018. *Coal Transition in China: Options to Move from Coal Cap to Managed Decline under an Early Emissions Peaking Scenario*. IDDRI and Climate Strategies.

Global Insight. 2019. ReX-explorer database. Pretoria: Global Insight.

Marais, L. and De Lange, A. 2021. Anticipating and planning for mine closure in South Africa. *Futures*, 125, 102669.

Matebesi, S. 2020. *Social Licensing and Mining in South Afric*a. London: Routledge.

McCall, B., Burton, J., Marquard, A., Hartley, F., Ahjum, F., Ireland, G. and Merven, B. 2019. *Least-cost Integrated Resource Planning and Cost-optimal Climate Change Mitigation Policy: Alternatives for the South African Electricity System*. Cape Town: Energy Research Centre, University of Cape Town.

MMSD (Mining, Minerals and Sustainable Development). 2002. *Breaking New Ground: Mining, Minerals and Sustainable Development*. London: Earthscan.

Morrison-Saunders, A., McHenry, M. P., Sequeira, A., Gorey, P., Mtegha, H. and Doepel D. 2016. Integrating mine closure planning with environmental impact assessment: Challenges and opportunities drawn from African and Australian practice. *Impact Assessment and Project Appraisal*, 34(2), 117–28.

Nkosi, M. 2017. *Black Workers, White Supervisors: The Emergence of the Labor Structure in South Africa*. Trenton: Africa World Press.

Obeng-Odoom, F. 2020b. *Property, Institutions and Social Stratification in Africa*. Cambridge: Cambridge University Press.

Obeng-Odoom, F. 2020a. *The Commons in the Age of Uncertainty: Decolonising Nature, Economy and Society*. Toronto: University of Toronto Press.

Owen, J. and Kemp, D. 2018. *Mine Closure and Social Performance: An Industry Discussion Paper*. Brisbane: Centre for Social Responsibility in Mining, Sustainable Minerals Institute, University of Queensland.

Pallagst, K., Wiechmann, T. and Martinez-Fernandez, C. 2014. *Shrinking Cities: International Perspectives and Policy Implications*. New York: Routledge.

Sartor, O. 2018. *Implementing Coal Transitions: Insights from Case Studies of Major Coal-consuming Economies*. IDDRI and Climate Strategies.

Sesele, K. 2020. Women and mine decline in the Free State Goldfields. Unpublished PhD thesis, University of the Free State.

Sesele, K., Marais, L., Van Rooyen, D. AND Cloete, J. 2021. Mine decline and women: Reflections from the Free State Goldfields. *The Extractive Industries and Society*. doi: 10.1016/j.exis.2020.11.006.

Simelane, T. and Abdel-Rahman, M. (eds) 2011. *Energy Transition in Africa*. Pretoria: HSRC Press.

Strambo, C., Burton, J. and Atteridge, A. 2019. *The End of Coal? Planning a Just Transition in South Africa*. Stockholm: Stockholm Environment Institute.

Vivoda, V., Kemp, D. and Owen, J., 2019. Regulating the social aspects of mine closure in three Australian states. *Journal of Energy and Natural Resources Law*, 37(4), 405–24.

World Bank. 2002. *It's Not Over When It's Over: Mine Closure around the World*. Washington, DC: World Bank Group Mining Department.

CHAPTER 4

Household Welfare in Emalahleni

Jean-Pierre Geldenhuys and Philippe Burger

Introduction

South Africa is one of the world's most unequal societies. The unemployment rate has exceeded 20% since truly nationally representative household surveys were first conducted in 1995. South African mineworkers, however, are comparatively well off. Although they are exposed to danger and often live far from their kin or in squalor in townships near the mines – a legacy of the colonial and apartheid migrant labour system – they are relatively well paid and well organised. (For recent discussion of the issues, see Bond and Mottiar, 2013; Baker, 2015; Forrest, 2015; Makgetla and Levin, 2016; Rajak, 2016.)

Abundant coal has made it possible for South Africa to generate electricity cheaply, and made the coal mining industry the mainstay of what is known as the minerals-energy complex (Fine and Rustomjee, 1996). The country's economic development required a steady supply of labour for the coal mines. However, recurring financial and operational woes at the country's state-owned electricity utility, Eskom, the falling costs of generating electricity from renewable sources, and the global push to reduce carbon emissions, are threatening the coal miners' relatively privileged position in the South African labour market.

In this chapter we compare household welfare in Emalahleni (in terms of income, spending, asset ownership and poverty levels) across mineworker households, non-mineworker households and non-employed households, and across two types of mineworker household: mine-employed and contractor-employed. We argue that mining has generated new forms of inequality and social stratification. These aspects are visible when comparing mineworkers with non-mineworkers and between households with full-time mine employees and households with contract workers. For example, mineworker households are much better off than other households in our sample of Emalahleni households: they have higher per capita levels of income, they spend more on food and are more likely to own television sets, personal computers, microwave ovens and motor cars, and their homes are more likely to have electricity, on-site piped water and flush toilets. They are also substantially less likely to be poor, and their subjective income rankings are much higher than those of other households. Of the two types of mineworker household, those employed directly by the mine are much better off than those sub-contracted to the mine. And, as expected, all types of household are better off than the non-employed households. Finally, we consider what we can learn from this analysis considering possible decline and closure. Decline and closure are likely to reinforce some historical inequalities and social stratification. Our findings also largely confirm similar work at a national scale in South Africa (Posel, Casale and Grapsa, 2020). Moreover, our finding emphasises the question asked by Brueckner et al. (2014), whether mining is a curse or cure to mining communities.

We use the following terms in this chapter. 'Mineworkers' means any people working at a mine, such as engineers, blasters, drillers, human resource officers, security guards and cleaners. A 'mineworker household' or 'mining household' is a household in which at least one member is a mineworker. A 'non-mineworker household' or 'non-mining household' is one that has at least one employed member, but no mineworkers. A 'non-employed household' is one where no member of the household is employed.[1] We distinguish two types of 'mineworker household' or 'mining household' as follows. A 'mine-employed household' or 'ME' is one where at least one member is a mineworker directly employed by a mine (these households can include contractor-employed members). A 'contractor-employed household' or 'CE' is one where at least one member is employed by a labour broker or contractor to work on a mine and no member is employed directly by a mine. Note that our classification of households is not related to the employment status of the household head.

Literature review

We review two topics covered by some studies of the economic effects of coal mining: the wage penalty suffered by workers employed by contractors and labour brokers, and the welfare of mineworker households compared with non-mineworker households.

Wage penalties faced by workers employed by contractors and labour brokers

The Marikana massacre of 16 August 2012 and the platinum miners' strike of 2014 brought into sharp relief the effect of labour brokers and outsourcing on South African mines in particular and the South African labour market in general. Since then, organised labour has made a sustained effort to outlaw labour-broking in South Africa, in response to workers' grievances about poor earnings and employment conditions. International and local studies find evidence that sub-contracted and temporarily employed service workers face an earnings penalty. Such penalties have been found in the United States (Houseman, 2001), the United Kingdom (Brown and Sessions, 2005), Germany (Pfeifer, 2012) and India (Saha, Sen and Maiti, 2013), and Makgetla and Levin (2016), Cassim and Casale (2018) and Burger and Geldenhuys (2018) find similar evidence in South Africa.

Makgetla and Levin (2016) found that mineworkers they interviewed in the North-West platinum belt believe that sub-contracted mineworkers (those employed by contractors and labour brokers) earn less and are treated less fairly than mineworkers employed directly by the mines. Makgetla and Levin also report that the cost of employing sub-contracted mineworkers is about 60% less than the cost of employing mineworkers directly (and they note also that the sub-contracted workers' take-home pay is substantially less than what the contractors and labour brokers charge the mines). Cassim and Casale (2018), using South African income tax data from the South African Revenue Service, show that labour broker employees' earnings are almost 50% lower than those of non-labour broker employees. This earnings penalty is reduced by about a third after controlling for individual-level fixed effects,[2] but the remainder is still higher in South Africa than in other countries. Most of this penalty is the result of lower benefit contributions made by labour brokers and contractors. Burger and Geldenhuys (2018), using data from a household questionnaire, found that mineworkers employed by the iron ore mines in Postmasburg earned substantially more and enjoyed many more benefits and protections (such as pensions, medical aid, unemployment insurance, bonuses and paid annual leave) than mineworkers sub-contracted to those mines.

If contractor-employed mineworkers face substantial earnings penalties, then we expect to find that household welfare levels are lower in mineworker households whose members are contract workers rather than mine-employed. The notion of contract workers is likely to reinforce social stratification (Obeng-Odoom, 2020). It is also essential to consider the historical reality of the mining industry's racial division of work (Nkosi, 2017). Contract work mostly reinforces this history.

Household welfare in South African mining towns

In emerging markets, and in South Africa in particular, relatively little is known about household welfare in mining communities (and in mineworker households in particular), as mineworkers are often underrepresented in national household surveys. The studies by Makgetla and Levin (2016) and Burger and Geldenhuys (2018) address this issue.

Makgetla and Levin (2016) found that housing, living conditions and government service delivery in the North-West platinum belt are poor. Despite high employment rates and (relatively) high cash incomes, many residents of the platinum belt were living in informal housing, without electricity, on-site piped water, flush toilets or refuse removal. Many respondents wondered who would want to live in conditions where there is no water or electricity and the sanitation is poor. Some Marikana widows, who were employed by the mines after their husbands were killed in 2012, said they could not bring their children to live with them in the squalor of the platinum belt.

Burger and Geldenhuys (2018) found that mineworker households in Postmasburg were much better off than non-mineworker households. They had higher levels of per capita spending, per capita income and per capita food spending, owned more types of assets and enjoyed more types of public services. Mine-worker households' subjective income rankings were higher than those of non-mineworker households, and those of mine-employed households were higher than those of contractor-employed households.

These two studies are particularly relevant to Emalahleni. At the time of writing, the city was in the middle of a coal-mining-led boom, with a high coal mining output and employment spilling over to other sectors of the city's economy. But a coal mining bust may be looming, for the reasons mentioned above.

Study methods

We used data on labour market outcomes, household income and spending, asset ownership and access to public services from the quantitative household survey of Emalahleni we conducted between October 2017 and January 2018 (see Chapter 1). Our cross-sectional survey gave us detailed information about the socio-economic circumstances of people living and working in Emalahleni. We cannot, of course, draw any causal inferences about the effects that mining, and coal mining in particular, have on household welfare in Emalahleni – to do that we would need longitudinal data on mining (including Emalahleni) and non-mining areas.

To compare the different types of household, we estimated the frequencies and proportions for categorical and binary variables (such as asset ownership and access to public services). For continuous variables (such as income and spending) we estimated means and medians,[3] as measures of central tendency, and standard deviations and interquartile ranges (IQR),[4] as the corresponding measures of variation. To limit the skewing effect that outliers (very small or very large values) can have on means and standard deviations (particularly of variables such as income and spending), we limited our analysis by excluding observations whose z-scores[5] were higher than three in absolute terms: the empirical rule states that 99.9% of the values of a normally distributed variable lie within three standard deviations of its mean. Observations with z-scores exceeding three therefore lie more than three standard deviations from the mean, and can be considered outliers (Anderson et al., 2017).

We also created two asset indices: a count asset index and a principal components asset index (along the lines of Burger and Geldenhuys, 2018). To construct these, we assigned each variable for ownership of a specific asset, or access to a particular service, a value of 1 if the household owned that asset, or had access to that service, and a value of 0 if not.[6] Asset indices are often used as proxies for household welfare in low- and middle-income countries where data on household income and spending are often unreliable or not collected (Booysen et al., 2008).

We constructed the count asset index simply by totalling the number of assets owned by households and the number of services that they have access to. Our count asset index, therefore, ranges from 0 (ownership of no assets and access to no services) to 11 (ownership of all of the assets and access to all of the services): higher values of the count index are therefore associated with higher levels of household welfare (see Harttgen, Klasen and Vollmer, 2013, for more details). We constructed the principal components analysis (PCA) asset index by obtaining first the z-score for each asset and service variable and then the correlation matrix, containing the pairwise correlation coefficients between the various asset and service variables. We used the PCA to extract a set of uncorrelated components from the correlation matrix, with each of these components consisting of linear, weighted components of the asset and service variables. We then obtained the inverses of these components, and used the first (principal) component as the asset index (as this component explains most of the covariation between the asset and service variables). Higher values of the asset index (which could be negative, because we standardised the asset and service variables) indicate higher household welfare levels. For more details (and a more technical discussion), see Vyas and Kumaranayake (2006) and Harttgen, Klasen and Vollmer (2013). The advantage of using the PCA index over the count index is that, while the count index assigns an equal (and unitary) weight to each asset and service included in the index, the PCA index estimates the weights that should be assigned to each asset or service to be added, based on how strongly that asset's ownership (or that service's access) is correlated with the ownership of or access to other assets and services in the index.

In our analysis of household welfare we also examined the extent and depth of household poverty across the different types of household. We did this by comparing the Foster-Greer-Thorbecke (FGT) poverty measures or indices (Foster, Greer and Thorbecke, 1984). We estimated the FGT measures using $P_\alpha = \frac{1}{N} \Sigma \left(\frac{G_i}{z}\right)^\alpha$, where $\alpha \geq 0$, and P_α is the poverty index of interest, with the three most commonly estimated and used indices being the poverty headcount, the poverty gap,[7] and the squared poverty gap: $\alpha = 0$, $\alpha = 1$ and $\alpha = 2$ respectively. N denotes the number of households, $G_i = z - y_i$ if $z > y_i$, $G = 0$ otherwise, z is an official or chosen poverty line, and y_i is an indicator of household welfare (such as household income and spending per capita). Larger values of P_α denote greater poverty. The poverty headcount (P0) indicates the percentage of households that are poor, the poverty gap (P1) indicates how much it would cost to lift households out of poverty, as a percentage of the poverty line, and the squared poverty gap (P2) indicates inequality among the poor (Haughton and Khandker, 2009).

To estimate the FGT poverty indices, we used two poverty lines – the upper-bound poverty line of R1,183[8] per month and the food poverty line of R531[9] per month, both in 2017 prices (Stats SA, 2018a); and three measures of household welfare – per capita household income, per capita household spending and per capita household food spending.

Results

In this section we discuss household welfare levels in our sample of Emalahleni households. Specifically, we compare household incomes, spending, asset ownership, poverty and subjective relative income rankings for our five types of household. Mineworker households (and particularly mine-employed households) have the highest levels of household income, household spending, asset ownership and access to public services, and non-employed households the lowest.

Table 4.1 presents demographic information about the five types of household in Emalahleni. We compare household size, household composition, and characteristics of the household head between mineworker, non-mineworker and non-employed households. We also compare these outcomes between ME and CE mineworker households.

Mean household size is just over two members per household, across all types of household (with the exception of CE households, which have fewer than two members per household on average). The household dependency ratio also does not differ markedly across the five household types, indicating that their household composition does not differ much. Non-employed households have the highest dependency ratio, while the dependency ratio for CE households is 50% lower than for ME households. There are marked differences in the proportion of single-person households across the five types: almost half of the mineworker households are in this category but just over a third of the non-employed households. CE households are 50% more likely to be single-person households than ME households.

In the 2016 Community Survey conducted by Statistics South Africa, the average household size in Emalahleni was three persons and the proportion of single-person households was 30%. The large differences between the household sizes and proportion of single-person households in our sample and those reported in the 2016 Community Survey could be due to differences in sampling approach: our sample included a large proportion of formal backyard dwellings, occupied by single persons in areas of Emalahleni where mineworkers are believed to live.[10] Furthermore, our fieldworkers also strictly administered separate household questionnaires to people if they indicated that they belonged to different households, even if they were living on the same stand (also known as 'erf' in South African law) as other people, and if they sometimes shared resources with them. Our definition of a household therefore differs from Statistics South Africa's definition, and could mean we found systematically more households, smaller households, and more single-person households in the same area. Our fieldworkers did not prompt respondents to indicate which household they belonged to, so as not to impose on respondents a preconceived definition of who or what constitutes a household. In addition, our fieldworkers did not go into informal settlements they considered to be dangerous. Because our sample may thus not be representative of all types of household in Emalahleni, care should be taken not to generalise our results.

Table 4.1 Household size, composition and characteristics of head, by type of household

Household characteristics	Full sample (n = 902)	Non-employed (n = 119)	Non-mineworker (n = 238)	Mineworker (n = 545)	CE (n = 211)	ME (n = 330)
Household size	n = 902	n = 119	n = 238	n = 545	n = 211	n = 330
Mean (SD)	2.25 (1.52)	2.21 (1.20)	2.45 (1.69)	2.17 (1.51)	1.79 (1.26)	2.39 (1.56)
Median (IQR)	2 (1)	2 (2)	2 (2)	2 (2)	1 (1)	2 (2)
Household dependency ratio	n = 887	n = 119	n = 235	n = 533	n = 207	n = 322
Mean (SD)	10.63 (20.20)	13.49 (27.15)	10.54 (19.45)	10.03 (18.64)	6.25 (14.77)	12.33 (20.35)
Median (IQR)	0 (17)	0 (0)	0 (20)	0 (17)	0 (0)	0 (25)
Single person household (freq (%))	405 (45%)	43 (36%)	95 (40%)	267 (49%)	130 (62%)	137 (42%)
Household head characteristics						
Male	636 (71%)	46 (39%)	151 (63%)	439 (81%)	177 (84%)	259 (78%)
Race: African	873 (97%)	114 (96%)	225 (95%)	534 (98%)	208 (99%)	322 (98%)
Race: Coloured	15 (2%)	3 (3%)	7 (3%)	5 (1%)	3 (1%)	2 (1%)
Language: Zulu	500 (55%)	62 (52%)	130 (55%)	308 (57%)	114 (54%)	193 (58%)
Language: Sotho	54 (6%)	9 (8%)	14 (6%)	31 (6%)	11 (5%)	20 (6%)
Age	n = 902	n = 119	n = 238	n = 545	n = 211	n = 330
Mean (SD)	38.52 (12.01)	45.92 (15.32)	40.21 (12.53)	36.17 (10.03)	34.50 (9.64)	37.16 (10.15)
Median (IQR)	35 (16)	44 (24)	38 (19)	33 (13)	32 (11)	34 (13)
Lived in town in 2007	634 (70%)	97 (82%)	163 (69%)	374 (69%)	131 (62%)	240 (73%)
Education	n = 854	n = 105	n = 222	n = 527	n = 206	n = 317
Mean (SD)	11.29 (2.67)	8.63 (4.18)	10.99 (2.76)	11.95 (1.73)	11.97 (1.68)	11.96 (1.72)
Median (IQR)	12 (2)	10 (6)	12 (2)	12 (1)	12 (1)	12 (1)
Employed (freq (%))	730 (81%)	NA	199 (84%)	531 (97%)	208 (99%)	320 (97%)

Notes: freq = frequency; SD = standard deviation; IQR = interquartile range, NA = not applicable. Dependency ratio = number of dependants (age < 15 or > 65) to number of working-age adults.

As Table 4.1 shows, mineworker households have fewer members (and are more likely to be single-person households) than non-mineworker households; in turn, CE households have fewer members (and are more likely to be single-person households) than ME households. One reason for this may be that mineworkers are more likely to be migrants than non-mineworkers, and CE mineworkers are more likely to be migrants than ME mineworkers. Mineworkers are less likely to report being born in the province of Mpumalanga and less likely to report having lived in Emalahleni in 2007 than non-mineworkers; CE mineworkers, in turn, are less likely to report being born in Mpumalanga and are less likely to report having lived in Emalahleni in 2007 than ME mineworkers.

The age, sex and other characteristics of the household head can have an effect on household welfare. About 60% of non-employed households are headed by a woman,[11] while 80% of mineworker households are headed by a man; CE households are slightly more likely to be headed by a man than ME households. Across all types of household, more than half of all household heads are Zulu first language speakers. Heads of mineworker households are about 10 years younger, on average, than the heads of non-employed households; CE household heads are on average slightly younger than ME household heads. More than 80% of non-employed households' heads and just under 70% of employed and mineworker household heads had lived in Emalahleni in 2007. CE household heads are about 10 percentage points less likely to have lived in Emalahleni in 2007 than ME household heads. In mineworker households, almost all heads are employed, while about 17 out of 20 heads of non-mineworker households are employed.

Table 4.2 compares household welfare levels, in terms of household income and spending, asset ownership and access to public services, across the five types of household. Surprisingly, non-response rates were higher for household spending than for household income across all five. Household spending and income per capita in non-employed households are about a third to half those of non-mineworker households, while per capita household spending and income in non-mineworker households are about two fifths those of mineworker households. Per capita food spending is also highest in mineworker households, followed by non-mineworker and non-employed households. The share of food spending in total spending is more than 40% in non-employed households, in contrast with just over 18% in mineworker households. Mineworker households have much higher asset indices (for both the PCA and count asset indices) than non-mineworker and non-employed households; non-mineworker households have higher asset indices than non-employed households, but the differences between the mean asset indices are not as stark as the spending and income differences between those two types of household.

Figure 4.1 shows that the difference between ME and CE households' means for household per capita spending and income is not statistically significant, but in the case of non-employed and non-mineworker households, non-employed

Table 4.2 Household welfare, by type of household

	Non-employed		Non-mineworker		Mineworker		CE		ME	
	n	mean (SD)	n	mean (SD)	n	mean (SD)	n	mean (SD)	n	mean (SD)
Income per capita	104	1601.7 (2094.3)	194	4687.0 (5088.7)	442	11722.9 (8438.7)	170	10957.1 (6806.8)	269	12281.6 (9310.7)
Median (IQR)		1000 (1125)		3000 (4750)		10000 (12000)		10000 (9750)		10000 (13000)
Spending per capita	92	1662.7 (1984.6)	168	3572.3 (3338.0)	333	8653.5 (5706.5)	145	8463.2 (5276.1)	187	8834.8 (6024.8)
Median (IQR)		1000 (1125)		2500 (4000)		7500 (8500)		7500 (7200)		7600 (10000)
Food spend per capita	108	578.6 (457.9)	233	896.6805 (587.1)	535	1236.8 (581.9)	213	1132.2 (517.8)	319	1309.9 (612.3)
Median (IQR)		500 (333.3)		800 (583.3)		1000 (667.7)		1000 (700)		1166.7 (291.7)
Food share (%)	76	40.54791 (15.4)	153	31.22952 (17.3)	314	18.31183 (10.8)	137	17.6 (11.0)	176	18.7 (10.4)
Median (IQR)		40 (20)		28.57143 (25.7)		15.83333 (14)		15 (13.1)		16.8 (13.1)
Asset index: PCA	119	-1.56	246	-1.16	558	0.86 (1.39)	217	0.41 (1.76)	337	1.14 (0.99)
Median (IQR)		0.32 (6.25)		0.98 (6.59)		1.33 (0.94)		0.98 (1.04)		1.36 (0.73)
Asset index: Count	119	6.25 (3.65)	246	6.91 (3.80)	558	9.44 (1.87)	217	8.73 (2.25)	337	9.90 (1.42)
Median (IQR)		8 (7)		9 (8)		10 (2)		9 (2)		10 (2)
Uses electricity (cook, light, or heat)	120	79 (66%)	248	167 (67%)	561	528 (94%)	218	194 (89%)	339	330 (97%)
Flush toilet in yard	120	73 (61%)	248	153 (62%)	560	515 (92%)	217	186 (86%)	339	325 (96%)
Piped water on site	120	83 (69%)	248	176 (71%)	561	525 (94%)	218	194 (89%)	339	327 (96%)
Dwelling is formal	120	85 (71%)	248	173 (70%)	560	535 (96%)	218	206 (95%)	338	325 (96%)
Owns TV	120	73 (61%)	248	172 (69%)	561	529 (94%)	218	193 (89%)	339	332 (98%)
Owns computer	119	19 (16%)	246	70 (28%)	561	257 (46%)	218	74 (34%)	339	183 (54%)
Owns mobile phone	120	115 (96%)	248	242 (98%)	561	558 (99%)	218	218 (100%)	339	336 (99%)
Owns car	120	11 (9%)	248	67 (27%)	561	323 (58%)	218	83 (38%)	339	239 (71%)
Owns oven	120	76 (63%)	248	181 (73%)	561	533 (95%)	218	202 (93%)	339	327 (96%)
Owns microwave	120	56 (47%)	248	141 (57%)	561	457 (81%)	218	150 (69%)	339	304 (90%)
Owns fridge	120	75 (63%)	248	167 (67%)	561	533 (95%)	218	203 (93%)	339	326 (96%)

Notes: freq = frequency; SD = standard deviation; IQR = interquartile range; PCA = principal component analysis. Because there were outliers, we trimmed the data (at z-scores exceeding 3 in absolute value – see text) for income per capita, spending per capita and food spending per capita. We obtained the food share in total spending by dividing reported food spending by reported overall household spending (while imposing an upper limit of 1, i.e. 100%, on the ratio).

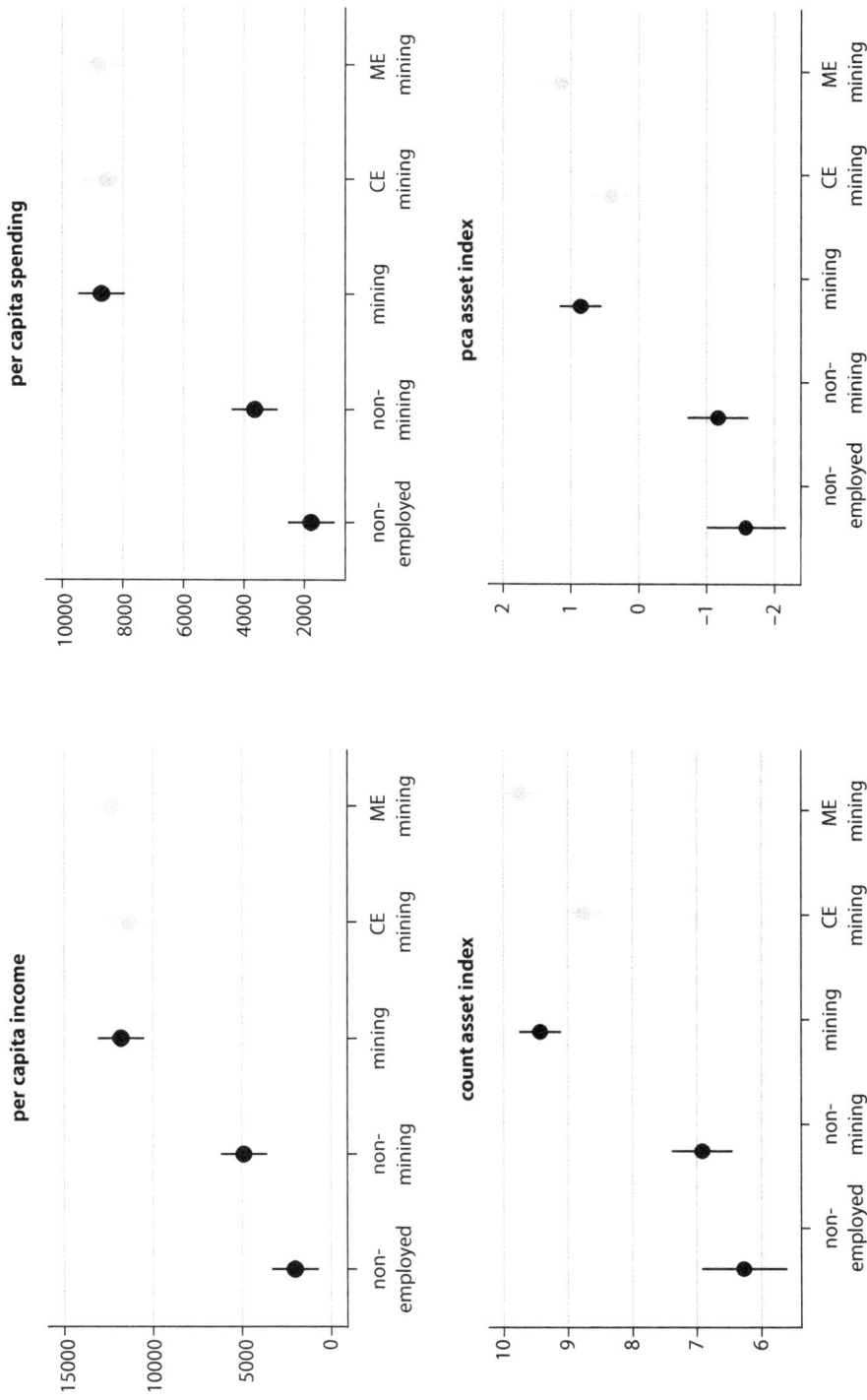

per capita income

per capita spending

count asset index

pca asset index

Figure 4.1 95% confidence intervals for means of per capita household income, per capita household spending, count asset index and PCA asset index, by type of household.

and mineworker households, and non-mineworker and mineworker households the differences are statistically significant. The figure also shows that the difference between the non-employed and non-mineworker households' means for the count and PCA asset indices is not statistically significant, but in the case of mineworker and non-employed households, mineworker and non-mineworker households, and CE and ME households the differences are statistically significant.

Ownership of assets and access to public services are useful indicators of welfare levels. Mineworker households have higher ownership and access to services than the other two types of household. The differences are much smaller between non-mineworker households and non-employed households. Non-mineworker households are better off across all types of assets and services than non-employed households, with the exception of living in a formal dwelling: the latter are slightly more likely to live in a formal dwelling.

While majorities (above 60%) of all five types of household report owning almost all of the assets, and having access to all the services listed in Table 4.2, it seems that ownership of personal computers (PCs), cars and microwave ovens differs sharply between the five types: 16%, 28% and 46% of non-employed, non-mineworker and mineworker households, respectively, own a PC, while the corresponding car ownership rates are 9%, 27% and 58%. More than 80% of mineworker households own a microwave oven, which is more than 25 and 33 percentage points higher than non-mineworker and non-employed households, respectively. Ownership of these assets also differed sharply between ME and CE households, with the former being 20, 21 and 30 percentage points more likely to own a PC, a microwave oven and a car, respectively, than the latter.

As Table 4.2 shows, differences in per capita household income, spending and food spending are not markedly different between ME and CE households, though ME mineworker households have higher levels of per capita income and spending on average. ME mineworker households have higher count and PCA asset index values than CE households, while ME mineworker households are more likely to have access to each type of service, and are more likely to own each asset listed in Table 4.2, with the exception of mobile phones, than CE households (but mobile phone ownership is practically ubiquitous across all five types of household).

Table 4.3 reports the poverty headcount, poverty gap and squared poverty gap, estimated using the FGT poverty measures, using two poverty lines (the upper-bound poverty line of R1,183 per month and the food poverty line of R531 per month) and three measures of household welfare (per capita income, per capita spending and per capita food spending).

As expected, given the results for household income, household spending and household asset ownership presented in Table 4.2, the prevalence (headcount, P0) and depth (poverty gap, P1) of poverty are substantially lower in mineworker than non-mineworker and non-employed households, and much lower in

Table 4.3 FGT poverty indices for household income and spending, by type of household

	Non-employed	Non-mineworker	Mineworker	CE	ME
HH income					
P(0)	0.558	0.196	0.066	0.075	0.058
P(1)	0.302	0.110	0.067	0.073	0.057
P(2)	0.219	0.083	0.065	0.072	0.057
HH spending					
P(0)	0.544	0.280	0.078	0.069	0.077
P(1)	0.268	0.130	0.066	0.061	0.065
P(2)	0.185	0.090	0.063	0.060	0.062
HH food spending					
P(0)	0.667	0.377	0.040	0.063	0.022
P(1)	0.260	0.135	0.013	0.019	0.009
P(2)	0.152	0.071	0.008	0.012	0.004

Notes: P(0) = poverty headcount; P(1) = poverty gap; P(2) = squared poverty gap; HH = household. SA line = South African (national, upper-bound) poverty line; national line = R1,183 (2017, Stats SA, 2018a) and R531 for HH food spending.

non-mineworker than non-employed households. Irrespective of the measure of household welfare that we used, less than 8% of mineworker households are poor, while between 20 and 38% of non-mineworker households and between 55 and 67% of non-employed households are poor. The poverty gaps and squared poverty gaps are also the highest for non-employed households, followed by non-mineworker households, indicating that poor non-employed households lie furthest from the poverty line, and that inequality among poor non-employed households is the greatest. With the exception of household spending, ME households are slightly less likely to be poor than CE households, while poor ME mineworker households lie slightly closer to the poverty line (i.e. P1, the poverty gap, is lower for these households), and exhibit less inequality (i.e. P2, the squared poverty gap, is lower for these households), than poor CE households.

To conclude our analysis of household welfare in Emalahleni, we also analysed the subjective income rankings of households in Emalahleni (Table 4.4). Household respondents ranked their household's income level, today, 5 years ago and 10 years ago, relative to that of other South African households, on a six-step ladder (step 1 being the lowest rung, step 6 the highest) representing the South African income distribution.

Table 4.4 Subjective income rankings of households, relative to SA households, today, 5 years ago and 10 years ago

	Non-employed	Non-mineworker	Mineworker	CE	ME
Rung of ladder today					
Mean (SD)	2.33 (1.05)	2.93 (1.14)	3.64 (0.86)	3.42 (0.75)	3.79 (0.89)
Median (IQR)	2 (1)	3 (2)	4 (1)	3 (1)	4 (1)
Rung of ladder 5 years ago					
Mean (SD)	2.53 (1.10)	2.74 (1.01)	3.26 (0.78)	3.07 (0.72)	3.39 (0.78)
Median (IQR)	2 (1)	3 (1)	3 (1)	3 (1)	3 (1)
Rung of ladder 10 years ago					
Mean (SD)	2.42 (1.03)	2.47 (1.06)	2.74 (0.90)	2.54 (0.81)	2.87 (0.93)
Median (IQR)	2 (1)	2 (1)	3 (1)	3 (1)	3 (1)

Notes: step 1 = lowest rung of ladder; step 6 = highest rung of ladder; SD = standard deviation; IQR = interquartile range.

The results of this exercise confirmed the picture of household welfare and poverty presented in Tables 4.2 and 4.3 above. Mineworker households placed their current household incomes about 0.7 rungs (on average) higher on the income ladder than non-mineworker households, while non-mineworker households placed theirs about 0.6 rungs higher (on average) than non-employed households. Mineworker households also placed their household incomes 5 and 10 years ago on a higher rung of the income ladder than non-mineworker households, who, in turn, placed theirs higher than non-employed households. Both mineworker and non-mineworker households believed that their household incomes were improving (relative to those of other South African households) over time: both types of household placed their recent incomes higher on the ladder than their previous incomes. However, non-employed households seemed to believe that their household incomes had moved down the ladder over the past 5 years. ME households placed their current and past income levels (slightly) higher on the ladder than CE households, while respondents in both types of mineworker household placed their recent incomes higher than their previous incomes, indicating that these households believed they were moving up the ladder over time.

Figure 4.2 shows statistically significant differences in the mean subjective income rankings between all pairs of households for current income, while the only statistically insignificant difference for the mean rankings of incomes from 5 years ago is between non-employed and non-mineworker households. For incomes from 10 years ago, we find statistically significant differences in the mean rankings between CE and ME households, as well as between mineworker and non-mineworker households, and mineworker and non-employed households. The figure

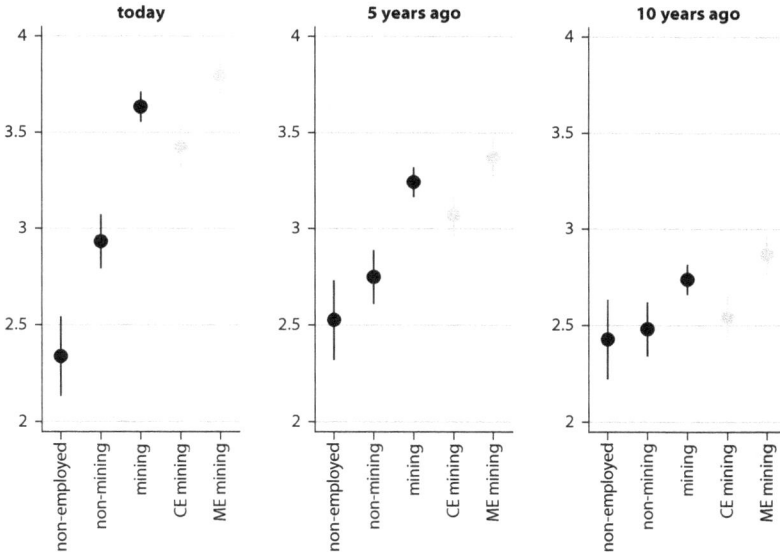

Figure 4.2 95% confidence intervals for the mean rung (on a six rung ladder) on which respondents rank their households' income today, 5 years ago and 10 years ago, by type of household.

also shows that mineworker households (and both CE and ME households) believe that their relative positions on the ladder are improving over time.

Finally, we also asked household respondents to rank their current household incomes relative to those of other households in their neighbourhood, suburb or village. The percentage of households who believed their household incomes were at least equal to the average in their area were as follows: mineworker households 86%, non-mineworker households 45%, non-employed households 17%, ME households 92% and CE households 79%. Households' subjective income rankings therefore show some agreement with their reported incomes: ME households are most likely to report income levels that lie above the sample mean and also most likely to rank their incomes as above average. Non-employed households are least likely to report incomes above the mean and also least likely to rank their incomes as above average.

Conclusion

In this chapter, we used data from our 2017–18 household survey to describe household welfare levels in Emalahleni. We distinguished between five types of household, on the basis of the members' employment status: mineworker households, non-mineworker households and non-employed households, and mineworker households were further divided into mine-employed mineworker households and contractor-employed mineworker households.

Our findings largely agree with those obtained by Burger and Geldenhuys (2018) in a similar study of households in Postmasburg, an iron-ore mining town. However, we note again that, like the Postmasburg study, our study of Emalahleni is a cross-sectional local case study which should not be used to draw causal inferences about the effects of the mining industry on labour market outcomes and household welfare.

We found that mineworker households had higher levels of per capita household income, household spending and household food spending than non-mineworker households, which, in turn, had higher levels of per capita household income, spending and food spending than non-employed households. Mineworker households were also more likely than non-mineworker households (which, in turn, were more likely than non-employed households) to own assets like televisions, cars, personal computers and microwave ovens, and to have access to public services like electricity, on-site piped water and flush toilets. They were much less likely than non-mineworker and non-employed households to be poor, and they ranked their households' relative income level higher than those households did. Likewise, we found that mine-employed mineworker households had higher household welfare levels than contractor-employed mineworker households. There are indications of social stratification because of mining. For example, our sample showed that most contract workers are black. The inequalities are therefore, not only racial but also between black mineworkers and contract workers.

Therefore, we conclude that although their working and living conditions are often far from ideal, mineworker households in Emalahleni, particularly those whose members are employed directly by the mines rather than contracted to work for them, are better off than other households in Emalahleni. Mine decline and closure are likely to reinforce inequalities and social stratification in Emalahleni.

References

Anderson, D., Sweeney, D., Williams, T., Freeman, J. and Shoesmith, E. 2017. *Statistics for Business and Economics*, 4th edn. Andover: Cengage Learning EMEA.

Baker, L. 2015. Renewable energy in South Africa's minerals-energy complex: A 'low carbon' transition? *Review of African Political Economy*, 42(144), 245–61.

Bond, P. and Mottiar, S. 2013. Movements, protest and massacre in South Africa. *Journal of Contemporary African Studies*, 31(2), 283–302.

Booysen, F., Van der Berg, S., Burger, R., Von Maltitz, M. and Du Rand, G. 2008. Using an asset index to assess trends in poverty in seven sub-Saharan African countries. *World Development*, 36(6), 1113–30.

Brown, S. and Sessions, J. G. 2005. Employee attitudes, earnings and fixed-term contracts: International evidence. *Review of World Economics*, 141(2), 296–317.

Brueckner, M., Durey, A., Mayes, R. and Pforr, C. 2014. *Resource Curse or Cure? On the Sustainability of Development in Western Austrlia*. Heidelberg: Springer.

Burger, P. and Geldenhuys, J. 2018. Work, wages and welfare in Postmasburg. In P. Burger, L. Marais and D. van Rooyen (eds), *Mining and Community in South Africa: From Small Town to Iron Town*. London: Routledge.

Cassim, A. and Casale, D. 2018. How large is the wage penalty in the labour broker sector? Evidence for South Africa using administrative data. WIDER Working Paper 2018/48. UNU-WIDER, Helsinki.

Fine, B. and Rustomjee, Z. 1996. *The Political Economy of South Africa: From Minerals-Energy Complex to Industrialisation.* Boulder, CO: Westview.

Forrest, K. 2015. Rustenburg's labour recruitment regime: Shifts and new meanings. *Review of African Political Economy*, 42(146), 508–25.

Foster, J., Greer, J. and Thorbecke, E. 1984. A class of decomposable poverty measures. *Econometrica*, 52(2), 761–6.

Harttgen, K., Klasen, S. and Vollmer, S. 2013. An African growth miracle? Or: what do asset indices tell us about trends in economic performance? *Review of Income and Wealth*, 59(S1), S37–S61.

Haughton, J. and Khandker, S. R. 2009. *Handbook on Poverty and Inequality*. Washington, DC: World Bank.

Houseman, S. N. 2001. The benefits implications of recent trends in flexible staffing arrangements. Upjohn Institute Working Paper 02-87. W. E. Upjohn Institute, Kalamazoo, MI.

Makgetla, N. and Levin, S. 2016. A perfect storm: Migrancy and mining in the North West Province. Working Paper TIPS (Trade and Industrial Policy Strategies), Pretoria. www. tips.org.za/research-archive/inequality-and-economic-inclusion/item/3099-a-perfect-storm-migrancy-and-mining-in-the-north-west-province (last accessed 21 April 2021).

Nkosi, M. 2017. *Black Workers, White Supervisors: The Emergence of the Labor Structure in South Africa.* Trenton: Africa World Press.

Obeng-Odoom, F. 2020. *Property, Institutions and Social Stratification in Africa*. Cambridge: Cambridge University Press.

Pfeifer, P. 2012. Fixed-term contracts and wages revisited using linked employer–employee data. Journal for Labour Market Research, 45(2), 171–83.

Posel, D., Casale, D. and Grapsa, E. 2020. Household variation and inequality: The implications of equivalence scales in South Africa. *African Review of Economics and Finance*, 12(1), 102–22.

Rajak, D. 2016. Hope and betrayal on the Platinum Belt: Responsibility, violence and corporate power in South Africa. Journal of Southern African Studies, 42(5), 929–46.

Rogan, M. 2014. Poverty may have declined, but women and female-headed households still suffer most. Econ3x3, May 2014. Available at www.econ3x3.org/article/poverty-may-have-declined-women-and-female-headed-households-still-suffer-most (last accessed 21 April 2021).

Saha, B., Sen, K. and Maiti, D. 2013. Trade openness, labour institutions and flexibilisation: Theory and evidence from India. Labour Economics, 24, 180–95.

Stats SA (Statistics South Africa). 2018a. National Poverty Lines 2018. Statistical Release P030.1. Pretoria: Statistics South Africa.

Stats SA (Statistics South Africa). 2018b. Provincial Profile: Mpumalanga. Report 03-01-13. Pretoria: Statistics South Africa.

Stats SA (Statistics South Africa). 2018c. Quarterly Labour Force Survey, Quarter 4: 2017. Statistical Release P0211. Pretoria: Statistics South Africa.

Vyas, S. and Kumaranayake, L. 2006. Constructing socio-economic status indices: How to use principal components analysis. *Health Policy and Planning*, 21(6), 459–68.

Notes

1. Non-employed households consist of people who are not economically active (unwilling or unable to work), or people who are unemployed (willing and able to work, but unable to find employment), or a combination of the two.
2. Individual-level fixed effects allow econometricians to control for unobserved time-invariant characteristics in panel data (see Cassim and Casale, 2018, for more details).
3. The median of a variable is the value that is larger than 50% of the values of that variable.
4. The interquartile range (IQR) of a variable measures the range (or spread) of the middle 50% of values of that variable (i.e. it is the difference between the values in the 75th and 25th percentiles).
5. An observation's z-score is given as $z = \frac{x_i - \bar{x}}{s_x}$, where x_i is the observed value of variable x, $\bar{x}$ is the sample mean of x, and s_x is the standard deviation of x.
6. The following variables were included in the construction of the asset indices: ownership of a television set, cell phone, personal computer, car, oven/stove, refrigerator, microwave oven, and access to piped water on site, a flush toilet in the yard, the use of electricity for either cooking, lighting or heating and whether the dwelling that the household resides in can be regarded as a formal dwelling.
7. It is known as the poverty gap because it measures the distance or gap between a poor household's income and the poverty line.
8. USD $89.08 (at the average exchange rate of 1 USD − 13.28 ZAR between October 2017 and January 2018).
9. USD 39.98.
10. Unfortunately, to the best of our knowledge, publicly available data from other household surveys conducted in Emalahleni at around the time of our survey, which could be used to benchmark our findings, are in short supply: publicly available data from Statistics South Africa for the fourth quarter of the 2017 Quarterly Labour Force Survey (Stats SA, 2018c) does not include an indicator that would allow us to identify non-metro municipalities like Emalahleni, which would then allow us to benchmark our reported household sizes and dependency ratios, and rates of unemployment and absorption (ratio of number of employed to working-age population). Data on many of the same variables that we collected in our household survey were collected by the Southern African Labour and Development Research Unit (SALDRU) at the University of Cape Town during 2017 as part of the fifth wave of the longitudinal National Income Dynamics Study (NIDS): publicly available data unfortunately allow us to identify only the district municipality in which a household in the NIDS sample lives. This is not ideal for benchmarking purposes: Emalahleni is one of six local municipalities that make up the Nkangala District Municipality. Lastly, the most recent national Census was conducted in 2011, which, as Emalahleni is a rapidly changing and fast-growing municipality, is probably too long ago to use for benchmarking. But in the 2016 Community Survey (Stats SA, 2018b), the mean household size in Emalahleni was found to be 3.0, and the proportion of single-person households was found to be 30% (noticeably higher and lower, respectively, than our results indicate).
11. As Table 4.2 shows, non-employed households have the lowest household welfare levels, and this corresponds well with the observation that female-headed households are more likely to have lower household welfare levels than male-headed households (see e.g. Rogan, 2014).

CHAPTER 5

Work and Life Satisfaction of Mining Employees

Petrus Nel and Tina Kotzè

Introduction

Many rural families move to a mining town in the hope of finding a job, or a better paying job, for at least one of the household's working adults. Working on a mine is financially advantageous, but it has its downsides, in the form of long working hours, pressure to meet production targets and often dangerous working conditions. Women may be affected too: a woman may leave her job to go with her husband to the mining town, be unable to find a new job, and end up relegated to the household chores (Sesele et al., 2021). Mining families need to be aware that the social and psychological implications of moving can outweigh the economic benefits. Life satisfaction, 'a global assessment of a person's quality of life according to his chosen criteria', or more simply 'satisfaction with life as a whole' (Diener et al., 1985), can be negatively affected by work–home conflict.

About half of South Africa's coal mining is underground and about half is open-cast. The latter is more mechanised, more capital intensive, and the workers are better paid than those who work underground. Most of the country's open-cast collieries are in Emalahleni. Concerns have been raised about the number of mine accidents and the long-term implications of coal mining for the health of mineworkers and their families (Munnik, 2010). Some mineworkers are migrant labourers, working on the mines far away from their families. Those whose families can live with them mostly live in informal settlements or improved compounds supplied by the mines (Cronje, 2014). The mines do not provide housing to workers employed by a contractor (Marais, 2018). There is also evidence that the historical racial division of work continues, with supervisors being white and the labourers being black (Nkosi, 2017). Furthermore, the quality of work (defined in the broadest possible terms) is central to addressing work inequalities and lower-paid individuals have lower levels of decent work (Mackett, 2020).

In this chapter we look at how supervisory support, work–home conflict and commitment to the company affect the life satisfaction of mineworkers in Emalahleni. We consider the effects of trade union membership and employment type (permanent staff or contract worker). We obtained our data from 393 responses to a questionnaire survey of mineworkers in the area. Formal mineworkers have better work conditions and life satisfaction than contract workers. This disparity suggests that mining employment could be viewed as both a curse and a cure to South Africa's employment and unemployment problem (Brueckner et al., 2014).

Work–home interference

Work and home are the two most important life roles for most employees. They must constantly juggle the demands of the two roles, which can be difficult when the demands of one make it difficult to satisfy the demands of the other. Work–home conflict can make it difficult for families to balance the responsibilities of the two domains, especially if employers do not try to minimise the negative effects of their business practices on their employees' home life.

Frone, Russell and Cooper (1992) suggest that to understand work–home conflict we need to look at spillover from one domain into the other and identify the predictors of the conflict. Work–home conflict is bi-directional. When work-related problems and responsibilities limit the employee's ability to deal successfully with family problems and responsibilities, the result is work-to-family conflict, and the reverse is family-to-work conflict. Frone et al.'s work–family interface model identifies predictors of work-to-family conflict such as job and family stressors and the degree of psychological involvement in the job or the family. Stress in one domain is likely to result in irritability and fatigue, making it difficult to cope with the demands of the other domain. An employee who is psychologically more involved in one domain than the other will devote more time to it, to the neglect of the other. Work-to-family conflict will damage the family's health and well-being; family-to-work conflict will mean job-related stress and burnout for the employee.

To balance their work and home responsibilities, employees need to move effortlessly between the two domains. If this is achieved, there are benefits not only for the employee and the family but also for the employer. Wayne et al. (2013) observe that employees who perceive their employers as family supportive are more likely to be happy in their work and committed to the company and less likely to be on the lookout for another job.

The work–home resources model

The work–home resources model proposed by ten Brummelhuis and Bakker (2012) supplements Frone et al.'s theory discussed above. It represents the interaction between demands (at work and home) and resources (at work and home) that will lead either to work–family conflict (where the demands outweigh the resources) or work–family enrichment (where the resources outweigh the demands). When employees and their family perceive that the demands from one of the domains constantly outweigh their ability (i.e. their resources) to deal with those demands successfully, work–family conflict is a likely outcome. The consequence is that employees and their families are likely to sacrifice the needs of the family to meet the demands of the employees' work. In essence, the demands of the working environment deplete the personal resources required to balance the demands of the two domains.

In this model, contextual demands consist of the physical, emotional and cognitive demands of both domains. For example, conflict as a result of overtime may put an emotional strain on a marriage or partnership. To cope with these demands, employees and their spouses or partners can access several contextual resources. Support from both the employee's manager and the employee's spouse or partner is a resource that is likely to lead to more positive perceptions of work–home enrichment. Instrumental resources (such as time and money) are also likely to enhance work–family enrichment. Autonomy (being able to decide when, where and how tasks at work and home are to be completed) can also lead to work–family enrichment. Some other personal resources that can help employees and their families manage work–family demands are intellectual resources, such as knowledge and skills that enable them to perform their work and home tasks efficiently, and emotional resources such as a positive attitude towards work and their spouse or partner.

Employees and families who successfully develop and use their contextual and personal resources to deal with demands are likely to experience three kinds of positive outcome both at work and home: production, behavioural and attitudinal outcomes. Employees with well-developed personal resources can generate good production outcomes at work while still being able to help with household chores and responsibilities when they are home. Some behavioural outcomes are lower levels of absenteeism and higher levels of safety at work and being available for important family events at home. Attitudinal outcomes at work are such things as a positive attitude towards the organisation, commitment to the organisation, and job satisfaction, and at home attitudinal outcomes are improved family satisfaction and family commitment.

Shift work and work–home interference (contextual demand)

Some work schedules, such as night shifts and rotating shifts, have a tendency to increase work–family conflict. In terms of the work–home resources model described above, we can treat irregular shift work as a contextual demand, since it places a physical demand on the employee to be at work during specific periods. Individuals working for a mine are likely to be absent from their families for long hours due to work-related responsibilities. Inconvenient working hours, such as weekend work and shifts, are likely to have a negative effect on work–family relationships, leading to conflict and reducing the well-being of the worker and the family. An irritable and often unavailable employee is not good for family relationships. Shift work may oblige the spouse or partner to take on the roles of both mother and father when raising a family, leading to role overload (Heiler, 2002). When mineworkers do have leisure time, many of them spend more time with their fellow mineworkers than with their families (Collis, 1999). The demands placed on mine employees make it challenging for them to integrate work and family responsibilities.

The financial benefits of mine work may be offset by the disruption that shift work causes to families. However, when flexible shift work schedules are allowed, the employee can be more 'in sync' with family life, leading to higher levels of family satisfaction and lower levels of work-to-family conflict. Wilson et al. (2007) found that family involvement, and family support such as rescheduling family activities to accommodate the shift worker, counterbalanced the negative influence of shift work and reduced work–family conflict.

Job security and work–home interference (contextual resource)
Job insecurity, which tends to result when a job is temporary or based on a fixed-term contract rather than permanent employment, increases the stress on both employees and their families and can cause problems at work and decrease life satisfaction.

Contracting companies are often smaller than mining companies and offer lower salaries and fewer training opportunities. Mineworkers who work for a contractor usually do so because they cannot find permanent employment at the mine or because they want only short-term employment. Contract workers usually provide support services to mines, such as transport, drilling and earth moving. Their working hours are different from those of permanent employees. The number of hours they work in a week can be classified as a work-related situational predictor of work-to-family conflict. The more time the employee spends at work, the less time is available to fulfil home-related responsibilities.

Family supportive supervisory behaviour (contextual resource)
The extent to which an organisation supports and values work–family integration reflects its work–home culture. A supervisor who allows employees to change or modify their work schedule to attend to family responsibilities is likely to be perceived as supportive, and employees may interpret this support as coming from the organisation and reflecting its views. When formal organisational policies and informal supervisory discretion allow modification of work schedules, this gives employees 'boundary flexibility', enabling them to move from one domain to another (work to family and vice versa) (Ferguson, Carlson and Kacmar, 2015). Boundary flexibility can be treated as a contextual resource in the work–home resources model. Supervisory instrumental support reflects how willing the employees perceive the organisation to be in helping them manage their work and home responsibilities, including dealing with scheduling conflicts. This kind of support can reduce both the role overload experienced by an employee and work–family conflict and improve family and life satisfaction. Employees who can negotiate their work schedules to deal with family responsibilities experience less work–home conflict.

Union membership (contextual resource)

Workers join unions to obtain benefits, such as medical aid and pension funds, better working conditions, job security and higher wages, that they cannot obtain individually. Iverson and Maguire (2000) found that involving unions during negotiations over such matters as remuneration and working conditions had a positive influence on life satisfaction. Unions represent the interests of mineworkers regarding changes to work practices that increase employees' levels of job satisfaction, ultimately leading to higher life satisfaction.

Organisational commitment (positive attitudinal outcome)

In the work–home resources model, organisational commitment is a positive attitudinal outcome associated with work–family enrichment. It can be argued that when an employee has access to contextual resources (such as a supportive supervisor who allows the employee time off to deal with family-related responsibilities), it becomes easier to manage the boundaries between work and family successfully, resulting in higher levels of organisational commitment. Ultimately, being committed to the organisation gives the employee continued access to such resources and support that will facilitate work–family enrichment. Kirchmeyer (1995) found that employees are more committed to organisations that are willing to accommodate their multiple roles associated with work and home domains.

Satisfaction with life (positive attitudinal outcome)

Work–family conflict has been found to be negatively related to life satisfaction. The development and implementation of contextual and personal resources leads to the various positive attitudinal outcomes associated with work–family enrichment. Satisfaction with life is one such positive attitudinal outcome.

This section was drawn largely from the following sources: Greenhaus and Beutell (1985), Ashford, Lee and Bobko (1989), Frone, Russell and Cooper (1992), Kirchmeyer (1995), Collis (1999), Iverson and Maguire (2000), Fenwick and Tausig (2001), Heiler (2002), Parker et al. (2002), Rhoades and Eisenberger (2002), Visser (2002), Beach, Brereton and Cliff (2003), Beauregard (2006), Wilson et al. (2007), Jacobs, Mostert and Pienaar (2008), Kaczmarek and Sibbel (2008), Hammer et al. (2009), Beutell (2010), Sharma (2010), McDonald, Mayes and Pini (2012), ten Brummelhuis and Bakker (2012), Carr and Chung (2014), Tummers and Bronkhorst (2014), Vojnovic et al. (2014), Ferguson, Carlson and Kacmar (2015), Misan and Rudnik (2015) and Robinson, Magee and Caputi (2016). The reader will find these sources useful for background to the chapter, for more detail and for research on problems experienced by mining families.

Survey methods

Sample
Fieldworkers collected usable data from 393 Emalahleni mineworkers, 60% mine employees and 40% contract workers. Sixty-four per cent were trade union members.

Measurement
We measured supervisory instrumental support using three items from Hammer et al. (2009); work–home conflict using five items from Netemeyer, Boles and McMurrian (1996); organisational commitment using three items of the organisational commitment scale from Meyer, Allen and Smith 1993); and satisfaction with life using the five items of the satisfaction with life scale from Diener et al. (1985).

Data analysis
We used Pearson's product moment correlation and stepwise multiple regression to determine the influence of supervisory instrumental support, work–home conflict and organisational commitment on satisfaction with life. We used the Mann–Whitney U test to explore possible differences between the above variables regarding union membership and type of employment (permanent employment on the mine or contract work). Reliability estimates of .7 and higher, as found in the present study, indicate good reliability (Field, 2005).

Results

Overall levels of supervisory instrumental support, work–home conflict, organisational commitment and life satisfaction
We found that our sample of mineworkers was fairly satisfied with their lives (see Table 5.1). They were very satisfied with the instrumental support they received from their supervisors and highly committed to their employers. They seemed to experience only minimal work–home conflict.

Table 5.1 Descriptive statistics (n = 393)						
Variable	Mean	Min. score	Max. score	Std. dev.	Reliability	No. of items
Supervisory instrumental support	5.159	1	7	1.220	.717	3
Work–home conflict	3.37	1	7	1.42	.892	5
Organisational commitment	5.50	1	7	1.06	.777	3
Satisfaction with life	4.42	1	7	1.26	.790	5

Correlations

Table 5.2 shows that in our sample of mineworkers all the independent variables (supervisory instrumental support, work–home conflict and organisational commitment) had significant correlations with satisfaction with life. Organisational commitment had the strongest positive correlation ($r = .408$) and work–home conflict had a significant negative correlation ($r = -.168$).

Stepwise multiple regression: Predictors of satisfaction with life

Table 5.3 shows that there were only two significant predictors of satisfaction with life in this sample of mineworkers: organisational commitment ($\beta = .430$, $p = .000$) and work–home conflict ($\beta = -.228$, $p = .000$). This regression model was statistically significant ($F = 54.362$, $p = .000$) and explained 22% of the variance in satisfaction with life. Organisational commitment contributed 17% and work–home conflict 5% of the variance in satisfaction with life.

Differences: Mine employee or contract worker

Table 5.4 shows that mine employees were significantly more satisfied with the supervisory instrumental support they received, more committed to the mine,

Table 5.2 Correlations

Variable	Satisfaction with life	p-value
Supervisory instrumental support	.130	.010
Work–home conflict	-.168	.001
Organisational commitment	.408	.000

Table 5.3 Significant predictors of satisfaction with life (stepwise multiple regression)

Variable	Standardised beta coefficients	t-value	p-value
Organisational commitment	.430	9.566	.000
Work–home conflict	-.228	-5.065	.000

Table 5.4 Differences: Mine employees and contract workers

Variable	Employment	Mean rank	Mann–Whitney U	p-value
Supervisory instrumental support	Mine	217.05	-4.692	.000
	Contract	164.35		
Work–home conflict	Mine	215.72	-3.626	.000
	Contract	174.05		
Organisational commitment	Mine	216.67	-4.058	.003
	Contract	170.93		
Satisfaction with life	Mine	214.46	-2.927	.000
	Contract	180.32		

Table 5.5 Differences: Trade union membership				
Variable	Union membership	Mean rank	Mann–Whitney U	p-value
Supervisory instrumental support	Yes	193.05	-1.290	.197
	No	208.14		
Work–home conflict	Yes	221.96	-4.612	.000
	No	166.87		
Organisational commitment	Yes	203.19	-.513	.608
	No	197.18		
Satisfaction with life	Yes	220.16	-3.693	.000
	No	175.41		

and more satisfied with their lives than contract workers. In contrast, they experienced significantly more work–home conflict than the contract workers. However, overall the level of work–home conflict was minimal.

Differences: Trade union membership

Table 5.5 shows that those who belonged to a union were significantly more satisfied with their lives than those who did not, but experienced significantly more work–home conflict than the non-members. Again, however, it seems that overall there was only minimal work–home conflict.

Discussion and recommendations

Overall, the mineworkers in our sample were fairly satisfied with their lives. They were of the opinion that they had most of the important things they wanted in life and that the conditions of their lives were acceptable. As part of the household survey, respondents were asked how happy they were with their living conditions. Most (59%) said they were happy. The role that supervisory support plays is important. The respondents were satisfied with the support they received from their supervisors in helping them if their work schedules clashed with home responsibilities and finding creative ways of resolving the conflict between work and family demands. Given that they receive such support from their supervisors, their levels of commitment to the company they worked for were fairly high. Being committed to their employer gives them access to resources (such as possible bonuses or promotion) that will probably increase their life satisfaction. In contrast, they did experience some degree of work–family conflict, but only a minimal amount. The amount of time they spent at work could make it difficult to fulfil home responsibilities. It is also possible that work demands may influence their home and personal lives. However, it is likely that the kind of support they received from their supervisors may have mitigated their overall experiences of work–family conflict. These results point to the social embeddedness of labour practice. The introductory chapter outlined the substantial change in labour practice since the early 1990s brought about by the focus on productivity by multinationals but also because labour unions have bought into these changes. The high levels of commitment to mine employers point to the social embeddedness of neoliberalism.

Although all the variables were significantly related to these employees' levels of life satisfaction, only two (organisational commitment and work–home conflict) predicted their satisfaction with life. The strongest predictor of life satisfaction was higher levels of organisational commitment. It is much easier for employees to be committed to an employer who helps them to manage the demands between work and family responsibilities successfully. Being committed to one's employer is likely to mean job security and thus increased satisfaction with life.

The second strongest predictor of life satisfaction for this sample was low levels of work–home conflict. Experiencing fewer job-related demands enables the mineworker to deal with home-related duties successfully and to spend quality time with family, ultimately leading to higher levels of life satisfaction. When the mineworker's job interferes unduly with home and personal life, lower levels of life satisfaction are to be expected.

In this sample of mineworkers, those belonging to a union were significantly more satisfied with their lives than the non-members. Unions represent the interests of mineworkers regarding changes to work practices that could affect their levels of job satisfaction. However, in exchange for improvements in work practices and remuneration, the mine is likely to expect employees to increase their levels of productivity. This may lead to more work-related demands that are likely to interfere with their ability to deal with home-related responsibilities. In short, it seems that union membership is a contextual resource that may have unintended consequences, leading to an increase in contextual demands (higher productivity and possible work–home conflict).

We found that those who were employed directly by the mines rather than doing contract work were significantly more satisfied with their lives, had higher levels of organisational commitment, and experienced more supervisory support to help them deal with work–home conflict. Our findings are important, considering the larger debates about decent work in South Africa (Mackett, 2020). However, they experienced more work–home conflict than those employed by a contractor. Contract work does not provide the same benefits and working conditions as those offered by the mines. Employment is temporary, the remuneration is often lower and the workers almost exclusively black.

On the basis of our survey findings we have some recommendations to make. The South African coal mining industry should provide the necessary support (for example, supervisors who understand the impact of work schedules on family-related responsibilities) that will increase employees' contextual resources and thus ultimately improve their levels of organisational commitment and life satisfaction. Formal changes to the work domain could include flexible working schedules and the provision of childcare facilities to lessen the mineworkers' family demands. In this way the coal mining industry will empower their employees to balance the demands of both the work and family domains. The families of mining employees can also be assisted to identify and use the resources at their disposal to cope with the employee's work demands. Spouses or partners who are willing to listen to mineworkers' job-related problems can provide emotional support that acts as a contextual resource. Research has found that such emotional support is more effective in alleviating work–family conflict than if the mineworker takes on additional family responsibilities (instrumental support). To counteract the negative influence of isolation, the spouse or partner of the mining employee can identify social events that offer support during difficult times. Increasing the degree of family cohesion (including dealing with unmet expectations and sharing family-related responsibilities) can be used as another resource by mining families to improve their overall well-being and life satisfaction. And if the spouse or partner can find meaningful employment, feelings of isolation and depression will be reduced and overall satisfaction with life will be increased.

More research needs to be done to investigate what mine work does to families, focusing on the individual and environmental factors that affect life satisfaction.

References

Ashford, S. J., Lee, C. and Bobko, P. 1989. Content, causes, and consequences of job insecurity: A theory-based measure and substantive test. *Academy of Management Journal*, 32, 803–29.

Beach, R., Brereton, D. and Cliff, D. 2003. Workforce turnover in FIFO mining operations in Australia: An exploratory study. Centre for Social Responsibility in Mining, Sustainable Minerals Institute, University of Queensland, Brisbane.

Beauregard, T. A. 2006. Predicting interference between work and home: A comparison of dispositional and situational antecedents. *Journal of Managerial Psychology*, 21, 244–64.

Beutell, N. J. 2010. Work schedule, work schedule control and satisfaction in relation to work–family conflict, work–family synergy, and domain satisfaction. *Career Development International*, 15, 501–18.

Brueckner, M., Durey, A., Mayes, R. and Pforr, C. 2014. *Resource Curse or Cure? On the Sustainability of Development in Western Austrlia*. Heidelberg: Springer.

Carr, E. and Chung, H. 2014. Employment insecurity and life satisfaction: The moderating influence of labour market policies across Europe. *Journal of European Social Policy*, 24, 383–99.

Collis, M. 1999. Marital conflict and men's leisure: How women negotiate male power in a small mining community. *Journal of Sociology*, 35, 60–72.

Cronje, F. 2014. *Digging for Development: The Mining Industry in South Africa and Its Role in Socioeconomic Development*. Johannesburg: South African Institute for Race Relations.

Diener, E. M., Emmons, R. A., Larson, R. J. and Griffin, S. 1985. The satisfaction with life scale. *Journal of Personality Assessment*, 49, 71–5.

Fenwick, R. and Tausig, M. 2001. Scheduling stress: Family and health outcomes of shift work and schedule control. *American Behavioral Scientist*, 44, 1179–98.

Ferguson, M., Carlson, D. and Kacmar, K. M. 2015. Flexing work boundaries: The spillover and crossover of workplace support. *Personnel Psychology*, 68, 581–614.

Field, A. 2005. *Discovering Statistics Using SPSS*, 2nd edn. Thousand Oaks, CA: SAGE.

Frone, M. R., Russell, M. and Cooper, L. 1992. Antecedents and outcomes of work–family conflict: Testing a model of work-family interface. *Journal of Applied Psychology*, 77, 68–78.

Greenhaus, J. H. and Beutell, N. J. 1985. Sources of conflict between work and family roles. *The Academy of Management Review*, 10(1), 76–88.

Hammer, L. B., Kossek, N. L., Bodner, T. E. and Hanson, G. C. 2009. Development and validation of a multidimensional measure of family supportive supervisor behaviors. *Journal of Management*, 35, 837–56.

Heiler, K. 2002. *The Struggle for Time: A Review of Extended Shifts in the Tasmanian Mining Industry*. Overview report prepared for the Tasmanian Government, UOS and ACIRRT.

Iverson, R. D. and Maguire, C. 2000. The relationship between job and life satisfaction: Evidence from a remote mining community. *Human Relations*, 53, 807–39.

Jacobs, D., Mostert, K. and Pienaar, J. 2008. The experience of work–life interaction in the Northern Cape mining industry: An exploratory study. *South African Journal of Economic and Management Sciences*, 11, 17–36.

Kaczmarek, E. A. and Sibbel, A. M. 2008. The psychosocial well-being of children from Australian military and fly-in/fly-out (FIFO) mining families. *Community, Work and Family*, 11, 297–312.

Kirchmeyer, C. 1995. Managing the work–nonwork boundary: An assessment of organisational responses. *Human Relations*, 48, 515–36.

Mackett, O. 2020. The measuring of decent work in South Africa. A new attempt at studying the quality of work. *African Review of Economics and Finance*, 12(1), 203–47.

Marais, L. 2018. Housing policy in mining towns: Issues of race and risk in South Africa. *International Journal of Housing Policy*, 18, 335–45.

McDonald, P., Mayes, R. and Pini, B. 2012. Mining work, family and community: A spatially-oriented approach to the impact of the Ravensthorpe Nickel Mine closure in remote Australia. *Journal of Industrial Relations*, 54, 22–40.

Meyer, J. P., Allen, N. J. and Smith, C. A. 1993. Commitment to organizations and occupations: Extension and test of a three-component conceptualisation. *Journal of Applied Psychology*, 78, 538–51.

Misan, G. M. and Rudnik, E. 2015. The pros and cons of long-distance commuting: Comments from South Australian mining and resource workers. *Journal of Economic and Social Policy*, 17, 1–37.

Munnik, V. 2010. *The Social and Environmental Consequences of Coal Mining in South Africa*. Cape Town: Environmental Monitoring Group.

Netemeyer, R. G., Boles, J. S. and McMurrian, R. 1996. Development and validation of work–family conflict and family–work conflict scales. *Journal of Applied Psychology*, 81(4), 400–10.

Nkosi, M. 2017. *Black Workers, White Supervisors: The Emergence of the Labor Structure in South Africa*. Trenton: Africa World Press.

Parker, S. K., Griffin, M. A., Sprigg, C. A. and Wall, T. D. 2002. Effect of temporary contracts on perceived work characteristics and job strain: A longitudinal study. *Personnel Psychology*, 55, 689–719.

Rhoades, L. and Eisenberger, R. 2002. Perceived organizational support: A review of the literature. *Journal of Applied Psychology*, 87, 698–714.

Robinson, L. D., Magee, C. and Caputi, P. 2016. Burnout and the work–family interface: A two-wave study of sole and partnered working mothers. *Career Development International*, 21, 31–44.

Sesele, K., Marais, L., Van Rooyen, D. and Cloete, J. 2021. Mine decline and women: Reflections from the Free State Goldfields. *The Extractive Industries and Society*. doi: 10.1016/j. exis.2020.11.006.

Sharma, S. 2010. The impact of mining on women: Lessons from the coal mining Bowen Basin of Queensland, Australia. *Impact Assessment and Project Appraisal*, 28, 201–15.

ten Brummelhuis, L. L. and Bakker, A. B. 2012. A resource perspective on work–home interface: The work–home resources model. *American Psychologist*, 67, 545–56.

Tummers, L. G. and Bronkhorst, B. A. C. 2014. The impact of leader–member exchange (LMX) on work–family interference and work–family facilitation. *Personnel Review*, 43, 573–91.

Visser, J. 2002. Why fewer workers join unions in Europe: A social custom explanation of membership trends. *British Journal of Industrial Relations*, 40, 403–30.

Vojnovic, P., Michelson, G., Jackson, D. and Bahn, S. 2014. Adjustment, well-being and help-seeking among Australian FIFO mining employees. *Australian Bulletin of Labour*, 40, 242–61.

Wayne, J. H., Casper, W. J., Matthews, R. A. and Allen, T. D. 2013. Family-supportive organization perceptions and organizational commitment: The mediating role of work–family conflict and enrichment and partner attitudes. *Journal of Applied Psychology*, 98(4), 606–22.

Wilson, M. G., Polzer-Debruyne, A., Chen, S. and Fernandes, S. 2007. Shift work interventions for reduced work–family conflict. *Employee Relations*, 29, 162–77.

CHAPTER 6

Informal Settlements in the Mining Context

Lochner Marais, John Ntema, Maléne Campbell,
Jan Cloete and Molefi Lenka

Informal settlements and complexity

The way policymakers view informal settlements has changed remarkably over the past century. Before the Second World War, they saw them as hotbeds of crime, drug abuse and disease. By the 1950s they had begun to see them as a temporary by-product of urbanisation. By the 1970s, influenced by the modernist town planning of the 1920s, they were treating them as a permanent feature of towns. In the 1980s they emphasised structural causes, arguing that global capital, legal systems and government policies were largely responsible for the development of informal settlements. Now in the 2000s they emphasise the agency of the poor, seeing these settlements springing up because households 'assess their situation and decide actively to connect their lives to the city or its fringes' (Huchzermeyer, 2011: 26).

The apartheid state was intolerant of informal urban settlements (Harrison, 1992). Right from its beginning in 1948 it enforced influx control and demolished such settlements. But the larger towns and cities always had some form of informality. When influx control was lifted in 1985, informal settlement increased rapidly. When the policy of orderly urbanisation was dismantled in the early 1990s, the urbanisation rate increased and informal settlements sprawled even further. During the transition phase (1990–4) the apartheid government introduced the Independent Development Trust to finance site and services for a 100,000 stands via a capital subsidy. The post-apartheid government mostly continued with this response. However, initially they did not make much progress with upgrading informal settlements because of the inflexible approach linked to the capital subsidy (Huchzermeyer, 2004). By 2004, the government had introduced a new and flexible informal settlement upgrading strategy. The new programme was more flexible, accepted an incremental approach to informal settlement upgrading and emphasised participatory development. However, informal settlement upgrading has found limited application in mining towns. Furthermore, this chapter focuses on understanding how informal dwellers make a living and benefit from informality (Stillwell, 1992; Obeng-Odoom, 2011), instead of focusing on structural concerns in the building environment (Obeng-Odoom, 2016). This focus on understanding informality is often overlooked by the mainstream work on policy and informal settlement upgrading programmes (Stillwell, 1992), as it concentrates on either the policy dimensions or the structural political-economic considerations (Bryceson and Potts, 2006). Yet poor living conditions are often the basis of social upheaval across South Africa (Matebesi, 2017).

A just transition requires a focus on informal settlements, as these settlements are dominated by black people, mostly migrants, women, poor black South Africans, and black people in general. Only a small amount of research has been done on informal settlement development in mining areas (Rubin and Harrison, 2016; Marais, Cloete and Denoon-Stevens, 2018), although some has been done on mineworker housing in general (Marais and Venter, 2006; Bezuidenhout and Buhlungu, 2011; Cloete and Denoon-Stevens, 2018; Pelders and Nelson, 2018). For a wide-ranging discussion of informal settlement upgrading and transformation in South Africa, against a global background, see Cirolia et al. (2016). This chapter looks at informal settlements in Emalahleni against a background of structural constraints caused by the dominance of capital and misguided government policies. We ask how informality links to mining and how people use informality to deal with mining risks. In addition, we ask what the contributing reasons for developing informal settlements in mining towns are (see also Cloete and Marais, 2020). We use data collected from interviews with households living in informal housing, from Statistics South Africa, police crime statistics and newspaper articles. First, we consider how complexity theory can help explain agency in this mining community.

Informal settlements and complex adaptive systems

Complexity theory originates from the natural sciences, but recently social scientists have used it to explain social systems (Byrne, 1998). It has its roots in a variety of theories, such as systems theory, network theory and chaos theory. Fundamentally, complexity theory challenges the linearity of Newtonian thinking. In this chapter we use it to help us understand the mining town of Emalahleni as a complex adaptive system.

Numerous scholars have offered definitions of a complex adaptive system (Hollings, 2001; Healey, 2006; Teisman, Van Buuren and Gerrits, 2009; Innes and Booher, 2010; Batty and Marshall, 2012). We do not intend to enter the debate. In this chapter, we use some concepts associated with the idea of a complex adaptive system, such as production systems, diversity of agents, multiple interactions, self-learning, emergence and co-evolution, non-linearity, discontinuities and path dependency, and lack of equilibrium. A complex adaptive system results where many parts of a system respond to the behaviour of other parts of the system. It is an open system that responds to interactions between the parts, making it difficult to predict the behaviour and the nature of interactions. Agents are prominent and can interact with one another and adapt to the environment. Systems can retain the status quo or change, but self-organisation remains dominant and often leads to the reorganisation of the system. The self-organisation process has four characteristics: it is not strategically driven and often changes quickly; it is open to influence from outside but takes place in a specific environment; it often survives outside a set equilibrium; and it is unplanned. Often, agents compete on the basis of a cost–benefit analysis. Feedback into the system produces different patterns. Some patterns are path dependent, but often they are unpredictable, non-linear and reflect adaptive behaviour. Often self-organisation is driven by 'a small number of controlling processes' rather than being dependent on a large number of factors (Hollings, 2001: 391). A complex adaptive system can adapt and in the social context people do this through learning, thinking, forecasting and creating agency.

Researchers apply the concept of a complex adaptive system in housing and planning. However, the initial complexity theory work in the urban environment was more linked to systems theory. The emphasis was on equilibrium in closed systems and the assumption was that the whole is equal to the sum of its parts. Urban studies increasingly recognise that the environment is unpredictable and that there are multiple actors, who are often in conflict with one another or the environment. Although equilibrium is still possible, it is more dynamic than imagined initially in systems theory. Urbanisation (including the development of informal settlements) and climate change are often cited as examples of complex problems in urban settings. Innes and Booher (2009) identified four lessons from complex adaptive systems and self-organisation for urban systems and planning: simplification is not always necessary and may be counterproductive; the relationship between cause and effect is often neither linear nor traceable; change occurs from learning and interaction in a system; and an incremental change may have implications for the system and therefore grandiose plans may be inappropriate. See Graham and Healey (1999) and De Roo (2010) for more detail on the application of the complex adaptive system notion to housing and planning.

In this chapter we assess the informal settlements in Emalahleni as a complex adaptive system. We demonstrate three ways in which these settlements may be viewed as a system of this kind. First, we show that they develop despite rational policy decisions by mining companies, government or unions to improve the mineworkers' living conditions. Their development is a non-linear outcome of policy. Second, we argue that informal settlements in mining communities are a rational response by residents to the mining environment. Despite the abrupt and spontaneous way in which these settlements develop, they exhibit some logic and rationality. They represent people's agency (i.e. capacity to act) in dealing with uncertainty and transition. Third, we acknowledge, in line with complexity theory, that we do not fully understand the cause–effect mechanisms involved in informal settlement development in mining communities.

Mine housing policy and informal settlements: The rational response and the non-linear outcome

As is well known, under apartheid black mineworkers were mostly housed in high-density compounds, a policy that fitted into the dominant model of migrant work, which viewed black workers as temporary sojourners in urban areas. Their white counterparts usually rented family housing from the mines, and many received a living-out allowance. By the mid-1980s, mine companies had started to consider privately owned housing for both the black and white mineworkers (Crush, 1989). Mining companies ventured into this new approach as mining profits came under pressure and they wanted to avoid long-term liabilities. They transferred the rental housing to individual households, but both they and the government made only slow progress in finding ownership housing for the black mineworkers.

The post-apartheid government, being keen to dismantle the compound and replace it with single quarters, largely proceeded on this track (Marais, 2018). It also wanted to discourage company towns and promote the integration of mining and non-mining communities. Homeownership thus became the dominant policy discourse. The labour unions mostly agreed with this policy. They fought energetically for parity between black and white mineworkers. By the end of the 1990s, mining companies had managed to provide black mineworkers with a living-out allowance (Kane-Berman, 2018). The critical point to note here is that where the government and mining companies had previously been in control of the housing options, suddenly thousands of mineworkers had agency and could make their own choices. This agency in the hands of mineworkers resulted in substantial informal settlement development in mining towns (Rubin and Harrison, 2016). The outcomes did not match expectations and the resulting housing was poor (Marais and Venter, 2006). However, as we discuss further below, and as research has already noted, it was not only mineworkers or people looking for a job on the mines who landed up in informal settlements.

The mining environment is continually changing. Neoliberal production systems and new labour regimes have changed the way mines operate. Outsourcing and shift work are now common. Many mineworkers are not employed directly by the mine but through contractors or labour brokers. Contract workers tend to earn lower salaries and have lower levels of access to medical aid and lower levels of union membership (Burger and Geldenhuys, 2018). They are also likely to be more poorly housed. Shift work, with four days on and three days off, has meant that migrant labour continues, although this was never the intention. Shift work and neoliberal policies contribute to informal settlement development because they emphasise impermanency. Considering the above reality, informal settlements and backyard living are for many miners a rational solution, particularly in view of the mining industry's volatility. Mine employees are aware of boom and bust cycles and the risk of mine downscaling or closure. Informal settlement, which co-develops with formal housing in mining communities, may well be a self-organising strategy for avoiding investing in a town with an uncertain future.

Growth of informal settlements in Emalahleni, 1996–2016

As is common in mining towns in South Africa, a large portion of Emalahleni's population live in informal settlements. Table 6.1 shows that in 2016 nearly one in four households was living in an informal house (on a separate stand or in a backyard). The number of households in informal settlements has grown nearly threefold since 1996. Figure 6.1 shows the location of these informal settlements.

Figure 6.1 Location of informal settlements in Emalahleni.

Table 6.1 House types in Emalahleni, 1996–2016								
	1996		2001		2011		2016	
House type	N	%	N	%	N	%	N	%
Formal	39,634	70.4	50,254	67.1	92,597	77.2	111,914	74.2
Informal	12,901	22.9	19,514	26.0	23,138	19.3	36,108	23.8
Traditional	2,952	5.2	4,851	6.5	2,721	2.3	2,398	1.4
Other	199	0.4	299	0.4	1,419	1.2	1,242	0.6
Unspecified	603	1.1	0	0.0	0	0.0	0	0.0
Total	56,289	100.0	74,918	100.0	119,875	100.0	150,662	100.0

Source: Stats SA (2013)

The 24% of people living in informal settlements in Emalahleni outstrips the national percentage of about 14%. The growth of informal settlements here is the result of the boom in the economy in the 2000s and, to some degree, the decline since the global financial crisis in 2008/9. It is also said to be the result of mining companies relinquishing their historical role in providing mine housing. But is such a direct interpretation valid or are there also more complex reasons? Some questions to be considered are what the relationship is between informal dwellers and mineworkers, whether the informal dwellers are new migrants, and how informal dwellers differ from formal dwellers.

Profile of informal settlers' households and housing

Informal settlements, the mines and migration

Informal settlements resulted from the mining boom of the 2000s, but they had been building up in the area since the mid-1980s. Family members who wanted to live close to migrant workers in compounds rented shacks on farms near the mines – commonly known as 'shack farming' (*The Citizen*, 1987). Reports on informal settlement development feature from the mid-1980s, with approximately 2,000 informal houses being reported near Witbank (Lukhuleni and Anders, 1988). Our survey found that one of the main increases in informal settlements occurred after the 2008 boom. This increase can be seen in the graph in Figure 6.2, which is based on the dates respondents said they had settled in a specific house. The rapid increase since 2009 is remarkable. Approximately 50% of the informal dwellers had settled in their current house since 2011. The figure also shows a rapid increase in formal housing since 1998, probably the result of the

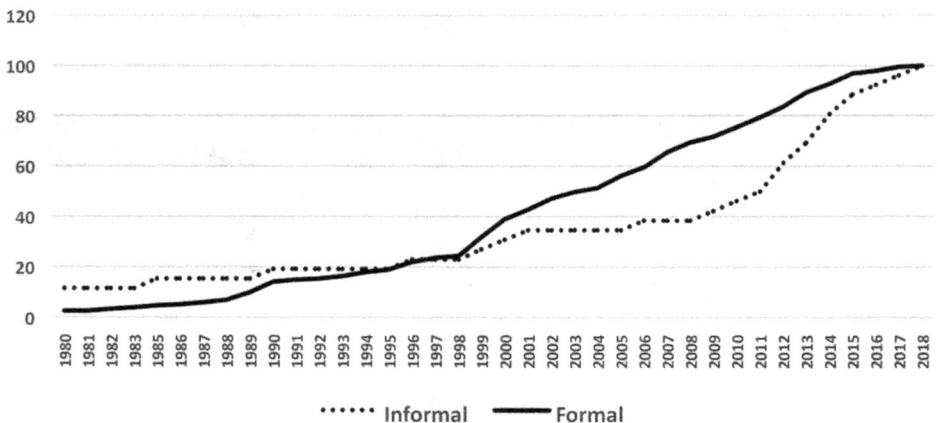

Figure 6.2 Increase in the percentage of people living in informal and formal housing, 1980–2017.

mines' housing assistance programmes and an increase in jobs at Eskom (the South African electricity provider).

Three other mining-related factors have contributed to informal settlement development in South Africa: the dismantling of the compounds, the unions' demand for a living-out allowance, and the systematic closure of company towns since the mid-1990s. The resistance against compounds increased from the mid-1980s. In 1987, some mineworkers invited their family members to the compounds as part of the resistance against the single-sex compound. Mineworkers who were crowded out of the compounds by the families then settled in informal houses near the mines or in Witbank's former black township, KwaGugu (Botes, 1987). Anglo-American, which owned a substantial number of coal mines in the mid-1980s, was the first mining company to consider alternatives to the compound (Crush, 1989). The company introduced homeownership programmes, but these had limited success as unaffordability hampered uptake. In 1994 the post-apartheid government promoted the conversion of single-sex compounds into family units or at least to one-person-one-room quarters. This policy approach further contributed to the creation of informal settlements, as the compounds had to be de-densified. At the same time, unions started to advocate for living-out allowances for all workers. Historically, living-out allowances had been available only to the white workforce.

The living-out allowance did not necessarily improve the black mineworkers' living conditions. For example, some of them chose to receive a living-out allowances and live in an informal settlement. In addition to homeownership programmes and living-out allowances, by the early 1990s mining companies were beginning to reconsider their role in peripheral activities like housing (Marais et al., 2018). In effect, the companies reconsidered their commitment to the many company towns in Emalahleni Local Municipality. The mining boom which had started by the late 1990s gave further impetus to the dismantling of company towns. Many towns were on top of existing coal reserves and the mining companies had good reason to provide incentives for people to move. The introduction of the living-out allowance aimed to relocate people from these towns. Consequently, the coal industry pays some of the highest housing allowances (Kane-Berman, 2018).

Despite the above background, our sample showed that only 19% of the Emalahleni households living in informal settlements worked on the mines. We expected this figure to be much higher. This finding means that the mines and the policies described above are unlikely to be the main contributors to the development of informal settlements. Of this 19%, 80% were contract workers.

Household characteristics

Table 6.2 provides a summary of the household statistics from our survey. We recognize that the uneven numbers of informal and formal households surveyed (respectively 135 and 796) to some extent limit the validity of our comparisons.

Table 6.2 Characteristics of houses and households, informal and formal, from household survey, Emalahleni 2017

Characteristics	Informal houses n = 135	Formal houses n = 796
% HHs with no one employed by mines	81	32
% HHs with someone employed by mines	10	41
% HHs doing contract work for mines	9	26
House size	1.85	4.48
Household size	1.7	2.4
% single-person HHs	61	41
% HHs with no member employed	29.6	11.5
% HHs receiving old age grants	5	8
% HHs receiving child support grants	16	16
% HHs sending money elsewhere every month	40	53
Average monthly rental (ZAR 2017 values)	442	1678
House value (ZAR 2017 values)	30,800	645,000
Price of house when bought (ZAR 2017 values)	10,200	365,000
% HHs who invested in repairs in past 2 years	10	25
% HHs unhappy about their housing	70	16
% HHs who received housing assistance from mine	0	9
% HHs who received government housing assistance	4	29
% HHs who own another house	3	4
% HHs with piped water in house	4	71
% HHs with piped water on stand	24	95
% HHs who treat their drinking water	27	50
% HHs who drink bottled water	40	78
% HHs whose water supply was disrupted in past 6 months	57	87
% HHs with flush toilet	13	92
% HHs with pit toilet	61	8
% HHs with bucket toilet	7	<1
% HHs sharing toilet facility	68	51
% HHs with moderate/strong wish to leave Emalahleni	60	19

Note: HH = household.

Our survey found that households in Emalahleni's informal settlements differ considerably from those in formal houses. Informal settlement households are small, having an average of 1.7 members, compared with an average of 2.4 in formal houses, and 61% are single-person households, compared with 41% in formal houses, which suggests a high level of mobility, as single-person households are usually mobile.

The two types of household also differ economically: 30% had no employed members, compared with 12% of formal households, and, as mentioned above, only 19% had a member employed on the mines, compared with 67% of those in formal houses. A smaller percentage are dependent on old age grants (5% compared with 8% in formal housing), but the same percentage of households said they received child support grants (16%). Many of Emalahleni's households send money elsewhere every month: 40% of the informal households do this, and 53% of the formal. This implies a heavy dependence on migrant labour for the whole area.

We asked respondents to rank their household income level on a scale of 1 to 6, with 1 representing the poorest people they knew and 6 the wealthiest, for their current situation (2017) and for 5, 10 and 15 years ago. Figure 6.3 shows the percentage of ratings at point 3 or below, indicating poverty. Over the four periods, 90% of the informal respondents rated themselves as poor. For the formal households, this percentage had dropped considerably, from 90% fifteen years ago to about 54% at the time of the survey in 2017. These figures indicate the

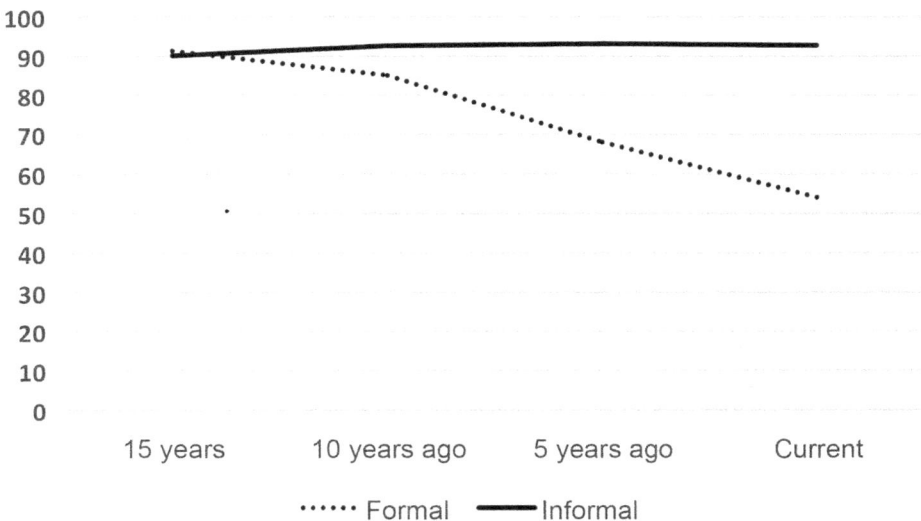

Figure 6.3 Percentage of respondents who perceive themselves as poor (based on scores of 3 or below on a scale of 1 to 6).

positive role that mining has played in taking people out of poverty by enabling them, through a mining salary, to own a house. What they do not convey is the risks for those who have benefited and the fact that it has not done so for all households.

The people who settle in informal settlements are mostly young and mobile, which accounts for the high percentage of single-person households. Although some of them work in the mining industry (mainly as contract workers), most are either unemployed or work outside the mining industry. Informal settlements have sprung up not just because people are seeking jobs on the mines but also as a response to the uncertainty of getting or keeping a job. Structural factors, such as the country's high unemployment levels and the cyclical nature of mining, also contribute to the complexity of the situation.

Housing characteristics

We found that the informal houses were much smaller than the formal houses, at 1.85 rooms per house compared with 4.48. Only about half (56%) of households living in informal housing said they paid rent, at an average monthly rental of R442. The average rental paid for formal housing was R1,678 per month. Those who had bought a shack and perceived ownership had paid on average R10,200 for it, in 2017 values. A formal house would have cost R365,000. Respondents estimated the current value of a formal house at R645,000 and an informal house at R30,800. Those in formal houses were also more likely to have done repairs in the past two years: 25%, compared with 10% in informal houses. Respondents living in informal houses were generally discontented with their housing situation, with 70% choosing the third of the three options 'very happy', 'satisfied' and 'unhappy'. Only 16% of those in formal housing chose that option.

We also asked respondents whether they had received assistance from the government or the mines. Of the formal house respondents, 29% had received assistance from the government and 9% from the mines. The corresponding figures for informal housing were 4% and 0%. Only 3% (four respondents) in informal houses said they owned another house. The figure for formal housing was 4%. Three of these houses were in KwaZulu-Natal and one was in the Eastern Cape provinces.

The standard of services in the informal houses was poor. Only 4% had piped water in the house and 19% had this service on the stand. A further 12% had access to water from a communal tap and 42% from a tanker or carrier. Consequently, 27% of the informal households said they treated their drinking water (by boiling it) either always or sometimes, and 50% of the formal households also treated it, as they were suspicious about the quality of the water from their taps. Bottled water was another alternative: 40% of the respondents in the informal settlements use it (always or sometimes) and 78% of those in the formal settlements. The municipality's inability to provide proper basic services is evident, and the consequences for people in informal settlements are glaringly obvious. Nearly 87% of respondents in formal houses and 57% in informal houses said their water supply had been interrupted in the past six months. The sanitation conditions for the informal settlers were extremely bad, with only 13% having a flush toilet, while 61% had to use an unventilated pit toilet, and 7% had nothing but a bucket system. Sharing of toilet facilities, reported by 67% of informal settlement households, constitutes a critical health risk. The 51% of respondents in formal houses also sharing toilet facilities is the result of large numbers of people living in formal backyards. The findings of our survey make it clear that the residents of Emalahleni's informal settlements have much poorer housing conditions, are more dissatisfied with their housing, and are more mobile than those who live in formal housing. On the one hand, this illustrates the marginalisation of people on the fringes of the city and the structural constraints. But on the other, it illustrates their agency in dealing with uncertainty by not making huge investments in an area where job security is limited, showing they are not just victims of their situation.

Social cohesion
Mining communities often suffer from a lack of social cohesion, partly because of the high levels of population mobility. Researchers use the concepts of place attachment and social disruption to explain social dynamics in mining communities (Ntema et al., 2017). One of the leading indicators of social disruption is crime levels or the perception of crime in an area.

Our survey found that Emalahleni's informal settlement dwellers had very little place attachment. This came as a surprise. Place attachment in informal settlements is usually high. The fear of eviction usually mobilises communities to actively prevent eviction or resettlement. A large proportion of the informal dwellers in Emalahleni were clearly not attached to the place, with 60% indicating a moderate or strong preference to leave. The corresponding figure for those in formal housing was 19%. The desire for house ownership was not strong in the informal settlements: 80% of the informal households who did not own a house said they did not want to own a house. The corresponding percentage for formal houses was 45%. This implies there is a close relationship between living in an informal settlement and the need to be mobile. Informality and not owning a house ensure mobility and adaptability. Informal settlements thus represent a complex adaptive system.

We tested the degree to which formal and informal dwellers differ in respect of their perceptions of crime. Respondents were asked to imagine they had lost their wallet with R200 in it and then to estimate the chance of getting it back – first, if someone who lived close by found it, and second, if a complete stranger found it. The likelihood of return was not rated very high by either group: 7% of formal dwellers considered the return of the wallet likely in the first scenario and 0.5% considered it likely in the second. The corresponding percentages for informal dwellers were 1% and 0%. These answers indicated a very high degree of mistrust by both types of household, but particularly the informal ones, and thus a low degree of social cohesion.

We followed this with a range of crime-related questions (see Table 6.3). There were no statistically significant differences between these two types of household. However, in their responses to all six questions the informal dwellers rated the incidence of crime higher than the formal dwellers. This pattern is evident even in the 'very common' column (except for the question on gangsterism, where the percentage for both formal and informal was 9%). The residents are not imagining things. Crime Stats South Africa (2018) has rated Emalahleni one of the top 10 crime hotspots in South Africa, recording large increases. From 2009 to 2018, common robbery increased from 210 cases to 326, robbery with aggravated circumstances from 426 cases to 821, and drug-related crime from 101 cases to 457. And these are only the cases that were reported to the police; actual figures are probably considerably higher.

The lack of social cohesion in the informal settlements coupled with the limited place attachment further confirms the high levels of mobility among Emalahleni's informal settlers. This, in turn, points to some kind of self-organisation, but a kind which is mobile, does not require place attachment and is essentially seeking economic opportunities.

Table 6.3 Formal and informal residents' perceptions of crime in Emalahleni, 2017

Frequency in neighbourhood	Type of housing	Never (%)	Very rare (%)	Not very common (%)	Fairly common (%)	Very common (%)	Average /5
Burglaries etc.	Formal	5.0	17.5	23.3	37.2	17.0	3.4
	Informal	0.7	26.1	17.2	29.1	26.9	3.6
Domestic violence?	Formal	13.9	23.8	32.7	20.0	7.5	2.77
	Informal	8.2	23.9	31.3	26.1	10.4	3.07
Violence between different HHs?	Formal	2.4	25.1	40.7	18.7	6.6	2.83
	Informal	0.7	8.2	44.0	29.1	8.2	3.07
Gangsterism?	Formal	3.4	19.0	36.8	29.7	9.0	3.16
	Informal	3.0	18.7	33.6	34.3	9.0	3.23
Murder, shootings or stabbings?	Formal	4.4	32.2	37.0	18.2	6.4	2.84
	Informal	0.7	34.3	27.6	29.9	6.7	3.05
Drug or alcohol abuse?	Formal	0.0	1.9	10.1	27.1	59.9	4.42
	Informal	0.0	2.2	11.9	20.1	64.9	4.46

Note: HH = household.

Conclusion

We conclude by recapping the points this chapter makes. First, we set out to show that informal settlements develop despite rational responses to prevent them. The mines, the government and the unions have been actively advocating for homeownership, the demise of the company town and the implementation of a living-out allowance. This was the linear response to the inhumane compound system and the inequality between black and white mineworkers. To be implemented the policy had to develop good formal housing for mineworkers. Our evidence shows that informal settlements develop despite these rational policies and that some Emalahleni mineworkers (mainly black) live in these informal houses (although a smaller percentage than we expected). The development of informal settlements is a non-linear outcome of policy. Despite the modernist intent of this policy (formality and homeownership), it gave mineworkers and other citizens the agency to make their own decisions about housing. The complexity lies in the provision of agency to mineworkers. Historically, government and the mining companies determined the housing patterns. Living-out allowances now mean that thousands of mineworkers can make those decisions themselves.

Second, informal settlements in mining communities are a rational response by residents to the context in which mining takes place. Informality is a rational housing response in an area whose long-term economic viability is questionable. Our survey found that a large percentage of households in informal settlements are single-person households and they have limited place attachment. The unpredictability of the economic environment is a critical contributor to informal settlement development. The government, mining companies and unions seem unaware of, or disregard, this unpredictability. Informal settlement dwellers recognise it. The impermanency of their living arrangements is their way of adapting to reality. Informal settlements develop along with the mining sector as a system that enables mineworkers to adapt to changing realities. At the same time, we acknowledge that a fair amount of informality is also because of economic volatility. For contract workers (predominantly black), who mostly live in informal settlements, there is a particularly high uncertainty of continued employment. Formal households also face risks: in the case of mine decline or closure they will have to deal with their outstanding mortgage and are likely to lose heavily in the process. A just transition would have implications for both groups: contract workers in informal housing and mineworkers in formal housing.

Third, we acknowledge, in line with complexity theory, that we do not fully understand the cause–effect mechanisms responsible for informal settlement development in mining communities. Some of it has to do with the unpredictability of the mining environment. Mobility is crucial in uncertain times. It also has to do with where informal dwellers perceive their home to be. They may have family responsibilities in another area, thus migrant labour continues. For black workers and other black residents, an informal house in 2018 has many unintended similarities with the compound in 1980. There is little evidence that mining cured the housing problems in Emalahleni, much as it has failed to do in other mining contexts across the world (Brueckner et al., 2014). At the same time, it does provide for flexibility and mobility in the case of mine decline or closure.

References

Batty, M. and Marshall, S. 2012. The origins of complexity theory in cities and planning. In J. Portugali, H. Meyer, E. Stolk and E. Tan (eds), *Complexity Theories of Cities Have Come of Age: An Overview with Implications to Urban Planning and Design*. Heidelberg: Springer.

Bezuidenhout, A. and Buhlungu, S. 2011. From compounded to fragmented labour: Mineworkers and the demise of compounds in South Africa. *Antipode*, 43(2), 237–63.

Botes, M. 1987. *Groeigebied nie ontein* [Group areas not expropriated]. *Die Transvaler*, 11 March, 7.

Brueckner, M., Durey, A., Mayes, R. and Pforr, C. 2014. *Resource Curse or Cure? On the Sustainability of Development in Western Australia*. Heidelberg: Springer.

Bryceson, D. and Potts, D. (eds) 2006. *African Urban Economies. Viability, Vitality or Vitiation*. London: Palgrave Macmillan.

Burger, P. and Geldenhuys, J. 2018. Work, wages and welfare in Postmasburg. In L. Marais, P. Burger and D. van Rooyen (eds), *Mining and Community in South Africa: From Small Town to Iron Town*. London: Routledge, 173–98.

Byrne, D. 1998. *Complexity Theory and the Social Sciences: An Introduction*. New York: Routledge.

Cirolia, L., Gorgens, T., van Donk, M., Smit, W. and Drimie, S. (eds) 2016. *Upgrading Informal Settlements in South Africa: A Partnership-based Approach*. Cape Town: UCT Press.

Cloete, J. and Denoon-Stevens, S. 2018. Mineworker housing. In L. Marais, P. Burger and D. van Rooyen (eds), *Mining and Community in South Africa: From Small Town to Iron Town*. London: Routledge, 141–56.

Cloete, J. and Marais, L. 2020. Mine housing in the South African coalfields: The unforeseen consequences of post-apartheid policy. *Housing Studies*. doi: 10.1080/02673037.2020.1769038.

Crime Stats South Africa. 2018. Crime statistics per area, South African Police Services. www.crimestatssa.com/.

Crush, J. 1989. Accommodating black miners: Home ownership on the mines. In *South African Review 5*. Johannesburg: Ravan Press, 335–47.

De Roo, G. 2010. Being or becoming? That is the question! Confronting complexity with contemporary planning theory. In G. De Roo and E. Silva (eds), *A Planner's Encounter with Complexity*. Farnham: Ashgate, 19–40.

Graham, S. and Healey, P. 1999. Relational concepts of space and place: Issues for planning theory and practice. *European Planning Studies*, 7(5), 623–46.

Harrison, P. 1992. The policies and politics of informal settlement in South Africa: A historical background. *Africa Insight*, 22(1), 14–22.

Healey, R. 2006. Relational complexity and the imaginative power of strategic spatial planning. *European Planning Studies*, 14(4), 525–46.

Hollings, C. 2001. Understanding the complexity of economic, ecological, and social systems. *Ecosystems*, 4, 390–405.

Huchzermeyer, M. 2004. *Unlawful Occupation: Informal Settlements and Urban Policy in South Africa and Brazil*. Trenton: Africa World Press.

Huchzermeyer, M. 2011. *Cities with 'Slums': From Informal Settlement Eradication to a Right to the City in Africa*. Cape Town: UCT Press.

Innes, J. and Booher, D. 2009. Consensus building and complex adaptive systems: A framework for evaluating collaborative planning. *Journal of the American Planning Association*, 65(4), 412–23.

Innes, J. and Booher, D. 2010. *Planning with Complexity: An Introduction to Collaborative Rationality for Public Policy*. London: Routledge.

Kane-Berman, J. 2018. *Mining and People: The Impact of Mining on Tte South African Economy and Living Standards*. Johannesburg: South African Institute of Race Relations.

Lukhuleni, W. and Anders, T. 1988. Witbank squatters offered houses they can't afford. *The Star*, 6 February, 3.

Marais, L. 2018. Mining policy in mining towns: Issues of race and risk in South Africa. *International Journal of Housing Policy*, 18(2), 335–45.

Marais, L. and Venter, A. 2006. Hating the compound, but . . . Mineworker housing needs in post-apartheid South Africa. *Africa Insight*, 36(1), 53–62.

Marais, L., Cloete, J. and Denoon-Stevens, S. 2018. Informal settlements and mine development: Reflections from South Africa's periphery. *Journal of the Southern African Institute of Mining and Metallurgy*, 118, 1103–11.

Marais, L., Haslam McKenzie, F., Deacon, L., Nel, E., Van Rooyen, D. and Cloete, J. 2018. The changing nature of mining towns: Reflections from Australia, Canada and South Africa. *Land Use Policy*, 76, 779–88.

Matebesi, S. 2017. *Civil Strife Against Local Governance: Dynamics of Community Protests in Contemporary South Africa*. Berlin: Barbara Budrich Publishers.

Ntema, J., Marais, L., Cloete, J. and Lenka, M. 2017. Social disruption, mine closure and housing policy: Evidence from the Free State Goldfields. *Natural Resources Forum*, 41(1), 31–40.

Obeng-Odoom, F. 2011. *Reconstructing Urban Economics Towards a Political Economy of the Built Environment*. London: ZED Books.

Obeng-Odoom, F. 2016. The informal sector in Ghana under siege. *Journal of Developing Societies*, 27(3/4), 355–92.

Pelders, J. and Nelson, G. 2018. Living conditions of mine workers from eight mines in South Africa. *Development Southern Africa*. doi: 10.1080/0376835X.2018.1456909.

Rubin, M. and Harrison, P. 2016. An uneasy symbiosis: Mining and informal settlement in South Africa with particular reference to the Platinum Belt in North West Province. In L. Cirolia, T. Gorgens, M. van Donk, W. Smit and S. Drimie (eds), *Upgrading Informal Settlements in South Africa: A Partnership-based Approach*. Cape Town: UCT Press, 145–74.

Stats SA (Statistics South Africa). 2013. Census 2011 data. Pretoria: Stats SA.

Stillwell, F. 1992. *Understanding Cities & Regions: Spatial Political Economy*. Leichhardt: Pluto Press.

Teisman, G., Van Buuren, A. and Gerrits, L. 2009. *An Introduction to Understanding and Managing Complex Process Systems*. New York: Routledge.

The Citizen. 1987. Mineworkers' families move into hostels. *The Citizen*, 4 April, 10.

CHAPTER 7

Coal and Water: Exploiting One Precious Natural Resource at the Expense of Another?

Surina Esterhuyse and Falko Buschke

Coal mining and water resources

Approximately 72% of South Africa's primary energy needs are currently met by coal. The country's most productive coalfield is the Emalahleni-Witbank coalfield on the Mpumalanga Highveld, where coal mining began in 1895. The highest density of collieries is concentrated here. Although the national significance of the Emalahleni-Witbank coalfield is indisputable, the environmental sustainability of coal extraction is less clear. This is especially true for natural water sources, which can be severely degraded by coal mining activities.

The impacts of coal mining on water resources are of four kinds: *direct, indirect, induced* and *cumulative* (Buschke et al., 2018). Coal mining directly degrades water resources by polluting natural waterways. It has indirect effects in the form of secondary damage from mining activities. The induced impacts are damage not directly attributable to mining activities but a likely consequence. The cumulative impacts are those resulting from the combined impacts of past, current or future mining. In Emalahleni, indirect impacts result from the transformation and degradation of natural habitats to the extent that they no longer provide ecosystem services (benefits that humans gain from the natural environment), such as water purification. The most common induced impacts are from the nature of urbanisation and urban sprawl, which increase the pressure on water resources and further degrade natural habitats. And because there are so many collieries around Emalahleni, the water resources also suffer the cumulative impacts caused by synergies between multiple smaller impacts. In this chapter, we argue that land use change resulting from mining could have a much larger impact than climate change on the supply of clean water to Emalahleni. Long-term environmental degradation will likely be present long after coal mining stops. Despite benefits like cleaner air, those remaining behind will have to live with the long-term environmental implications after mine closure. Poor urban and communal rural areas will likely be the most affected (Obeng-Odoom, 2020).

To fully appreciate the damage that coal mining does to water resources around Emalahleni, it is necessary to step back and evaluate the four types of impact holistically. Such a broad approach could have major implications for the governance and long-term sustainability of coal mining. South African mining generally has left a legacy of environmental degradation because many operations were established before the current environmental legislation, without any formal consideration of the consequences. However, new mining operations, even when they have done environmental impact assessments, have tended to focus on direct impacts (which are more easily attributable to mining activities) and overlook the other types (Edwards et al., 2013). We assessed the total impact of coal mining on the pollution levels of Emalahleni's water bodies. We synthesised data on levels of common chemical pollutants from coal mining and simulated the effects of land use around Emalahleni on the ecosystem's natural function of water purification. Furthermore, we assessed the induced impacts on municipal water supply by summarising data from a household survey about water usage by Emalahleni residents. Our simulation also allowed us to quantify the cumulative impacts of changing rainfall patterns anticipated under climate change as well as some scenarios of continued ecosystem degradation or restoration. Our case study offers a comprehensive overview of the challenges facing the water–energy nexus and demonstrates how integrating the water and energy sectors is essential for our pursuit of a more sustainable future.

Mines polluting water resources

Most of South Africa's coal reserves are shallow, largely unfaulted and lightly inclined, making their exploitation suitable for open-cast and mechanised mining. Open-cast mining removes large volumes of soil and rock overburden to get to the workable coal seams, destroying regional aquifers in the process and producing large volumes of solid waste. Acid leachate that percolates through the mine workings and waste heaps often causes widespread contamination of underground and surface water.

Emalahleni is located on the water divide between several quaternary catchments in the Olifants water management area (Figure 7.1). Coal is mined in all of these, as well as in other upstream catchments. This means that all the run-off from upstream coal mines drains through the Emalahleni Local Municipality. We obtained water quality monitoring data from the Department of Water and Sanitation (DWS) to evaluate the effects of coal mining pollutants on water resources.

We looked at six variables of water quality: pH, a measure of the acidity; electrical conductivity (EC), an indicator of the salt content; the sulphate (SO_4^{2-}) content; and the concentrations of the heavy metals arsenic (As), iron (Fe) and manganese (Mn). These end products of a complex set of chemical reactions are reliable indicators of acid mine drainage associated with coal extraction.

The main cause of acid mine drainage is the oxidation of sulphide mineral ores, which are exposed to the environment by intensive mining activities. Among the metal sulphides, pyrite ore (FeS_2, commonly known as 'fool's gold') is one of the main minerals responsible for acid mine drainage because it oxidises easily when exposed to oxygen, water and micro-organisms. The disturbance of the coal strata during mining introduces oxygen into the coal deposits, which oxidises the pyrite in the deposits. Pyrite in waste rock heaps can also be oxidised. During the oxidation of pyrite, sulphur is oxidised to sulphate and ferrous iron. Sulphuric acid is also released and the water turns more acidic (reflected as lower pH). The acidic water mobilises an array of heavy metals, such as As, Fe and Mn, from the coal deposits and rock heaps. Because of this increase in heavy metals and minerals in the water, the electrical conductivity (salt content) of the water is usually also high.

We compared the levels of these six variables of Emalahleni's water resources to the South African SANS 241 standards for drinking water (SABS, 2015). We categorised the DWS monitoring sites as having good water quality that is within those standards, marginally acceptable water quality, or poor water quality that is considerably below the standards. These are symbolised respectively as squares, diamonds and circles in Figure 7.1.

The monitoring data demonstrated the direct negative impacts of coal mining on these water resources (Figure 7.1). The pH of the water was generally

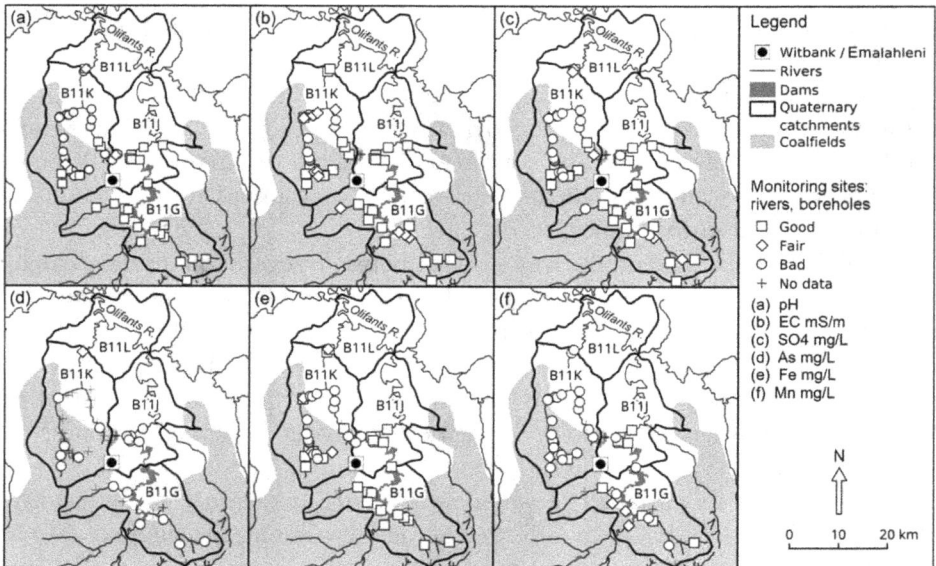

Figure 7.1 Monitored water quality in the aquatic system around Emalahleni.
Water quality monitoring results for pH (a), EC (b), SO_4^{2-} (c), As (d), Fe (e) and Mn (f), for the quaternary catchments of the Olifants River and its tributaries, Klipspruit, Blesbokspruit and Klip rivers. The condition of these rivers downstream from the coal mining area indicates the direct effect of coal mining on the region's water resources. The symbols used in the maps indicate the national water quality standards.

well below water quality standards, indicating the effects of acid mine drainage (Figure 7.1a). Controlling acid mine drainage is one of the most significant environmental challenges facing coal mines, particularly in the Emalahleni area, where the coal seams are very shallow. Monitoring data showed that the pH of the river water was lower in downstream sites (i.e. north of Emalahleni), which indicates the cumulative effects of acid mine drainage from many mining operations. The high EC from the monitoring sites (Figure 7.1b) indicates the high salt content from dissolved salts (such as sulphate, Figure 7.1c) and heavy metals (such as arsenic, Figure 7.1d). Acid mine drainage exacerbates these high salt levels because the acidic water mobilises heavy metals and salts from the environment, mine waste and river sediments.

The signature of acid mine drainage was even more visible in the SO_4^{2}, Fe and Mn levels (Figures 7.1 c, e and f), which were well above the limits for acceptable drinking water quality. Arsenic (As) was of particular concern because every single monitoring site recorded unacceptably high levels of this element (Figure 7.1d). Such high levels of salts and heavy metals are notoriously difficult to remove from drinking water and can have dire human health consequences in Emalahleni. Witbank Dam acts as a sink for pollutants and Loskop Dam probably performs a similar function (Dabrowski and De Klerk, 2013), which may explain why pollution levels in these dams have increased steadily in recent decades (McCarthy and Pretorius, 2009). This finding is of particular concern because the Emalahleni municipality uses the Witbank Dam to supply water to residents and poor water quality will increase water treatment costs considerably.

Mines degrading nature's water filter

Coal mining is not the only source of water pollution: urbanisation, agriculture, industry and natural processes can also degrade water quality. However, nature has an uncanny ability to absorb pollution and purify water. This is especially true for the mesic highveld grasslands around Emalahleni. The dense cover of perennial grass species traps surface water, reducing run-off and allowing more time for water to percolate through the soil (SANBI, 2013). This slows the rate at which water moves through the landscape, giving more time for chemical elements to be taken up by vegetation or broken down by chemical reactions in the soil. Thus healthy grassland ecosystems supply the ecosystem water purification service, which is critical for the continued availability of good quality water for domestic, industry, agricultural and commercial use.

Unfortunately, the continued supply of water-related ecosystem services is being jeopardised by land use change. The two predominant ecosystem types around Emalahleni – the Eastern Highveld and Rand Highveld Grasslands – are both listed as *Vulnerable* because of irreversible habitat transformation (RSA,

2011). The natural habitats upstream of Emalahleni have mostly been trans-formed for agriculture, while urban expansion and mining are responsible for habitat loss around Emalahleni. This has meant that nature's ability to absorb pollutants is being eroded by human activities.

It is difficult to quantify the loss of ecosystem services due to habitat trans-formation because most of this transformation predates current methods for measuring these services. We lack reliable baselines of pre-industrial ecosystem services because the science of these services developed only towards the end of the twentieth century. Ecosystem service scientists therefore rely on hypothetical future scenarios based on likely ecological drivers or policy interventions (IPBES, 2016) which can be compared to the status quo. This approach provides the nec-essary context within which to interpret the current supply of ecosystem services.

We simulated nutrient loads from the tertiary river catchment around Emalahleni. Nutrients − total nitrogen and total phosphorous − can come from various sources, such as industrial effluent or discharges from water treatment plants, or fertilisers from cultivated lands. These nutrients flow through the landscape after rain and eventually find their way into natural water bodies. Currently, global nitrogen and phosphorous levels are exceeding nature's capac-ity to absorb these nutrients, which are contributing to the acidification and eutrophication of freshwater ecosystems (Breuer et al., 2008). Depending on the vegetation and soil characteristics, nutrients can be mobilised as above-ground run-off or through sub-surface infiltration. The interplay of rainfall, topography and land cover controls the flow of nutrients through a landscape. The nutrients become pollutants when an excess of them gets into the water bodies.

We used InVEST (Integrated Valuation of Ecosystem Services and Tradeoffs (https://naturalcapitalproject.stanford.edu/software/invest), a suite of open-source software models, to map the nutrient loads around Emalahleni. The nutrient deliv-ery ratio model in InVEST simulates nitrogen and phosphorous loads across a landscape based on precipitation data (as a proxy for nutrient run-off mobilisation), topography data (to determine the direction and rate of water flow across a land-scape) and land-cover data (where each land use class is parameterised according to nutrient loads, retention rates and infiltration rates). We then repeated these simulations for different future scenarios of climate and land use change.

Since topography remained unchanged across the scenarios, we used a sin-gle globally available digital elevation model obtained from the Shuttle Radar Topography Mission (SRTM: Jarvis et al., 2004). We used two different data sets for precipitation: one for current precipitation levels (BIOCLIM: Hijmans et al., 2005) and one for precipitation projected for 2050 by the Community Cli-mate System Model (CCSM) under the representative concentration pathway 60 (RCP60: http://worldclim.org/cmip5_30s). The RCP60 pathway assumes that greenhouse emissions will continue to rise until 2080. We also included three scenarios of land cover: the current conditions (from the European Space Agency Climate Change Initiative: http://2016africalandcover20m.esrin.esa.int/); a *degradation* scenario, where cultivated, bare ground and built-up areas increase by 10%; and a *restoration* scenario, where cultivated and bare ground decrease by 10% (we assumed that the extent of built-up areas cannot be reduced). In both future scenarios, we assumed that habitat degradation or restoration would happen at the edges of current land uses. Therefore, in the degradation scenario the degradation of natural habitat depended on the proximity to existing farms, mines or towns, and in the restoration scenario, previously degraded areas were restored to shrubland, which we assumed reflected the likely outcome of incomplete grassland restoration efforts.

Overall, if the climate change projections are correct, Emalahleni is likely to become wetter by 2050 (Figure 7.2A). If habitat transformation continues, the region might lose half of its wetlands and 10% of its natural grasslands (degradation scenario in Figure 7.2B). The ecosystem services model suggests that habitat transformation would have a much stronger effect than increased precipitation on increasing phosphorous (Figure 7.2C) and nitrogen (Figure 7.2D) loads.

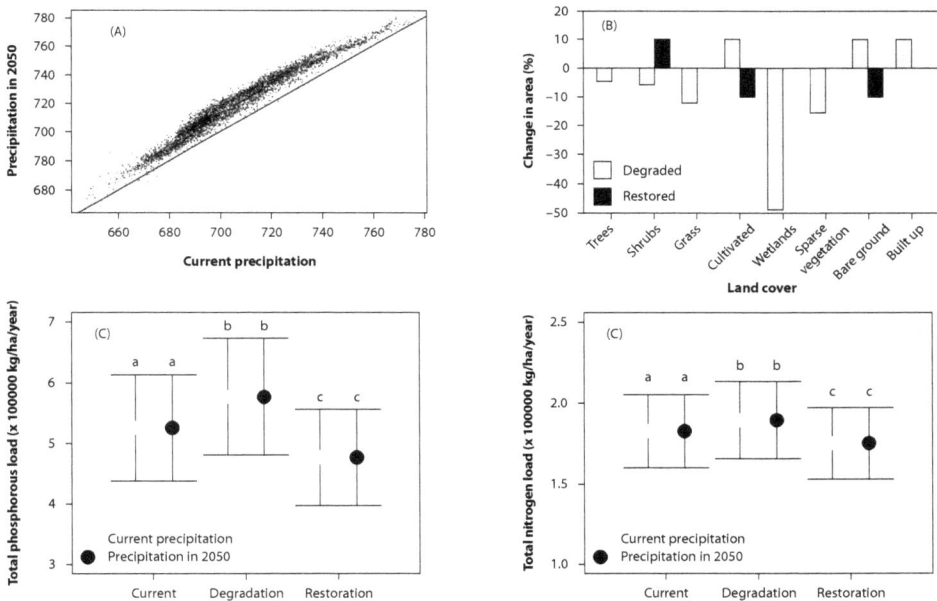

Figure 7.2 Modelling water purification ecosystem services in Emalahleni. (A) Increased precipitation by 2050 anticipated under climate change. Each point represents a 1 km² pixel in the tertiary river catchment around Emalahleni. The diagonal line represents perfect concordance between current and future rainfall. (B) Simulated land-use change relative to current extent for degradation (grey) and restoration (black) scenarios. (C) Means (points) and standard errors (bars) for total phosphorous loads in quaternary catchments for each scenario of climate and land-use change (a, b, c denote statistically different groups from a non-parametric Friedman test). (D) As for (C), but for total nitrogen loads.

Conversely, restoration of currently degraded land would reduce the nutrient loads (Figure 7.2C,D). Simulations do, however, show substantial variation in the nutrient loads from the different quaternary catchments within the main tertiary catchments (as reflected by the error bars in Figure 7.2C,D). In general, upstream agricultural activities tend to contribute higher nutrient loads, as is typical for this type of land use (e.g. Scanlon et al., 2007). It is therefore essential to maintain healthy grasslands upstream of Emalahleni to ensure that these high levels of agricultural nutrients are not exported downstream to the city.

Our ecosystem service simulation demonstrates that land use change could have a much larger impact than climate change on the supply of clean water to Emalahleni. This could have positive consequences for mitigation plans, because managing land use change through local spatial planning is more feasible than influencing climate change, which has global-scale drivers. Strategic investment in restoring the upper reaches of the Olifants River catchment would have positive consequences for water quality in Emalahleni. On average, the benefits of ecological restoration are 10 times greater than the costs (IPBES, 2018), and in South Africa the costs of such investments in ecological infrastructure are in the same order of magnitude as related built infrastructure such as dams, boreholes, water transfer schemes and water treatment plants (Mander et al., 2017).

Drinking water deterioration and supply interruptions

Environmental degradation is unlikely to inspire active intervention until humans are affected directly. The household survey of some 900 residents and interviews with key informants carried out in Emalahleni suggest that this point has been reached (see also Chapter 15). Residents are experiencing the effects of deteriorating water resources. Approximately 87% of respondents in the household survey said they receive water from the municipality. Although the municipality treats the water before distributing it to residents, half of the respondents said they treat the municipal water themselves before drinking it. This implies that they do not feel confident that the water from their taps is safe for consumption without first boiling or filtering it. Further supporting this lack of trust in the tap water, 73% of respondents said they had at some point bought bottled water.

These responses suggest that municipal water providers are unable to fully remove contaminants from natural water resources (see Chapter 15). Oberholster et al. (2017) reported widespread dysfunctional water treatment infrastructure in the Olifants River catchment. Emalahleni's water infrastructure is about 50 years old and has reached the end of its intended lifespan. Aging infrastructure may explain why most of the wastewater treatment plants in the Olifants River catchment are functioning at less than 30% of their full capacity (Oberholster et al., 2017). Failing infrastructure exacerbates the decline of water quality because untreated sewage from domestic sources enters natural water bodies, filling these ecosystems with phosphates and potentially leading to algal blooms.

Adding to the problems of polluted water sources and ageing infrastructure is the increased demand for water in Emalahleni. The local municipality had already exceeded its licensed abstraction limit of 90 ML/d from Witbank Dam a decade ago (Hobbs, Oelofse and Rascher, 2008). Rapid urbanisation and the growth of the mining and other industry sectors have put extreme pressure on the bulk infrastructure, leading to overutilisation, rapid deterioration of service infrastructure and considerable water losses.

These shortages are being felt by residents, as evidenced by the 78% of respondents who reported that their water supplies had been interrupted during the past six months. This corroborated the general impression during community participation meetings in 2016, where residents stated that insecure water supply was one of the city's main problems. In the case of complete system failure, the municipality supplies water to residents using water tankers, and 7.4% of respondents said these tankers were their main source of water.

This problem of contaminated water sources, increasing demands and failing infrastructure is not limited to Emalahleni but has a wider impact. Despite the large number of productive mines in this region, the Witbank coalfield has not yet reached its production peak (Hobbs, Oelofse and Rascher, 2008). The rapid establishment of new mines in the upper reaches of the Vaal catchment and the high number of pending mining applications for new coal mines to satisfy Eskom's increased demand will significantly increase water service providers' operational costs if pollution from these collieries cannot be curtailed.

One possible solution is to shift the burden of water provisioning away from municipalities and onto polluters, in line with the 'polluter pays' principle enshrined in national environmental legislation (RSA, 1998). Industry has stepped in to alleviate water provisioning pressures for the Emalahleni Local Municipality through the Emalahleni water reclamation plant. The Emalahleni coalfields produce 45 million m^3 of excess water per year during their operations (DWS, 2011). Currently, 30 Ml of this water is treated to potable standards and supplied to the municipality each day and the intention is to expand this plant to treat 50Ml/day, with a maximum capacity of 60Ml/day. All additional yields from such mine water reclamation plants are earmarked for the local municipalities in the coal mining areas (DWS, 2016). While this is a promising solution to a pressing problem, it does raise questions about the risks of shifting the water provisioning responsibility from the public to the private sector.

Tallying the total impact of coal mining

Determining the impact cost is often a complex exercise. Mining contributes to long-term environmental costs that are often not fully included on mines' balance sheets (Tambo and Theobald, 2018). These long-term environmental costs are essential for understanding the real costs of mining and the cost of the social unrest that goes with it (Matebesi, 2017, 2020). The *direct* impacts of coal mining in Emalahleni are clear: the natural aquatic systems in the area show unambiguous signs of acid mine drainage. The same is true for the *indirect* impacts, where the continued transformation of natural habitats will reduce the supply of ecosystem services and increase the nutrient loads that enter the water. The *induced* impacts of coal mining in Emalahleni can be seen in municipal water infrastructure that is struggling to treat polluted water and meet the growing demand for clean water. Of course, these problems cannot be ascribed to a single mining operation but rather to the *cumulative* impact of Emalahleni's coal mining industry as a whole.

Solving these problems will be complex, but the urgent need for solutions is indisputable. While the economic cost of interventions will be substantial, the cost of delaying action will be even greater. It is likely that the current impacts are only the tip of the iceberg because abandoned mines will still have latent impacts (Hobbs, Oelofse and Rascher, 2008). Mines may only start decanting acidic water 20 years after abandonment because geochemical reactions can result in delayed contamination. The need for immediate intervention is obvious. We propose four strategies to mitigate the negative impact of coal mining on water systems.

First, the Departments of Mineral Resources and Water and Sanitation must hold coal mines accountable for polluting water resources. This may seem obvious, but a report by the Centre for Environmental Rights (2016) illustrates the ineptitude of these government departments at upholding the law and meeting their constitutional mandate. The report, titled *Zero Hour: Poor Governance of Mining and the Violation of Environmental Rights in Mpumalanga*, describes how the Department of Mineral Resources unlawfully granted mining licences to companies that had already broken the law, disregarded appeals lodged by local communities, and failed to ban prospecting and mining in critical water source areas and critical biodiversity areas. It describes how the Department of Water and Sanitation issued water licences with weak or inappropriate licence conditions, although this point is largely theoretical, because enforcement of the conditions is negligible (Centre for Environmental Rights, 2016). These are serious obstacles to sustainability, but they are not unique to Emalahleni. Weak implementation and enforcement of legislation has been cited as the most significant weakness of South African water resources management by academia, government and the private sector (Buschke and Esterhuyse, 2012). However, applying the law should be the first step towards making the coal mining sector more environmentally sustainable.

Second, the Olifants River catchment needs to be the target of strategic ecological protection and restoration. The South African National Biodiversity Institute advocates against any further transformation of virgin mesic grasslands (SANBI, 2013). Since Emalahleni's grassland ecosystems are listed as vulnerable, continued transformation will lead to the loss of biodiversity, ecological functioning and supply of ecosystem services. In addition to avoiding transformation, concerted effort should be directed towards restoring the wider catchment. Restoration of coal mining areas has been shown to improve the supply of ecosystem services in other developing countries, such as Brazil (Rocha-Nicoleite, Overbeck and Müller, 2017) and China (Xiao et al., 2018). South Africa has a framework for investing in ecological infrastructure (SANBI, 2014), such as healthy river catchments, and this could have positive effects beyond improving ecological functioning. Most notably, restoration can be carried out through national initiatives like the Working for Wetlands expanded public works programme, which grew from the successful Working for Water programme (Turpie, Marais and Blignaut, 2008). Such initiatives create employment, particularly for marginalised community groups, thereby ensuring that public funds create both ecological and social benefits.

Third, there needs to be an immediate and extensive investment in water infrastructure. Of course, investment in reliable water treatment and distribution is urgently needed, but delaying big capital investments in water infrastructure can result in economic losses as high as 150% after five years, after accounting for reduced water revenue and the loss of jobs and production in the agricultural and industrial sectors due to water insecurity (Muller, 2018). Private investment by coal mining companies to treat polluted water, such as the Emalahleni Water Reclamation Plant, is a promising strategy to leverage investment from the private sector in improving water infrastructure. However, projects of this type should supplement, rather than supplant, public sector investment. The state is constitutionally obliged to provide citizens with access to sufficient water, and mining companies should invest in water treatment to fix the problem that they themselves have caused. Globally, the coal industry has used 'greenwashing' to maintain positive public sentiment and avoid reputational damage (Long et al., 2012). So, while mining companies should be lauded for their investment in the Emalahleni Water Reclamation Plant, this should not blind us to the fact that, on balance, coal mining has devastating impacts on water resources.

Fourth, concerted effort is needed to evaluate the sustainability of coal extraction from a holistic sector-wide perspective. Coal mining needs to be planned and monitored using a centralised framework, rather than case by case. The impacts of the multiple coal mines increase cumulatively because the environment's capacity to absorb the individual impacts becomes eroded and negative synergies exacerbate individual impacts. The Department of Mineral Resources currently grants mining rights while disregarding the cumulative environmental effects of coal mining which it is obliged by law to take into account (Centre for Environmental Rights, 2016). Clarity is needed on how cumulative impacts should be integrated into the decision-making process (Esterhuyse, Redelinghuys and Kemp, 2017). For example, when two mines are established in an area, both are responsible for the cumulative impacts, but only the second mine is likely to be held accountable. This can have detrimental environmental effects because it disproportionately punishes new mines and incentivises mining in previously pristine regions (Buschke and Vanschoenwinkel, 2014). Besides the impacts from coal mines that are currently operational, there are many derelict and ownerless mines in the area that add to the acid mine drainage problem and create long-term liabilities for Emalahleni. Therefore, we need a strategic landscape-level approach to planning and managing the area's coal mines.

Strategic assessment of the probable environmental impacts of planned future coal mines in the region – similar to the strategic environmental assessment for shale gas development that was performed in South Africa in 2016 – could pave the way for more sustainable coal extraction, especially considering the cumulative coal mining impacts already observed in the region. Such an assessment should include vulnerability mapping of biodiversity, sensitive water resources and socio-economic aspects (Esterhuyse et al., 2017). It should also assess the risk of possible future cumulative coal mining impacts and translate this scientific information into policy and regulations aimed at minimising the impacts. This is especially important because the Olifants river is a tributary of the Limpopo, so the acid mine drainage has a transboundary impact on the Limpopo watercourse, which is shared with neighbouring Zimbabwe and Mozambique.

The road forward

This chapter described the direct, indirect, induced and cumulative impacts of coal mining on water resources in the region of Emalahleni. There is a delicate balance between having sufficient energy and having sufficient water. In Emalahleni the emphasis on generating energy from coal has tipped the balance. The coal sector needs to wake up. Prompted by the Paris Agreement in 2016, rating agencies S&P and Moody's (which control 80% of the credit ratings market) have rated unregulated power generation, coal mining and coal terminals as having the highest levels of emerging financial risk (Mathiesen, 2018), largely because environmental factors could limit their future profitability. Unscrupulous coal mines could exploit the government's inability to enforce regulations to maintain profits. However, such a strategy would be viable only in the very short term because local communities are already feeling the effects of deteriorating water quality. If the coal mines in Emalahleni want to keep their social licence to operate and retain long-term profitability, they will have to restore the water–energy balance and ensure that they are not exploiting one precious natural resource at the expense of another.

Over the long term, the existing communities will have to manage water problems (acid mine drainage) and land problems (the reuse of contaminated land). The long-term environmental costs of mining are, however, seldom considered when permitting mining. A just transition after coal mine closure must therefore address these long-term consequences.

References

Breuer, L., Vaché, K. B., Julich, S. and Frede, H.-G. 2008. Current concepts in nitrogen dynamics for mesoscale catchments. *Hydrological Sciences*, 53, 1059–74.

Buschke, F. T. and Esterhuyse, S. 2012. The perceptions of research values and priorities in water resource management from the 3rd Orange River Basin Symposium. *Water SA*, 38, 249–53.

Buschke, F. T., Sommen, J., Seaman, M. T. and Williamson, R. D. 2018. Environmental legislation, mining and Postmasburg's ecosystems. In L. Marais, P. Burger and D. van Rooyen (eds), *Mining and Community in South Africa: From Small Town to Iron Town*. London: Routledge, 121–38.

Buschke, F. T. and Vanschoenwinkel, B. 2014. Mechanisms for the inclusion of cumulative impacts in conservation decision-making are sensitive to vulnerability and irreplaceability in a stochastically simulated landscape. *Journal of Nature Conservation*, 22, 265–71.

Centre for Environmental Rights. 2016. *Zero Hour: Poor Governance of Mining and the Violation of Environmental Rights in Mpumalanga*. Cape Town: Centre for Environmental Rights.

Dabrowski, J. M. and De Klerk, L. P. 2013. An assessment of the impact of different land use activities on water quality in the upper Olifants River catchment. *Water SA*, 39, 231–44.

DWS (Department of Water and Sanitation). 2011. Development of a reconciliation strategy for the Olifants river water supply system. Report No. WP10197, Department of Water Affairs, Pretoria.

DWS (Department of Water and Sanitation). 2016. Development of an integrated water quality management plan for the Olifants river system. Inception Report. Department of Water and Sanitation, Pretoria.

Edwards, D. P., Sloan, S., Weng, L., Dirks, P., Sayer, J. and Laurence, W. F. 2013. Mining and the African environment. *Conservation Letters*, 7, 302–11.

Esterhuyse, S., Redelinghuys, N. and Kemp, M. 2017. Unconventional oil and gas extraction in South Africa: Water linkages within the population–environment–development nexus and its policy implications. In J. E. Nickum, B. B. Brooks, A.Turton and S. Esterhuyse (eds), *The Water Legacies of Conventional Mining*, Routledge special issues on water policy and governance. London: Routledge, 86–102.

Esterhuyse, S., Sokolic, F., Redelinghuys, N., Avenant, M., Kijko, A., Glazewski, J., Plit, L., Kemp, M., Smit, A., Vos, A. T. and von Maltitz, M. J. 2017. Vulnerability mapping as a tool to manage the environmental impacts of oil and gas extraction. *Royal Society Open Science*, 4, e171044.

Hijmans, R. J., Cameron, S. E., Parra, J. L., Jones, P. G. and Jarvis, A. 2005. Very high resolution interpolated climate surfaces for global land areas. *International Journal of Climatology*, 25, 1965–78.

Hobbs, P., Oelofse, S. H. and Rascher, J. 2008. Management of environmental impacts from coal mining in the upper Olifants River catchment as a function of age and scale. *International Journal of Water Resources Development*, 24, 417–31.

IPBES (Intergovernmental Science-Policy Platform on Biodiversity and Ecosystem Services). 2016. *The Methodological Assessment Report on Scenarios and Models for Biodiversity and Ecosystem Services: Summary for Policymakers*. Bonn: IPBES.

IPBES (Intergovernmental Science-Policy Platform on Biodiversity and Ecosystem Services). 2018. *The Assessment Report on Land Degradation and Restoration: Summary for Policymakers.* Bonn: IPBES.

Jarvis, A., Rubiano, J., Nelson, A., Farrow, A. and Mulligan, M. 2004. Practical use of SRTM data in the tropics: Comparisons with digital elevation models generated from cartographic data. Working Document 198, International Centre for Tropical Agriculture, Cali, Colombia.

Long, M. A., Stretesky, P. B., Lynch, M. J. and Fenwick, E. 2012. Crime in the coal industry: Implications for green criminology and treadmill of production. *Organization and Environment,* 25, 328–46.

Mander, M., Jewitt, G., Dini, J., Glenday, J., Blignaut, J., Hughes, C., Marais, C., Maze, K., van der Waal, B. and Mills, A. 2017. Modelling potential hydrological returns from investing in ecological infrastructure: Case studies from the Baviaanskloof-Tsitsikamma and uMngeni catchments, South Africa. *Ecosystem Service,* 27, 261–71.

Matebesi, S., 2017. *Civil Strife Against Local Governance: Dynamics of Community Protests in Contemporary South Africa.* Berlin: Barbara Budrich Publishers.

Matebesi, S., 2020. *Social Licensing and Mining in South Africa.* London: Routledge.

Mathiesen, K. 2018. Rating climate risks to credit worthiness. *Nature Climate Change,* 8, 454–6.

McCarthy, T. S. and Pretorius, K. 2009. Coal mining on the highveld and its implications for future water quality in the Vaal river system. In Proceedings of the 2009 International Mine Water Conference, Water Institute of Southern Africa and International Mine Water Association, Pretoria, 56–65. www.imwa.info/imwa-proceedings/72-proceedings-2009.html (last accessed 21 April 2021).

Muller, M. 2018. Lessons from Cape Town's drought. *Nature,* 559, 174–6.

Obeng-Odoom, F. 2020. *The Commons in the Age of Uncertainty: Decolonising Nature, Economy and Society.* Toronto: University of Toronto Press.

Oberholster, P. J., Botha, A.-M., Hill, L. and Strydom, W. F. 2017. River catchment responses to anthropogenic acidification in relationship with sewage effluent: An ecotoxicology screening application. *Chemosphere,* 189, 407–17.

RSA (Republic of South Africa). 1998. *National Environmental Management Act (107/1998).* Gazette No. 19519. Pretoria: Government Printer.

RSA (Republic of South Africa). 2011. *National Environmental Management: Biodiversity Act (10/2004): National List of Ecosystems That Are Threatened and in Need of Protection.* Government Gazette No. 34809. Pretoria: Government Printer.

Rocha-Nicoleite, E., Overbeck, G. E. and Müller, S. C. 2017. Degradation by coal mining should be priority in restoration planning. *Perspectives in Ecology and Conservation,* 15, 202–5.

SABS (South African Bureau of Standards). 2015. *South African National Standard (SANS) (241) Drinking Water.* Pretoria: SABS Standards Division.

SANBI (South African National Biodiversity Institute). 2013. *Grassland Ecosystem Guidelines: Landscape Interpretation for Planners and Managers.* Compiled by C. Cadman, C. de Villiers, R. Lechmere-Oertel and D. McCulloch Pretoria: South African National Biodiversity Institute.

SANBI (South African National Biodiversity Institute). 2014. *A Framework for Investing in Ecological Infrastructure in South Africa.* Pretoria: SANBI.

Scanlon, B. R., Jolly, I., Sophocleous, M. and Zhang, L. 2007. Global impacts of conversions from natural to agricultural ecosystems on water resources: Quantity versus quality. *Water Resources Research,* 43, W03437. doi: 10.1029/2006WR005486.

Tambo, O. and Theobald, S. 2018. *Financial Provisioning for Rehabilitation and Mine Closure: A Study of South African Platinum and Coal Mining Companies.* Intellidex. https://fulldisclosure. cer.org.za/2018/wp-content/uploads/2018/06/Intellidex-financial-provisioning-for-rehabilitation-and-closure-in-SA-mining.pdf (last accessed 11 May 2021).

Turpie, J., Marais, C. and Blignaut, J. 2008. The working for water programme: Evolution of a payments for ecosystem services mechanism that addresses both poverty and ecosystem service delivery in South Africa. *Ecological Economics*, 65, 788–98.

Xiao, W., Fu, Y., Wang, T. and Lv, X. 2018. Effects of land use transitions due to underground coal mining on ecosystem services in high groundwater table areas: A case study in the Yanzou coalfield. *Land Use Policy*, 71, 213–21.

CHAPTER 8

The Health Impacts of Coal Mining and Coal-based Energy

Stuart Paul Denoon-Stevens and Katrina du Toit

Coal and health

The relationship between coal and capitalist development is not well established in the literature. At the same time, it has also come at a cost: climate change, land degradation and people's health (Obeng-Odoom, 2020). This chapter investigates the health impact of coal mining and asks whether there might be benefits to moving away from coal. These health concerns have not received adequate attention in the literature and a full consideration of the cost of coal should include health costs.

Emalahleni Local Municipality falls under the Nkangala District Municipality. This chapter is based on data from Nkangala because the district is the lowest level of health management data in South Africa. Nkangala faces considerable environmental health challenges. It is part of the Highveld Air Quality Priority Region, which, because of its many coal-fired power plants, frequently exceeds the pollution limits set for acceptable air quality. In a 2015 Department of Environmental Affairs review of progress in reducing air pollutants in this region, Witbank exceeded the World Health Organization limits (WHO, 2005) in all the years studied (2012–15), generating more than twice the permitted level of $PM_{2.5}$ (fine particulate matter) pollutants in 2012 and 2013 and nearly three times the permitted level in 2015. Similar levels were found for PM_{10} (coarse particulate matter), SO_2 (sulphur dioxide), NO_2 (nitrogen dioxide) and O_3 (ozone). The main contributor to these pollutants on the Highveld is coal-fired power generation, except for PM_{10}, which is mostly caused by mining.

The extensive coal mining places a considerable health burden on the region, both for miners and for those living in the current and former coal mining areas (Hendryx, 2015). In a systematic review of the literature, Cortes-Ramirez et al. (2018) found that coal mining was connected with a wide range of health problems, encompassing 78 ICD (International Classification of Diseases) categories in nine different groups, in particular cancer and birth defects. In Emalahleni, concerns about the health risks from coal mining and coal-based power generation stretch back to the early 1920s (Singer, 2011). Research has validated the concerns in South Africa. Naidoo et al. (2004), for example, found that around 2–4% of coal miners in their study had pneumoconiosis, and autopsies showed that coal miners had prevalence rates of silicosis, tuberculosis (TB), coal workers' pneumoconiosis and emphysema of 10.7%, 5.2%, 7.3% and 6.4%, respectively.

Against this background, this chapter discusses the health dynamics of Nkangala District Municipality. We find that despite the considerable disease burden resulting from mining and energy generation, the resources allocated to the district are irrationally low and the poor quality of healthcare, in particular with regard to screening for HIV/ AIDS and TB, is adding to the health burden. A just transition will require a plan to deal with the long-term health problems created by coal mining and energy generation in the area. We ask the following specific questions in the chapter:

- Is there an overinvestment by the mines to counter coal's health cost and could one expect this to continue after coal?
- Are there indications of poorer health in the area and is this related to coal?

Literature review

Mining, health and healthcare

Only a few studies investigate the link between mining and healthcare systems. Two cross-country studies found that resource dependency is detrimental to state expenditure on health care. Cockx and Francken (2014) found that greater accountability of state actors mitigated the effects of mining. Karimu et al. (2017) found a positive relationship between overall public expenditure and resource rents,[1] but a negative relationship between expenditure and health, implying that road and other infrastructure investments were responsible for the overall positive relationship. Contradicting those findings, El Anshasy and Katsaiti (2015) found that in economies dependent on mineral resources, expenditure on healthcare was higher, with a 10% increase in the mineral resources rent share equating to a 0.4% increase in public healthcare provision.

Other studies have looked at the connection between dependence on a resource and health outcomes. Here, the results are less contradictory. In a cross-country study of oil-rich and oil-poor countries, with a specific focus on HIV/ AIDS, De Soysa and Gizelis (2013) found that the rate of HIV/AIDS was higher in the oil-rich countries. They found that 'increasing oil rents per capita by one standard deviation, holding all other variables at their means, increases the prevalence of HIV/AIDS by roughly 10% of the mean value of the prevalence of HIV/AIDS' (De Soysa and Gizelis, 2013: 93). Additionally, in a similar cross-country study, Wigley (2017) found that oil-poor countries were more successful than oil-rich countries in reducing child mortality. In a study that challenges but does not contradict these findings, Kim and Lin (2017) found a significant and negative relationship between life expectancy and resource exports and specific resource dependence.

Coal mining and coal-based power generation

Bloch et al. (2018) found that a sample of 306,297 South African miners had a 20% higher mortality rate than the general population, which they attributed to the sample's higher HIV rate. Of relevance for our topic of Emalahleni, they found that coal miners had a substantially lower mortality rate than miners in other sectors: a rate of 6.2 per 100,000 years, compared with 23.1 for the full sample. However, this finding needs treating with caution, as it may have been an effect of underrepresentation of coal miners in the sample.

Coal mining also affects surrounding communities. For example, in a survey of 16,493 West Virginians, Hendryx and Ahern (2008) found that high levels of coal production correlated with higher rates of cardiopulmonary disease, chronic obstructive pulmonary disease, hypertension, lung disease and kidney disease. Similar studies were done by Ahern et al. (2011) and Hendryx (2015). We note, however, the caution raised by Boyles et al. (2017): 'the strong potential for bias in the current body of human literature'.

Other studies have investigated the health effects of the use of coal for energy. Two studies undertaken by the GBD MAPS working group project (2016, 2018) found that coal burning by industry and power plants and for domestic heating accounted for approximately 366,200 deaths in China in 2013, and 169,300 deaths in India in 2015.

In South Africa, the issue of coal mining and coal-based power generation has received considerable attention from the non-profit organisations Greenpeace and Groundwork. Myllyvirta (2014), Greenpeace coal and air pollution specialist, estimated that '2,200 to 2,700 premature deaths are caused each year by the air pollution emissions from Eskom's coal-fired power plants, including 200 deaths of young children'. Holland (2017), commissioned by Groundwork and building on Myllyvirta's findings, estimated that coal-fired power generation costs the South African economy USD 2,373 million and 996,628 lost working days annually. In other reports for Groundwork, Hallowes and Munnik (2016, 2017) provided a more qualitative review of these issues as they affect South Africa's Highveld region. Their 2016 report documents the damage that coal mining has done to this region, and their 2017 report, focusing on coal-generated electricity, documents some of the air pollution issues described at the beginning of this chapter, and also notes that the climate of the Highveld is particularly unsuited to air pollution dispersion, which exacerbates the already severe health impacts.

The health infrastructure of Nkangala

Public health facilities, budget and personnel

In terms of medical personnel employed in the public sector, Nkangala is significantly worse off than South Africa as a whole, with one medical practitioner (including specialists) per 4,703 uninsured people in Nkangala, compared to one per 2,471 at a national level. Put differently, medical practitioners in Nkangala have nearly twice as many potential patients as the average South African medical practitioner. Similar trends can be seen for every type of health professional listed in Table 8.1, with the sole exception of dental practitioners.

Nkangala has one tertiary hospital, seven district hospitals, and 13 other hospitals, including a specialist TB hospital, 79 public clinics, 7 private clinics and 23 community health centres[2] (HST, 2017). This equates to 15,419 uninsured people per clinic, which is 13% more than the South African average.[3] However, this is mitigated to some extent by the fact that Nkangala has 59% more community health centres per 100,000 individuals than the national average, and the difference is only 1.1% if clinics and community health centres are combined.

In terms of satisfaction with the clinics and hospitals in the area, the 2016 Community Survey showed that Nkangala did not measure up to the national average. Hospitals in Nkangala were rated good by only 29.5% of residents (national average 41.6%); 10.5% did not have access to hospitals (national average 6.5%); clinics were rated good by 37.2% (national average 41.8%); and 4.7% did not have access to a clinic (national average 3.8%) (Stats SA, 2016). On the ideal clinic index, 23.6% of clinics achieved silver or higher status (national average 29.8%) (see Table 8.3 below).

Nkangala's health budget is a matter for concern. Expenditure on primary healthcare was R767.24[4] per capita in 2016, which is 37.4% less than the national average of R1,054,28. Of South Africa's 52 districts, this is the second lowest per capita expenditure (the lowest was Alfred Nzo). Overall health expenditure (including spending on hospitals) was slightly better at R1,470 per capita, which is 17.4% less than the national average of R1,726. The district's poor stock of

Table 8.1 Number of individuals to one public health worker, by type, in Nkangala and South Africa, 2016		
	Nkangala	**South Africa**
Occupational therapists	55,367	36,244
Physiotherapists	50,753	34,647
Dental practitioners	35,826	41,496
Pharmacists	18,456	8,882
Medical practitioners	4,703	2,471
Enrolled nurses	4,129	1,481
Nursing assistants	3,593	1,341
Professional nurses	978	685
Community Health Workers	934	n/a

Sources: Stats SA (2016); Day and Gray (2017)

essential medicines is a further matter for concern: only 69% of primary health clinics had 90% of the essential medicines available, compared to the national average of 78.4% (HST, 2017; see Table 8.3).

Health services provided by mines and power stations in Nkangala
This section would be incomplete without recognition of the health services provided by the mines. There are seven occupational health centres at the various mines and power plants, and a further seven hospitals linked to the mines (HST, 2017). These health facilities typically provide healthcare services to employees at the mines, and occasionally their dependants. Over and above these facilities, the mines run health programmes for their employees. Anglo American, the largest mining group in the area, is particularly proud of its health systems and its HIV/AIDS programme. This programme has been running since 2002 and involves annual anonymous HIV counselling and testing campaigns, and a wellness programme for HIV-positive employees, including the provision of antiretroviral therapy (Meyer-Rath et al., 2015). This is not purely altruistic, as Anglo American has worked out that providing antiretroviral drugs (ARVs) in 2010 cost $126 per worker but resulted in savings of $219 (World Coal Association, 2012). In 2014, Anglo American had 8,808 workers on this programme, of whom 1,425 were HIV-positive (16.5%) (Brink and Pienaar, 2014).

The downside, however, is that the mines provide these health services only to their employees, not to contract workers. The household survey undertaken for this book found that contract workers and mineworkers supplied by labour brokers made up around a third of all mineworkers. These individuals typically do not receive good healthcare, despite working in the harsh conditions of the mines, and are reliant on the state for healthcare services.

One superior healthcare service is the recently introduced 'offsets' programme run by Eskom (the South African electricity provider). The aim of the programme is to improve air quality in areas close to coal-fired energy plants by reducing domestic fuel burning, such as burning coal and wood for heating or cooking. The intention is to offset some of the health damage caused by coal-based power plants by reducing household emissions rather than the emissions at the plants. This is done by helping households to move to cleaner sources of energy such as electricity, providing heating and cooking devices with lower emissions, and insulating houses to reduce the need for heating (Eskom, 2017). As the programme is only in the early implementation phase, it is too early to tell how effective it will be in the long term.

The health of Nkangala

To get a sense of the health problems that Nkangala, and by implication Emalahleni, is facing we analysed data from the Health Systems Trust District

Health Barometer 2016/2017 (HST, 2017), *South African Health Review* 2017 (Day and Gray 2017), the Statistics South Africa community survey (Stats SA, 2016) and the Statistics South Africa statistical release on mortality and causes of death (Stats SA, 2018). We note that the cause of death statistics in these three sources contain many errors. Findings based on these data sets must therefore be viewed with caution. We were obliged to use them because to date they remain the only data sets that list causes of death at district level.

The community survey (Stats SA, 2016) data show that the situation in Nkangala is worse than the national average, whereas the cause of death statistics (Stats SA, 2018) show the reverse. We used the community survey (Stats SA, 2016) rather than the cause of death statistics for mortality rates (Stats SA, 2018) because (a) the data are in line with the inpatient crude death rate[5] for Nkangala (HST, 2017), which is 23.71% higher than the national average (see Table 8.3), and (b) the data from the community survey (Stats SA, 2016) are more in line with the results we expected, given the statistics on the quality and quantity of healthcare in the district and the high levels of air pollution. For the purpose of this chapter we used the premature mortality rate and the age-specific mortality rate.

Premature mortality is calculated as follows:

$$\textit{Premature mortality rate} = \textit{(Number of individuals who died before reaching the age of average life expectancy / Total population alive) x 100,000}$$

The rate of premature mortality for Nkangala was 9.7% higher than for South Africa (650 deaths per 100,000 alive individuals, compared to 593). For men the rate was 8.4% higher, and for women 10.9% higher (Stats SA, 2016).

Age-specific mortality is calculated as follows:

$$\textit{Age-specific mortality rate} = \textit{(Number of deaths per age group / Total population alive per age group) x 100,000}$$

Figure 8.1 shows that Nkangala has a higher than average mortality rate for several age groups. The rate for children is noticeable, particularly the rate between the ages of 6 and 10, which is 41.1% higher than the national rate. There is a strong likelihood that this can be explained in part by Nkangala's severe air pollution. As evidence, the Health Systems Trust (HST, 2017) lists lower respiratory tract illnesses as the leading cause of death for children aged 5 to 14, and Albers et al. (2015) found that 34.1% of their sample of children aged 9 to 11 in Emalahleni and Steve Tshwete had respiratory health problems, and that this was level was elevated in households using non-electrical fuel sources.

For reasons that are not clear, young people aged 11 to 20 had a below average mortality rate, with those aged 11 to 15 having a rate 27.6% below the national average, and those aged 16 to 20 a rate 45.5% below. The rate for

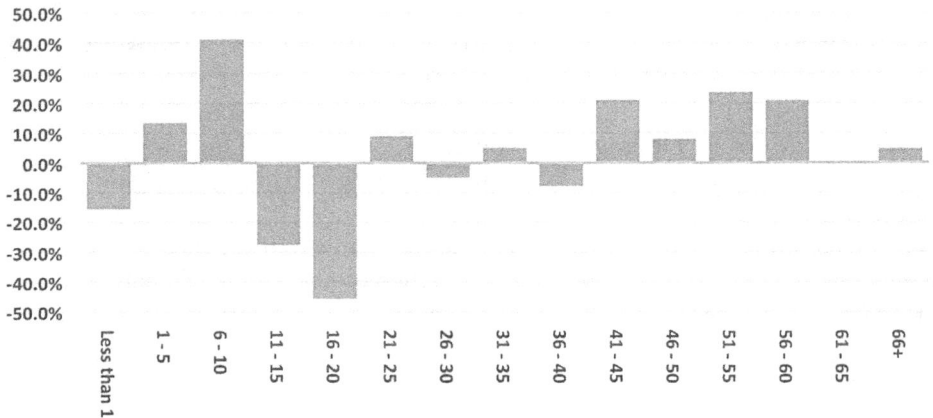

Figure 8.1 Age-specific mortality rates in Nkangala compared with South Africa as a whole.

adults aged 21 to 40 was very little different from the national average, but above the average for those aged 41 to 60. The Health Systems Trust data (HST, 2017) show that the leading causes of death in this age group are HIV/AIDS, TB and lower respiratory tract illnesses.

From the 2015 figures on population and the number of individuals with HIV/AIDS according to the 2017–22 integrated development plan (IDP) (Nkangala District Municipality, 2017), we estimated that the HIV/AIDS prevalence rate for the district is 15%, considerably higher than the national rate of 11%. De Soysa and Gizelis (2013) found a clear link between HIV/AIDS and mining (though this is contested by Sterck, 2016), so it is possible that this higher than average HIV/AIDS rate may be partly related to the mining in Nkangala. One explanation that has been suggested for the higher rate of HIV/AIDS among miners, for example by Corno and de Walque (2012), is the continuing use of migrant labour, which separates men from their families and creates the opportunity for multiple concurrent relationships.

Table 8.2 shows the 10 leading causes of death in Nkangala in 2016, compared with the average for all 52 district municipalities. Nkangala had the 10th highest number of deaths from respiratory diseases, with 12.1% of deaths being from this cause, compared to the average of 9.4%. The significantly higher portion of deaths from respiratory diseases points to the likely role of air pollution. See Mo et al. (2018) for strong evidence linking respiratory illnesses to air pollution in China.

The municipality's IDP lists the following specific causes of death, with the first five being respiratory illnesses: tuberculosis, pneumonia, acute respiratory infections, bronchitis, bronchopneumonia, immune suppression/HIV/AIDS, head injuries arising from motor vehicle accidents, gastro-cardiac conditions,

Table 8.2 Causes of death in Nkangala, 2016

Cause of death	% of all deaths	Rank	Diff. in rank from average district municipality
External causes of morbidity and mortality	13.4	4	-22
Diseases of the respiratory system	12.1	10	-16
Other natural causes	17.8	16	-10
Diseases of the circulatory system	18.7	28	2
Conditions originating in the perinatal period	1.8	28	2
Diseases of the blood and immune mechanism	2.4	33	7
Endocrine, nutritional and metabolic diseases	6.7	33	7
Infectious and parasitic diseases	17.7	34	8
Diseases of the digestive system	2.2	40	14
Diseases of the nervous system	1.8	43	17
Neoplasms (tumours, e.g. cancer)	5.3	45	19

Source: Stats SA (2018)

diabetes mellitus and stillbirths/prematurity (Nkangala District Municipality, 2017). A parliamentary question posted in 2018 to the Minister of Health, asking what the 10 leading causes of admission to a healthcare facility in Nkangala were in the 2016–17 financial year, received the following response: HIV/AIDS, TB, lower respiratory tract infections, hypertensive heart diseases, ischaemic heart diseases, cerebrovascular diseases, chronic obstructive pulmonary disease, diabetes, diarrhoeal diseases and road injuries (Minister of Health, 2018).

External causes of morbidity and mortality are also extremely high in Nkangala. The district ranked 4th out of the 52 municipalities, with this being the cause of 13.4% of deaths in the municipality, compared to the average of 11.2%. This could be partly because of occupational accidents at the mines and the power stations, and partly because of the high level of alcohol consumption in the area, as per the findings in the household survey.

Unusually, neoplasms (abnormal growths, such as cancer) were the cause of only 5.3% of all deaths, compared to an average of 9.3%, ranking Nkangala 45th out of the 52 district municipalities. One possible explanation for this is the shortage of oncology facilities in the area, with oncology patients being treated in Gauteng (Portfolio Committee on Health, 2014).

Table 8.3 provides evidence of the quality of medical care in Nkangala in recent years, compared with that of South Africa as a whole. Nkangala's high crude death rate is evident. Corroborating the data from the 2016 Community Health Survey (Stats SA, 2016), it was 23.7% higher than the national average.

The maternal mortality rate is a matter for concern, at 19.2% higher than the national average. This may partly explain why women in Nkangala have a higher premature mortality rate than men. Conversely, the rate of deaths of newborns within seven days of delivery is 14.5% lower than the average. Other contraceptive and reproductive issues are also a matter for concern. The percentage of infants who at 10 weeks are infected with HIV is 35.8% higher than the average. The percentage of women protected against pregnancy using modern contraceptive devices is 15.5% lower than the average. The male condom distribution rate is 13.2% lower than the average, and the male medical circumcision rate (which some research has suggested may act as a preventive measure against HIV/AIDS) is 80.97% lower than the average.

As regards finance, Nkangala has a below average expenditure for all given indicators, in particular expenditure per capita on primary healthcare, which is 37.4% below the average, and the second lowest in the country. Overall district health expenditure per capita is slightly better, though still 17.42% below the average. This is a long-running trend: Blecher et al. (2008) note that Nkangala had some of the lowest expenditure per capita in 2005/6, 2006/7 and 2007/8. They show that two reasons for this are lack of expenditure on community services and low local government contributions.

The district's screening performance is mixed. The screening of patients older than five years for TB is a disturbing 104.8% below the average. The HIV screening situation is less dire but still a worry, with the screening rate being 26.6% below the average. However, surprisingly, initiating HIV and TB patients on medication and following up with them is better than the average. For example, the percentage of GeneXpert-confirmed TB patients who started treatment is 16.8% above the average. The follow-up situation is more mixed. The 84.5% of drug-resistant TB patients lost to follow-up is below the average, but the percentage of drug-resistant TB patients cured plus those who completed treatment is 7.1% above the average. The percentage of TB patients overall lost to follow-up is 6.6% below the average. The percentage of people estimated to be living with HIV who remain on ART is only 2.6% below the average.

The overall picture shows that the district's health services are performing very poorly in terms of screening, but doing reasonably well in initiating TB and HIV patients on treatment. However, this is to be expected if only a small proportion of the actual cases of TB and HIV are being identified. Given that it is expected that this district will have a greater health burden than the typical district, because of the effects of coal mining and coal-based energy, this is highly problematic. The likelihood is high that, because of the low screening rate, many sick people are not being identified, which means that many of those affected by the coal mining and coal-based energy are not receiving the treatment they need.

Table 8.4 shows that in 2016 the district was also mostly underperforming with regard to child healthcare. Most worrying is that the proportion of

Table 8.3 Key indicators of quality of healthcare in Nkangala and South Africa (2016, and some earlier years)

Section	Indicator	Unit	Nkangala	South Africa	Difference (%)	Year
	Provincial expenditure on DHS sub-programmes (2.2–2.7) plus net local govt. expenditure on PHC divided by PHC headcount from DHIS	ZAR per capita	365.39	389.31	-6.55	2016
Finance	Provincial expenditure on all DHS sub-programmes (except 2.8, coroner services) plus net local govt. expenditure on PHC per uninsured pop.	ZAR per capita	1,470.04	1,726.12	**-17.42**	2016
	Provincial expenditure on sub-programmes of DHS (2.2 - 2.7) plus net local govt. expenditure on PHC per uninsured pop.	ZAR per capita	767.24	1,054.28	**-37.41**	2016
	PHC facilities, of all facilities that have conducted a status determination, with 90% of the tracer medicines available	%	68.97	78.40	-13.68	2016
Management of PHC	Fixed PHC facilities assessed on ideal clinic dashboard that achieved ideal clinic status (silver, gold, platinum or diamond)	%	23.6	29.80	**-26.30**	2016
	Admitted patients/separations who died during hospital stay	%	6.41	4.89	**23.71**	2016
	Beds occupied, expressed as proportion of all available bed days	%	73.30	63.90	12.82	2016
Management of inpatients	No. of patient days that an admitted patient spends in hospital before separation	Patient days	5.00	4.44	11.19	2016
	Average cost per patient per day seen in a hospital (ZAR per patient day equivalent)	ZAR per capita	2,544.83	2,568.43	-0.93	2016
	Women who die in a health facility as a result of childbearing, during pregnancy or within 42 days of delivery or termination of pregnancy, per 100,000 live births	Rate per 100,000	144.56	116.87	**19.15**	2016
Childbirth	Inpatient deaths within first 7 days of life per 1,000 live births	Rate per 1,000	8.67	9.93	-14.50	2016

Section	Indicator	Unit	Nkangala	South Africa	Difference (%)	Year
Prevention of mother-to-child transmission	Infants tested PCR-positive for follow-up test as proportion of infants PCR-tested around 10 weeks	%	2.07	1.33	**35.77**	2016
	Antenatal patients on ART as proportion of total no. of antenatal patients who are HIV positive and not previously on ART	%	96.38	95.13	1.29	2016
Reproductive health	Proportion of women 30 years and older who had Pap smear screening (according to national policy of screening all women in this age category every 10 years)	%	56.44	61.48	-8.93	2016
	Women using modern contraceptive methods, including sterilisation, as proportion of female pop. 15–49 years	%	60.83	70.24	**-15.47**	2016
	TB rifampicin-resistant confirmed patients started on treatment	%	92.89	67.95	**26.85**	2016
	GeneXpert-confirmed TB patients started on treatment	%	87.46	72.81	**16.75**	2016
	Positive TB tests that are rifampicin resistant	%	6.29	6.19	1.60	2016
	Patients 5 years and older screened for TB symptoms as proportion of PHC headcount	%	25.20	51.60	**-104.78**	2016
	HIV-positive TB cases (all TB) recorded as being on ART	%	94.85	88.27	6.94	2016
TB	TB patients (all types registered in ETR.net) cured plus those who completed treatment	%	84.89	80.96	4.63	2015
	TB patients (all types of TB registered in ETR.net) who died	%	6.57	6.58	-0.14	2015
	TB patients who were lost to follow-up as proportion of TB patients started on treatment	%	6.02	6.42	-6.63	2015
	TB patients (DR TB) cured plus those who completed treatment	%	50.81	47.23	7.05	2013
	TB patients (DR TB) who died	%	23.15	23.00	0.63	2014
	TB patients (DR TB) lost to follow-up	%	9.72	17.94	**-84.49**	2014

Section	Indicator	Unit	Nkangala	South Africa	Difference (%)	Year
	Patients (including ANC first and re-test patients) tested pos. for HIV	%	8.64	8.16	5.46	2016
	People living with HIV who remain on ARVs	%	53.63	55.00	-2.55	2016
HIV	No. of male condoms distributed to patients via the facility or via factories, offices, restaurants, NGOs or other outlets, per male 15 years and older	Per capita	42.02	47.54	-13.15	2016
	Patients HIV tested (ANC and other) as proportion of pop. 15–49 years	%	28.37	35.92	**-26.63**	2016+
	No. of female condoms distributed per female 15 years and older via the facility or via factories, offices, restaurants, NGOs or other outlets	Per capita	0.71	1.26	**-78.10**	2016

Notes: Differences in bold represent high values (more than 15% difference between the absolute values).

ANC = antenatal care, ART = antiretroviral therapy, ARV = antiretroviral (drug), DHS = district health services, DHIS = district health information system, DR TB = drug-resistant tuberculosis, ETR-net = electronic tuberculosis register, GeneXpert = machine that performs a chemical test to identify Mycobacterium tuberculosis, NCD = non-communicable disease, PCR = polymerase chain reaction, PHC = primary health care, Separation = when a patient leaves a hospital, including instances where the patient dies, is discharged or leaves against medical advice, or is transferred; Tracer medicine = 14 drugs used to monitor whether a healthcare facility has adequate stocks of essential medication.

Source: HST (2018)

Table 8.4 Key indicators of quality of child healthcare in Nkangala, 2016, in percentages			
Indicator	Nkangala	South Africa	Difference
Children under 5 yrs admitted with pneumonia who died	2.69	2.01	**25.18**
Children under 5 yrs admitted with diarrhoea who died	0.84	2.05	**-144.03**
Children under 5 yrs admitted with severe acute malnutrition who died	6.52	7.96	**-22.00**
Female Grade 4 pupils who received 1st HPV immunisation	77.01	78.00	-1.28
Female Grade 4 pupils who received 2nd HPV immunisation	60.27	60.80	-0.88
All children under 1 yr who completed primary course of immunisation	80.31	82.29	-2.47
Children who received 2nd measles immunisation (around 18 mths)	87.02	96.25	-10.61
Exclusively breastfed infants who received 3rd DTaP-IPV-Hib-HBV at 14 weeks	34.88	41.63	**-19.34**
Children 12–59 mths who received vitamin A 200,000 units, pref. every 6 mths	53.12	58.00	-9.19
Grade 1 pupils screened by a nurse in line with ISHP service package	28.80	33.00	-14.58
Grade 8 pupils screened by a nurse in line with ISHP service package	8.80	19.80	**-125.00**

Notes: Differences in bold represent high values (more than 15% difference between the absolute values).

DTaP-IPV-Hib-HBV = diphtheria, tetanus, acellular pertussis, inactivated polio vaccine, Haemophilus influenzae type B, hepatitis B (part of the standard vaccination schedule), HPV = human papillomavirus, ISHP = integrated school health policy, PHC = primary health care.

Source: HST (2018)

Grade 8 pupils screened by a nurse is 125% lower than the national average. The proportion of children under 5 years admitted with pneumonia who died is 25.2% higher than the average. This may be the effect of air pollution, and may explain the higher mortality rate. For example, Li et al. (2018) have shown a link between elevated levels of air pollution and hospital visits for pneumonia in children in Taipei, Taiwan.

The levels of the various immunisations were below the South African average, but mostly by a small to moderate margin. The one immunisation statistic that was significantly below the national average (a greater than 15% difference) was the proportion of exclusively breastfed infants who had received their third DTaP-IPV-Hib-HBV immunisation at 14 weeks (19.34% less than the national average).

Two indicators that showed Nkangala doing better than the average were the percentage of children under 5 years admitted with diarrhoea who died (144% lower than the average), and the percentage of children under 5 years admitted with severe acute malnutrition who died (22% lower than the average). The available data do not provide any answers on why this district is performing better in this regard, in particular given its overall performance.

As with the statistics for adult patients, the low screening rate means that sick children are probably not being identified. The elevated pneumonia rate provides some evidence of a link between the poor health of the district and air pollution.

Discussion and conclusion

Despite Nkangala's strong economic foundation,[6] its public health expenditure per capita is low. The district has a substantially higher premature mortality rate and crude death rate than the South African average. We also expect these impacts to be substantially more severe among black communities, which are generally poor (Talukdar, 2016). It also means that any attempt to a just transition requires an explicit reference to race.

The question is why there is this disparity between the wealth of the district and its health outcomes. For instance, Stuckler, Basu and McKee (2011) note that with each financial allocation the gap between health needs and funding widens, and they suggest that some of this disparity in healthcare in South Africa may be due to a historical lack of investment in healthcare in specific regions. Part of the problem may spring from the historical reliance on the mines to provide healthcare to their workers.

The data presented in this chapter provide tentative evidence for a link between coal mining and coal-based energy and the health outcomes experienced in Nkangala. In particular, the high rate of deaths attributable to respiratory illnesses can most likely be explained as the effect of the high levels of air pollution in the area.

Given the findings of this chapter, it would appear that the residents of Emalahleni are on the receiving end of a patently unfair situation, where the mines are polluting the air of the district and demonstrably causing respiratory health problems, and yet the residents are receiving substandard healthcare from the government. It is not sufficient for the government merely to talk about reducing the reliance on coal over the long term in South Africa (Department of Energy, 2018). Immediate action is needed to improve healthcare in Nkangala, to mitigate the harmful effects of air pollution.

This is key to achieving a just transition. It is likely that even as coal mining, and coal-based energy production, declines in importance, these communities will continue to suffer from the health impacts of coal mining and coal-based energy production. For example, people who have suffered from lower respiratory illnesses may have diminished lung capacity or structural damage, which may make them more susceptible to future respiratory illnesses. Furthermore, mines leave behind tailings and disturbed land, which can lead to acid mine drainage and air pollution (specifically, particulate matter), which will continue to affect the health of surrounding communities.

Given this situation, a just transition requires sustained effort on the part of the state to raise the level of healthcare in Nkangala. The district needs a medical system that is not simply on par with other district municipalities, but can cope with the higher health burden that coal mining and coal-based energy production imposes, both now and in the future.

References

Ahern, M., Mullett, M., MacKay, K. and Hamilton, C. 2011. Residence in coal-mining areas and low-birth-weight outcomes. *Maternal and Child Health Journal*, 15(7), 974–79.

Albers, P. N., Wright, C. Y., Voyi, K. V. and Mathee, A. 2015. Household fuel use and child respiratory ill health in two towns in Mpumalanga, South Africa. *South African Medical Journal*, 105(7), 573–7.

Blecher, M. S., Day, C., Dove, S. and Cairns, R. 2008. Primary health care financing in the public sector. In P. Barron J. and Roma-Reardon (eds), *South African Health Review 2008*. Durban: Health Systems Trust, pp. 179–94.

Bloch, K., Johnson, L. F., Nkosi, M. and Ehrlich, R. 2018. Precarious transition: A mortality study of South African ex-miners. *BMC Public Health*, 18(1), 862.

Boyles, A. L., Blain, R. B., Rochester, J. R., Avanasi, R., Goldhaber, S. B., McComb, S., Holmgren, S. D., Masten, S. A. and Thayer, K. A. 2017. Systematic review of community health impacts of mountaintop removal mining. *Environment International*, 107, 163–72.

Brink, B. and Pienaar, J. 2014. What makes a successful response to HIV/AIDS and TB? The Anglo American Coal SA example. https://mhsc.org.za/sites/default/files/public/publications/What%20makes%20a%20successful%20response%20to%20HIV%20%26%20TB.pdf (last accessed 27 April 2021).

Cockx, L. and Francken, N. 2014. Extending the concept of the resource curse: Natural resources and public spending on health. *Ecological Economics*, 108, 136–49.

Corno, L. and de Walque, D. 2012. Mines, migration and HIV/AIDS in southern Africa. *Journal of African Economies*, 21(3), 465–98.

Cortes-Ramirez, J., Naish, S., Sly, P. D. and Jagals, P. 2018. Mortality and morbidity in populations in the vicinity of coal mining: A systematic review. *BMC Public Health*, 18(1), 721.

Day, C. and Gray, A. 2017. Health and related indicators. In A. Padarath and P. Barron (eds), *South African Health Review 2017*. Durban: Health Systems Trust, pp. 217–340.

Department of Energy. 2018. Draft Integrated Resource Plan. http://www.energy.gov.za/IRP/irp-update-draft-report2018/IRP-Update-2018-Draft-for-Comments.pdf (last accessed 27 April 2021).

Department of Environmental Affairs. 2015. The medium-term review of the 2011 Highveld Priority Area (HPA): Air quality management plan. Draft review report. https://cer.org.za/

wp-content/uploads/2016/07/HPA-AQMP-Midterm-review-Draft-Report_February-2016.pdf (last accessed 27 April 2021).

De Soysa, I. and Gizelis, T. I. 2013. The natural resource curse and the spread of HIV/AIDS, 1990–2008. *Social Science and Medicine*, 77, 90–6.

El Anshasy, A. A. and Katsaiti, M. S. 2015. Are natural resources bad for health? *Health and Place*, 32, 29–42.

Eskom. 2017. Air quality offsets implementation plan for Nkangala District Municipality: Hendrina, Arnot, Komati, Kriel, Matla, Kendal and Duvha power stations: March 2017 update. http://www.eskom.co.za/AirQuality/Documents/AQoffsetPlanNkangalaMar17.pdf.

GBD MAPS Working Group. 2016. *Burden of Disease Attributable to Coal-Burning and Other Major Sources of Air Pollution in China*. Special Report 20. Boston, MA: Health Effects Institute.

GBD MAPS Working Group. 2018. *Burden of Disease Attributable to Major Air Pollution Sources in India*. Special Report 21. Boston, MA: Health Effects Institute.

Hallowes, D. and Munnik, V. 2016. *The Destruction of the Highveld part 1: Digging Coal.* http://www.groundwork.org.za/reports/gWReport_2016.pdf (last accessed 27 April 2021).

Hallowes, D. and Munnik, V. 2017. *The Destruction of the Highveld part 1: Burning Coal.* https://lifeaftercoal.org.za/wp-content/uploads/2017/11/FINAL-DoH-Part-2_gW-Report_16-Nov-2017.pdf (last accessed 27 April 2021).

Hendryx, M. 2015. The public health impacts of surface coal mining. *The Extractive Industries and Society*, 2(4), 820–6.

Hendryx, M. and Ahern, M. M. 2008. Relations between health indicators and residential proximity to coal mining in West Virginia. *American Journal of Public Health*, 98(4), 669–71.

Holland, M. 2017. *Health Impacts of Coal-fired Power Generation in South Africa.* https://cer.org.za/wp-content/uploads/2017/04/Annexure-Health-impacts-of-coal-fired-generation-in-South-Africa-310317.pdf (last accessed 27 April 2021).

HST (Health Systems Trust). 2017. District Health Barometer 2016/2017. Report and associated dataset. http://www.hst.org.za/publications/Pages/District-Health-Barometer-201617.aspx (last accessed 27 April 2021).

IndexMundi. 2018. Total natural resources rents (% of GDP). https://www.indexmundi.com/facts/indicators/NY.GDP.TOTL.RT.ZS (last accessed 27 April 2021).

Karimu, A., Adu, G., Marbuah, G., Mensah, J. T. and Amuakwa-Mensah, F. 2017. Natural resource revenues and public investment in resource-rich economies in sub-Saharan Africa. *Review of Development Economics*, 21(4), e107–e130.

Kim, D. H. and Lin, S. C. 2017. Human capital and natural resource dependence. *Structural Change and Economic Dynamics*, 40, 92–102.

Li, D., Wang, J. B., Zhang, Z. Y., Shen, P., Zheng, P. W., Jin, M. J., Lu, H. C., Lin, H. B. and Chen, K. 2018. Effects of air pollution on hospital visits for pneumonia in children: A two-year analysis from China. *Environmental Science and Pollution Research*, 25(10), 10049–57.

Meyer-Rath, G., Pienaar, J., Brink, B., Van Zyl, A., Muirhead, D., Grant, A., Churchyard, G., Watts, C. and Vickerman, P. 2015. The impact of company-level art provision to a mining workforce in South Africa: A cost-benefit analysis. *PLoS Medicine*, 12(9), e1001869. doi: 10.1371/journal.pmed.1001869.

Minister of Health (South Africa). 2018. Written reply to question number 785, asked by Ms Ms L Mathys. https://pmg.org.za/files/RNW785-180423.docx (last accessed 27 April 2021).

Mo, Z., Fu, Q., Zhang, L., Lyu, D., Mao, G., Wu, L., Xu, P., Wang, Z., Pan, X., Chen, Z. and Wang, X. 2018. Acute effects of air pollution on respiratory disease mortalities and outpatients in southeastern China. *Scientific Reports*, 8(1), 3461.

Myllyvirta, L. 2014. Health impacts and social costs of Eskom's proposed non-compliance with South Africa's air emission standards. https://cer.org.za/wp-content/uploads/2014/02/Annexure-5_Health-impacts-of-Eskom-applications-2014-_final.pdf (last accessed 27 April 2021).

Naidoo, R. N., Robins, T. G., Solomon, A., White, N. and Franzblau, A. 2004. Radiographic outcomes among South African coal miners. *International Archives of Occupational and Environmental Health*, 77(7), 471–81.

Nkangala District Municipality. 2017. Final 2017/18–2021/22 IDP. http://www.nkangaladm.gov.za/download/final-201718-202122-idp/ (last accessed 27 April 2021).

Obeng-Odoom, F. 2020. *The Commons in the Age of Uncertainty. Decolonising Nature, Economy and Society*. Toronto: University of Toronto Press.

OECD (Organisation for Economic Co-operation and Development). 2013. Glossary of Statistical Terms.

Portfolio Committee on Health. 2014. ATC140404: Report of the Portfolio Committee on Health on oversight visit to Mpumalanga Province from 16 to 17 September 2013, dated 12 March 2014. National Assembly (South Africa). https://pmg.org.za/tabled-committee-report/2076/ (last accessed 27 April 2021).

Quantec. 2016. EasyData Regional Database. Pretoria: Quantec Research.

Singer, M. 2011. Towards 'a different kind of beauty': Responses to coal-based pollution in the Witbank Coalfield between 1903 and 1948. *Journal of Southern African Studies*, 37(2), 281–96.

Stats SA (Statistics South Africa). 2012. South African Census 2011. Statistical Release P0301.4. Pretoria: Stats SA.

Stats SA (Statistics South Africa). 2016. Community Survey 2016: Provinces at a glance. Report 03-01-03. Pretoria: Stats SA.

Stats SA (Statistics South Africa). 2018. Mortality and causes of death in South Africa: Findings from death notification, 2016. Statistical Release P0309.3. Pretoria: Stats SA.

Sterck, O. 2016. Natural resources and the spread of HIV/AIDS: Curse or blessing? *Social Science and Medicine*, 150, 271–8.

Stuckler, D., Basu, S. and McKee, M. 2011. Health care capacity and allocations among South Africa's provinces: Infrastructure–inequality traps after the end of apartheid. *American Journal of Public Health*, 101(1), 165–72.

Talukdar, R., 2016. Hiding neoliberal coal behind the Indian poor. *Journal of Australian Political Economy*, 78, 132–58.

WHO (World Health Organization). 2005. *WHO Air Quality Guidelines for Particulate Matter, Ozone, Nitrogen Dioxide and Sulfur Dioxide: Global Update 2005*. http://apps.who.int/iris/bitstream/handle/10665/69477/WHO_SDE_PHE_OEH_06.02_eng.pdf;jsessionid=BBD342318FE5C03EC3FC2AF9B87C6D06?sequence=1 (last accessed 27 April 2021).

Wigley, S. 2017. The resource curse and child mortality, 1961–2011. *Social Science and Medicine*, 176, 142–8.

World Coal Association. 2012. Case study: South Africa – Anglo American HIV/AIDS program. https://www.worldcoal.org/file_validate.php?file=wca_anglo_american_case_study_final(06_02_2012).pdf.

Notes

1. A 'resource rent' is the difference between the price of a commodity and the average cost of producing it (IndexMundi, 2018).

2. A community health centre is like a clinic in that it provides first-contact care but has additional facilities such as emergency care, a short-stay ward and a 24-hour maternity service. Note that the total number of facilities is disputed. The HST District Health Barometer 2016/2017 lists 79 clinics, with names, whereas according to the Department of Health shapefile and the Mpumalanga Department of Health there are only 68. The HST figures are used for this chapter.
3. 'Uninsured population' is a rough measure which attempts exclude from the calculation the part of the population that uses private medical facilities.
4. 1 USD = 15.6565 ZAR (average), 1 June 2016.
5. The crude death rate is defined as 'the number of deaths occurring among the population of a given geographical area during a given year, per 1,000 mid-year total population of the given geographical area during the same year' (OECD, 2013).
6. Nkangala's GVA per capita was roughly 24.5% higher than South Africa's in 2011 (Stats SA, 2012; Quantec, 2016).

CHAPTER 9

Sustainability Reporting by Collieries

Cornelie Crous

Introduction

Against a background of climate change, declining biodiversity and the accelerated use of natural resources, companies are faced with demands to assess, measure and disclose sustainability practices. The number of international rating agencies that assess these practices has increased and international frameworks have been created to assess disclosure of the practices. Today's investors are increasingly interested in non-financial information that is reliable and easily understandable. Companies are typically recommended to cover economic, social and environmental aspects in their disclosures (Maubane, Prinsloo and Van Rooyen, 2014). Research shows that a 'triple context' disclosure improves a company's reputation (Azapagic, 2004; Cho and Patten, 2007; Farneti and Guthrie, 2009; De Villiers and Alexander, 2014; De Villiers, Low and Samkin, 2014; Christian, 2016).

Triple context reporting is often referred to as 'sustainability reporting' and, like integrated reporting, it is largely voluntary in nature. Companies, particularly those with a high environmental impact, usually disclose sustainability aspects related to energy, water and biodiversity. Approximately 90% of international companies that disclose sustainability aspects make use of the GRI (Global Reporting Initiative) Standards (KPMG, 2017). The GRI guidelines for sustainability reporting give companies, including environmentally sensitive companies in the mining industry, the tools to communicate with stakeholders and investors about only significant sustainability risks and opportunities the company faces (Maubane, Prinsloo and Van Rooyen, 2014; Torrence, 2017).

Corporate reporting in South Africa on aspects other than financial information has been guided by the various King Reports and Codes of Corporate Governance. In an attempt to align corporate reporting in South Africa to issues of climate change, pollution, scarce resources and biodiversity, the King II Report on Corporate Governance in South Africa proposed the disclosures of ESG (environmental, social and governance) aspects (IoD, 2002). Corporate reporting on ESG aspects, the triple-bottom-line disclosure principle, has become the norm for most South African listed companies (Carels, Maroun and Padia, 2013). The King III report (2009) and the King IV report (2016) testify to the importance of the ESG aspects, as both these reports continue to call for their disclosure (IoD, 2009, 2016). Moreover, the King IV report, which is applicable to all organizations, companies, non-profit organizations, close corporations, municipalities, and so on, with a financial year end starting on or after 1 April 2017, recommends that all companies make use of integrated reporting principles to report to stakeholders on ESG aspects, which include sustainability.

However, the disclosure of ESG aspects, as intended by the King Reports, has not been as successful as anticipated (Carels, Maroun and Padia, 2013), as most listed companies focus on financial sustainability. To remedy this defect in sustainability reporting, the Johannesburg Stock Exchange, as part of its listing requirements, encourages listed companies to apply international sustainability reporting guidelines (JSE, 2013, 2014). In 2004 the JSE created the SRI (Social Responsibility Index) to increase companies' environmental disclosures and 'foster good corporate citizenship and promote sustainable development' (Maubane, Prinsloo, and Van Rooyen, 2014; JSE, 2015a; Crous et al., 2021). In 2015, in partnership with the global index provider FTSE Russell, the JSE replaced the SRI with the FTSE/JSE Responsible Investment Index, which has similar goals (JSE, 2015b). The index has two categories: the top 30 companies that achieved the minimum ESG rating from FTSE Russell according to a market capitalisation weighted index, and the top 30 that achieved the minimum ESG rating according to an equally weighted index calculated on a real-time basis (JSE, 2015b). In 2018, four of the listed companies that have operations in Emalahleni-Witbank (South 32, Exxaro, Anglo American and Glencore) were listed in the first category of responsible investment companies, but only Anglo American was listed in the second.

Despite attempts like these to encourage sustainability and integrated reporting, implementing this kind of reporting remains a challenge because internationally it is largely voluntary (Morros, 2016), though the trend is for stock exchanges to shift from voluntary to mandatory disclosures (KPMG, 2017). Sustainability disclosures are still voluntary for South African listed companies, including mining companies. This chapter investigates the quality of the disclosures by the four listed companies that have operations in Emalahleni: South 32, Exxaro, Anglo American and Glencore. Because collieries have a high environmental impact, we focus on disclosures on Water, Effluents and Waste; Emissions; Occupational Health and Safety; Closure Planning; and Indigenous Rights. I argue that the quality of these reports is poor, with little disclosure of any substance being made. Although more can be done to improve disclosure standards, the disappointing results also point to how mining companies manipulate disclosure requirements to their benefit. These reports require rapid improvements to ensure that transparency and disclosure assist in the process of a just transition. Methodologically, the chapter uses content analysis of the sustainable reports of these four listed coal companies.

International sustainability reporting

Until recently, corporate reports consisted mostly of financial information. Environmental and sustainability information was published as stand-alone information, and these reports are now published on company websites, entitled 'sustainability report', 'social responsibility report', 'social and environmental report', and suchlike. There have been calls for the creation of standards to help companies prepare these reports in a standardised form.

It was to this end that the GRI was created in Boston, USA, in 1997 (GRI, 2021a). It was based on the Coalition for Environmentally Responsible Economics and had the support of UNEP (the United Nations Environment Programme). In 2002 the GRI moved to Amsterdam and issued the G2 guidelines (second generation reporting guidelines) at the World Summit on Sustainable Development in Johannesburg. The G3 guidelines (third generation reporting guidelines) were issued in 2006 as a result of a formal partnership between the UNGI (United Nations Global Impact) and the OECD (Organisation for Economic Co-operation and Development).

In 2008 the GRI issued the first sector supplement, for Financial Services, and followed this with three more sector supplements in 2010, for Mining and Metals, Airport Operators, and Construction and Real Estate. The GRI also introduced the GSDD (Global Sustainability Disclosure Database). This database, currently listing more than 24,000 global companies, makes it easy to find relevant information on a company's sustainability.

In 2014 the G4 (fourth generation) guidelines were issued, with the support of the UN Global Compact Initiative and the World Business Council for Sustainable Development. In 2017 the GRI issued the Global Standards for Sustainable Reporting, which made sustainability reporting more accessible to information users and investors. The modular format of the Standards combines the G4 guidelines and the G4 implementation manuals and its aim is to improve understanding and application of the Standards. The changes also make provision for greater flexibility and transparency in the use of the Standards. The GRI also issued an Excel document to help companies map the G4 guidelines to the new Standards. Although the new Standards were applicable only to reports issued on or after 1 July 2018, companies were encouraged to adopt them earlier (GRI, 2021b). Several companies, including Anglo America, Glencore and Exxaro, chose to adopt the Standards for their 2017 sustainability reporting.

Sustainability reporting has attracted some international criticism. The most severe critics have been Mark McElroy, Executive Director of the Center for Sustainable Organizations, and the Sustainability Context Group (www.sustycontext.org). One criticism is that the lack of clear guidance on the concept of context-based sustainability makes current reporting practices meaningless (McElroy, 2013). McElroy and the Sustainability Context Group plead for the inclusion of clarifying guidelines that would state, for example, thresholds and limits for vital resources and say how the resources should be allocated. Using the example of water, McElroy (2017) links the thresholds for sustainable water usage to the volume of renewable water available for consumption. To ensure sustainability, water usage should not exceed supply. He proposes that water use should be allocated to consumers according to the available supply in the area. This will make it possible to measure and monitor consumption. He argues that if a company is to uphold the GRI's Sustainability Context Principle, its reporting must disclose the thresholds and allocations, and these have not been included in the GRI Standards. Further criticism is that although the GRI Standards provide guidance on reporting, there is no uniformity in how sustainability aspects are to be disclosed (McElroy, 2013; Munoz, Zhao and Yang, 2017). Plainly, further clarification and standardisation of the sustainability reporting is needed.

For more detail on sustainability reporting internationally, see Brown, De Jong and Levy (2009), Cho et al. (2009), De Villiers and Van Staden (2011), Fonseca, McAllister and Fitzpatrick (2014), Maubane, Prinsloo and Van Rooyen (2014), Higgins, Milne and Van Gramberg (2015), Jarvie-Eggart (2015), Christian (2016), GRI (2021a, 2021b), De Villiers, Rinaldi and Unerman (2017), Miller, Fink and Proctor (2017), Torrence (2017) and Lampinen and Prahl (2018), and for critical views see McElroy (2013, 2017) and Munoz, Zhao and Yang (2017).

GRI standards and guidance for the Mining and Metals sector

The G4 reporting framework consists of 150 guiding principles, divided into 58 principles for general standard disclosures and 92 for specific standard disclosures, the latter divided into six categories: economic aspects (9 principles), environmental aspects (34 principles), labour practices (16 principles), human rights practices (12 principles), social practices (11 principles) and product responsibility and management practices (10 principles). Each principle contains detailed guidance on what should be disclosed.

Unlike the G4 reporting framework, the GRI Standards issued in 2017 were issued in 37 documents to accomplish the goals of improved understanding, flexibility and transparency. The documents are divided into five different groups. The first group contains only one document (GRI 101), which is the foundation of the Standards and explains the development of the Standards, how the Standards should be used and the basic principles of sustainability reporting. The second group consists of the GRI 102 and GRI 103 documents. GRI 102 contains guidance on how companies should report on their reporting context, and GRI 103 on how they should report on their management approach in identifying topics that are material for inclusion in the sustainability report. The last three groups, GRI 200, GRI 300 and GRI 400, provide guidance on reporting on economic, environmental and social aspects, respectively. Each of the topics in a group contains principles for the company's management approach and topic-specific disclosures. The management approach principles guide the company on how to explain why they consider topics to be material and how those material topics are to be managed and disclosed. To give companies extra help in applying the principles, some principles also contain examples and detailed guidance on issues or aspects a company can exclude from reporting. Companies that prepare reports in accordance with the G4 Guidelines will produce a balanced picture of topics material to the company's business. If a company uses the G4 Guidelines it should reference the selected GRI Standards in its report.

In addition to the GRI Standards, a mining and metals company that wishes to prepare a report in accordance with the G4 Guidelines should also use the Mining and Metals sector guidance first issued in 2010. This supplement, based on the G3 guidelines, was changed to conform to the G4 guidelines in May 2013. The changes, which make for a more streamlined document, include reorganisation of content, structure and recommendations (GRI, 2013). The supplement contains 10 additional principles, applicable specifically to the environment, labour practices and human rights, that mining and metals companies need to consider in their sustainability report. Against the background of South Africa's scarce natural water resources, its labour problems and human rights problems, and its continuing debates on land reform and redistribution, this chapter examines the Emalahleni-Witbank collieries' disclosures on these issues. Particular focus will be placed on the disclosures relating to occupational health and safety under labour disclosures and indigenous rights under human rights.

Environmental disclosures

Both the G4 and the GRI Standards guidelines contain 34 environmental disclosure principles, covering biodiversity and emissions, and the use of materials (virgin or recycled), water and energy. They also provide guidance on reporting on waste management, products and services, compliance with environmental legislation, transport, supplier assessment, and grievance mechanisms that are available for environmental aspects. The environmental information must be disclosed according to operational sites and should make it easy for a stakeholder to form an opinion of a company's environmental sustainability performance.

The Mining and Metals sector guidelines add three specific recommendations to the environmental disclosures. As part of their biodiversity disclosures, companies need to disclose the amount of land disturbed and rehabilitated and the total number of sites where plans are in place for biodiversity management. Under 'effluents and waste', the guidelines suggest that the total amount of overburden (rock or soil overlying a mineral deposit) and tailings (dumps of material, usually sludge, left over after the valuable part of the ore has been removed), with their associated risks, should be disclosed.

Labour practice disclosures

The G4 and GRI Standards guidelines contain 16 and 22 labour practice disclosure principles respectively, covering employment, labour and management relationships, occupation health and safety, training and education, diversity and equal opportunity, equal remuneration for men and women (Sesele et al., 2021), assessment of supplier labour practices, and grievance mechanisms. The Mining and Metals sector guidelines also cover strikes or lock-outs lasting more than one week. The GRI Standards contains additional guidance on occupational health and safety (OHS) disclosures and recommends specific disclosures of prevention and mitigation of safety incidents, work-related injuries and illnesses, and agreements made with formal bargaining units, which in South Africa would include the trade unions.

Human rights disclosures

Both the G4 and the GRI Standards guidelines contain 12 human rights disclosure principles, covering investment in human rights, non-discriminatory practices, freedom of association, child labour and forced labour, security practices, indigenous rights, assessment of human rights, assessment of supplier human rights and grievance mechanisms. Under indigenous rights disclosures, the Mining and Metals sector guidelines also recommend the disclosure of the number of operations adjacent to indigenous territories and whether an agreement has been made with the indigenous community on the use of the land. Disclosure of the impact of mine closures on the community is also recommended, including aspects such as the redeployment and re-employment of mineworkers and the overall financial provision for mine closures.

Sustainability disclosures in Emalahleni-Witbank

One of the costs of coal mining is the damage it does to the groundwater in Emalehleni-Witbank. According to Gausdal and Sharife (2011), mines in South Africa are responsible for 88% of the country's wastewater. Even the World Wide Fund for Nature has commented on the damage done to the Olifants River Basin (WWF, 2011). Mines are expected to mention this impact and their mitigating actions in their sustainability reporting. Besides dealing with groundwater pollution, the mines also have to find ways to reduce air pollution and the high levels of water usage (see Chapter 17, 'Is a Just Transition Possible?). Other unintended consequences of mining are health problems such as fevers, coughs and diarrhoea and even cancer (see Chapter 8, 'The Health Impacts of Coal Mining and Coal-based Energy'). Exacerbating the unintended consequences are the perceived inequalities between mineworkers, contract workers and the original inhabitants of Emalahleni. The impact of the mines on the indigenous peoples must also be taken into account in sustainability reporting.

The costs and problems described above create expectations that the mines in the area will recognise and address them in their reports. Part of the reporting responsibility of the mines is to disclose how they have dealt with these issues. But it is difficult to assess the content and quality of the reports because of the voluntary nature of the disclosures and the different types and number of reports published by companies on their websites. None of the four Emalahleni-Witbank coal mines – South 32, Exxaro, Anglo American and Glencore – has published a report that includes both environmental and other sustainability disclosures relating to social issues. South 32 has published 10 different reports, Exxaro three, Anglo American three and Glencore five. The length of the reports ranges from five to 220 pages.

These companies' current reporting practices do not achieve the GRI objective of more easily understandable and transparent reporting. The variety of the reports is, however, confirmation that the companies are making use of the flexibility of the GRI reporting standards. They include information about water usage, air pollution, groundwater, occupational health and safety and indigenous rights in stand-alone sustainability reports, integrated reports, sustainability data tables (also called data books), supplementary reports to integrated reports, and even a stand-alone 'environment emissions' report (see Table 9.1).

In these reports, less than half (46%) of the reports from the four collieries contain disclosures on water and effluents (EN8, EN9 and EN10), OHS (LA5), indigenous rights (HR8 and MM5) and mine closures (MM10). Notably lacking are disclosures on transport of hazardous waste (EN25), OHS and mining operations adjacent to indigenous communities. At first glance, the reporting by the four collieries on sustainability aspects looks acceptable and they appear to have applied the GRI Standards in their various types of reports (see Table 9.1). Detailed examination of some of the disclosures in the reports, however, showed that the quality of the reporting was poor.

With the exception of South 32, all the companies disclosed detailed information on closure plans. Exxaro included information on the Tshikandeni mine, Anglo American on the Sishen mine and Glencore on five mining operations in Australia but nothing on mine closures in South Africa or Emalahleni. The disclosures by these three companies included plans to accommodate and assist employees after mine closure. No detail was given of the content of the plans, however, which made it difficult to assess the adequacy of the plans. The following subsections discuss the quality of the environmental, labour practices (with focus on occupational health and safety) and human rights (with focus on indigenous rights) disclosures.

Environmental disclosures

In the course of a questionnaire survey that provided some of the material for this book, 73% of 897 Emalahleni householders said they either agreed or strongly agreed that coal mining leads to water pollution. This shows they are aware of the consequences and would thus expect the companies in Emalahleni-Witbank to say how their activities affect the water in the area and what they are doing to mitigate the risks of contamination by effluents, and also how much water they use, given its scarcity in the area.

Table 9.1 Disclosures by Emalahleni collieries

Category	GRI4 Indicator	GRI Standard	Principle	Management practices vs topic	South 32	Exxaro	Anglo American	Glencore
	EN8	303-1	Interactions with water as a shared resource	Management	DB	IR	SR	DB
	EN9	303-2	Management of water discharge-related impacts	Management	-	IR	-	-
Water and Effluents	EN10	303-3	Water withdrawal	Topic	DB	IR	-	DB
		303-4	Water discharge	Topic	-	-	-	-
		303-5	Water consumption	Topic	-	-	-	-
	EN15	305-1	Direct (scope 1) GHG emissions	Topic	DB	SUP	SR	DB
	EN16	305-2	Energy indirect (scope 2) GHG emissions	Topic	DB	SUP	SR	DB
	EN17	305-3	Other indirect (scope 3) GHG emissions	Topic	DB	SUP	SR	DB
	EN18	305-4	GHG emissions intensity	Topic	-	-	-	DB
Emissions	EN19	305-5	Reduction of GHG emissions	Topic	Environment Emissions	SUP	SR	
	EN20	305-6	Emissions of ozone-depleting substances (ODS)	Topic	-	SUP	SR	DB
	EN21	305-7	Other significant emissions	Topic	DB	SUP	SR	DB
	EN22	306-1	Water discharge by quality and destination	Topic	DB	-	SR	DB
	EN23	306-2	Waste by type and disposal method	Topic	-	SUP	SR	DB
	EN24	306-3	Significant spills	Topic	DB	SUP	SR	SR
Effluents and Waste	EN25	306-4	Transport of hazardous waste	Topic	-	-	-	-
	EN26	306-5	Water bodies by water discharge and/or run-off	Topic	-	-	-	-
	MM3	MM3	Total amounts of overburden, rock, tailings, and sludges and their associated risks		DB	-	-	DB
Employment	LA2	401-2	Benefits provided to full-time employees that are not provided to temporary or part-time employees	Topic	-	-	-	-

Category	GRI4 Indicator	GRI Standard	Principle	Management practices vs topic	South 32	Exxaro	Anglo American	Glencore
	LA5	403-1	Occupational health and safety system	Management	-	SUP	-	-
	LA6	403-2	Hazard identification, risk assessments and incident investigation	Management	DB	SUP	SR	DB
	LA7	403-3	Occupational health services	Management	DB	SUP	SR	SR
	LA8	403-4	Worker participation, consultation, and communication on occupational health and safety	Management	-	SUP	-	-
Occupational Health and Safety		403-5	Worker training on occupational health and safety	Management	-	-	-	-
		403-6	Promotion of worker health	Management	-	-	-	-
		403-7	Prevention and mitigation of occupational health and safety impacts directly by business relationships	Management	-	-	-	-
		403-8	Workers covered by an occupational health and safety management system	Topic	-	-	-	-
		403-9	Work-related injuries	Topic	-	-	-	-
		403-10	Work-related ill health	Topic	-	-	-	-
	HR8	411-1	Incidents of violations involving rights of indigenous peoples	Topic	DB	-	SR	SR
Indigenous Rights	MM5	MM5	Total number of operations taking place in or adjacent to indigenous peoples' territories, and number and percentage of operations or sites where there are formal agreements with indigenous peoples' communities		-	-	-	SR
Closure Planning	MM10	MM10	Number and percentage or operations with closure plans	Topic	DB	SUP	SR	SR

Notes: GHG = Greenhouse gases, IR = Integrated Report, SR = Sustainability Report, DB = Databook or Data Tables, SUP = Supplementary Report.

However, all four companies' disclosures on water and effluents (EN8–EN10) and effluents and waste (EN22–EN26) are substandard and incomplete. Although three of them explained how they interact with water (how water is drawn, consumed and discharged) as a shared resource and how much they consumed, only Exxaro disclosed the volume of water consumed per mine. None of the companies disclosed the amounts of surface water and groundwater they discharged. They did, however, disclose the volume of water that was recycled or reused.

The companies' disclosures on the transport of hazardous waste (some reports classify this as removal of hazardous waste) and disposal of other types of waste are also unsatisfactory. Three of them mentioned the transport of hazardous waste, but none disclosed the effects of hazardous waste and effluents on the water bodies in the area. Given the WWF's concerns about the pollution that coal mining activities in the Olifants River Basin in Mpumalanga create, in the form of an increase of sulphates in the water, this deficiency is alarming. It tends to support the findings by Atlatsa, a platinum mining company, that mining companies in South Africa significantly underprovide for environmental rehabilitation (Centre for Environmental Rights, 2018).

Asked to say whether they believed electricity generation from coal harms the environment, 81% of 921 Emalahleni householders believed it did, and 97% of 930 believed that coal mining leads to air pollution. As with the responses to the questions about water, they would expect the Emalahleni-Witbank collieries to disclose their contribution to emissions and air pollution in the area. In this case the companies met their expectations. The disclosures on emissions are fairly complete and of high quality. Only Glencore, however, disclosed the base year that it used to determine the reduction in emissions, and the reason for choosing that year. Glencore's emissions disclosures were the most complete and, unlike the other three companies, included both quantitative and qualitative information.

The inclusion of emission information by the mines may be attributable to the increased pressure on companies, by society and interest groups and investors, to be transparent and accountable for their use of natural resources and to disclose how they plan to sustain the resources in the short, medium and long term. The community pressure may be due to the air pollution created by the mining activities in the area that causes the area's air to be the dirtiest in the world (Goldswain, 2018).

Labour practices disclosures: Occupational health and safety
The majority of the community we sampled consists of mineworkers and their families. Of our respondents, 60% were employed on the mines. The benefits of mining to communities are well documented. Of 916 householders, 55% agreed that mining in Emalahleni-Witbank benefits the community. However, 94% of

929 agreed that coal mining led to health problems for the mineworkers. The average spent on healthcare in the month preceding the household question-naires was R432 for 207 householders. The average outlay on medical aid insur-ance for 289 households was R1,297 per month. For 78 households that said they did not have medical aid, the average out-of-pocket medical expenses amounted to R389 (ranging from R20 to R1,500). While these amounts are not very high (but high in proportion to the income level of the households), they indicate that the households may have had health problems, some of which may be attribut-able to the mining activities in the area. This again underlines the likelihood that the community will expect the companies to be transparent about health issues in their sustainability reports.

The increased focus on safety in mines in South Africa intensifies the need for occupational health and safety (OHS) disclosures. These disclosures provide a means for stakeholders (such as communities, employees, investors and gov-ernment) to gather information on health and safety issues on the mines and to discover what the companies are doing to minimise and remediate health risks for employees. The absence of a specific mention of an OHS system in the disclosures of three of the four collieries in Emalahleni-Witbank is therefore a matter for extreme concern. Although it was evident from their various reports that some form of the system does exist, the vagueness makes it difficult for a stakeholder to discover what this system entails.

A report entitled 'Health at South 32' discloses OHS-related illnesses and what support the company provides to its workers. A matter for concern, though, is that this report makes no reference to South 32's 'sustainability navigator' document. This company's compilation of stand-alone reports does not consider ease of use by stakeholders and investors. Exxaro discloses the existence and pro-cedures of a formal committee on worker participation and consultation in the OHS process, but not much else.

Human rights disclosures: Indigenous rights

The continuing debate in South Africa over land reform and land redistribu-tion creates the expectation that the listed companies in South Africa will rec-ognise South Africa's indigenous peoples and their rights. However, none of the Emalahleni-Witbank collieries said anything about indigenous rights in their sus-tainability reports, in whichever form they choose to report. A report entitled 'Communities and Society at South 32' disclosed how this company is managing human rights and how it interacts with indigenous peoples. Anglo American disclosed how it manages indigenous rights in its Canadian operations and Glen-core did the same for its Canadian and Australian operations. None of the four companies made satisfactory disclosures on indigenous rights in South Africa, indicating that they are more concerned about indigenous rights in countries other than South Africa.

Conclusion

This chapter evaluated the nature and scale of disclosure by South African coal companies in Emalahleni. Disclosure and transparency are crucial ingredients for a just transition. The results of this analysis are disappointing. Although international guidelines exist that are intended to help companies disclose sustainability-related information, in South Africa the lack of legal requirements for disclosures makes it easy for companies to omit information. The fact that the sustainability reports are voluntary means that they are also not required by law to be audited. This lack of statutory assurance may, furthermore, contribute to the incompleteness or absence of information. Only when sustainability disclosures are made mandatory will it be possible to trust companies' reports to be complete, accurate and within the context of the company's activities.

Our survey between November 2017 and January 2018 found that although the four listed mining companies in Emalahleni-Witbank do apply some sustainability disclosure guidelines according to the GRI Standards, the quality of their reports leaves much to be desired. The incompleteness of the information makes it difficult for stakeholders and investors to compare the companies. This chapter's analysis of the information supplied by these four companies supports previous studies' findings that companies in environmentally sensitive industries tend to disclose more sustainability information than companies not in these industries. However, it differs from those studies in finding that the quality and completeness of these companies' disclosures were unsatisfactory. This supports the criticism that the GRI Standards offer a list of detailed recommendations rather than guidance on context-based reporting, and that the current practices in sustainability disclosures are meaningless and lacking in context (McElroy, 2013; Munoz, Zhao and Yang, 2017). The provision of detailed principles may further confuse companies that are trying to report on sustainability, and they may elect to use the list as a box-ticking exercise. The disclosure recommendations may need to be revised and simplified with guidance on how to apply the principles in context. The inadequacy of the GRI Standards guidelines may partially explain the large differences between the four Emalahleni collieries' disclosures.

The lack of, or incomplete, information on water effluents, occupational health and safety, and indigenous rights means that the disclosures do not attain the GRI goals of transparency. This, along with the proliferation of different types of reports, complicates the task of investors and stakeholders wanting to form an opinion of these four collieries' sustainability risks and opportunities. Appropriate disclosure and transparency on these issues are essential to understanding fully the environmental concerns associated with a just transition.

The voluntary nature of sustainability disclosures internationally may very well impede the goal of transparency in disclosures, as companies may be tempted not to disclose information that could damage their reputation. Perhaps the international trend of making sustainability disclosures compulsory for listed companies would be the correct move for South Africa and provide a basis for managing a just transition.

References

Azapagic, A. 2004. Developing a framework for sustainable development indicators for the mining and minerals industry. *Journal of Cleaner Production*, 12, 639–62.

Brown, H. S., De Jong, M. and Levy, D. L. 2009. Building institutions based on information disclosure: Lessons from GRI's sustainability reporting. *Journal of Cleaner Production*, 17, 571–80.

Carels, C., Maroun, W. and Padia, N. 2013. Integrated reporting in the South African mining sector. *Corporate Ownership and Control*, 11(1), 957–71.

Centre for Environmental Rights. 2018. The truth about mining rehabilitation in South Africa. https://fulldisclosure.cer.org.za/companies/atlatsa-resources-corporation (last accessed 27 April 2021).

Cho, C. H. and Patten, D. M. 2007. The role of environmental disclosures as tools of legitimacy: A research note. *Accounting, Organizations and Society*, 32, 639–47.

Cho, C. H., Phillips, J. R., Hageman, A. M. and Patten, D. M. 2009. Media richness, user trust, and perceptions of corporate social responsibility. *Accounting, Auditing and Accountability Journal*, 22 (6), 933–52.

Christian, J. 2016. Differences between environmental disclosures in various corporate reports. Unpublished Master's thesis, University of Pretoria.

Crous, C., Owen, J., Marais, L., Khanyile, S. and Kemp, D. 2021. Public disclosure of mine closures by listed South African mining companies. *Corporate Social Investment and Environmental Management*. doi: 10.1002/csr.2103.

De Villiers, C. and Alexander, D. 2014. The institutionalisation of corporate social responsibility reporting. *British Accounting Review*, 46, 198–212.

De Villiers, C., Low, M. and Samkin, G. 2014. The institutionalisation of mining company sustainability disclosures. *Journal of Cleaner Production*, 84, 51–8.

De Villiers, C., Rinaldi, L. and Unerman, J. 2017. Integrated reporting: Insights, gaps and an agenda for future research. *Journal of Management Control*, 28(3), 275–320.

De Villiers, C. and Van Staden, C.J. 2011. Where firms choose to disclose voluntary environmental information. *Journal of Accounting and Public Policy*, 30, 504–25.

Farneti, F. and Guthrie, J. 2009. Sustainability reporting by Australian public sector organisations: Why they report. *Accounting Forum*, 33, 89–98.

Fonseca, A., McAllister, M. and Fitzpatrick, P. 2014. Sustainability reporting among mining corporations: A constructive critique of the GRI approach. *Journal of Cleaner Production*, 84, 70–83.

Gausdal, L. and Sharife, K. 2011. Quick and dirty – but not cheap: South Africa's minerals-energy complex. Paper presented at Pre-COP 17 Meeting, Durban, 25–26 November, Centre for Civil Society Online Library, University of KwaZulu-Natal, Durban. http://ccs.ukzn.ac.za/files/Quick%20and%20Dirty%20-%20But%20Not%20Cheap_Sharife-Gausdal.pdf (last accessed 27 April 2021).

Goldswain, Z. 2018. We have the dirtiest air in the world. *Witbank News*. https://witbanknews.co.za/116572/dirtiest-air-world/ (last accessed 27 April 2021).

GRI (Global Reporting Initiative). 2013. Sustainability Reporting Guidelines. https://www. globalreporting.org/standards/g4/Pages/default.aspx (last accessed 7 May 2021).

GRI (Global Reporting Initiative). 2021a. About GRI, Mission and History. https://www. globalreporting.org/about-gri/mission-history/ (last accessed 7 May 2021).

GRI (Global Reporting Initiative). 2021b. How to use the GRI standards. https://www. globalreporting.org/how-to-use-the-gri-standards/ (last accessed 7 May 2021).

Higgins, C., Milne, M. J. and Van Gramberg, B. 2015. The uptake of sustainability reporting in Australia. *Journal of Business Ethics*, 129, 445–68.

IoD (Institute of Directors). 2002. The King Report on Corporate Governance for South Africa 2002 (King II). *LexisNexis.* Johannesburg, South Africa.

IoD (Institute of Directors). 2009. The King Code of Governance for South Africa 2016 (King III). *LexisNexis.* Johannesburg, South Africa.

IoD (Institute of Directors). 2016. The King Report on Corporate Governance for South Africa (King IV). *LexisNexis.* Johannesburg, South Africa.

Jarvie-Eggart, M. E. 2015. *Responsible Mining: Case Studies in Managing Social and Environmental Risks in the Developed World*. Englewood, CO: Society for Mining, Metallurgy and Exploration.

JSE (Johannesburg Stock Exchange). 2013. JSE guidance letter on integrated reporting. Johannesburg: JSE.

JSE (Johannesburg Stock Exchange). 2014. JSE listing requirements. Johannesburg: JSE.

JSE (Johannesburg Stock Exchange). 2015a. JSE SRI Index. https://www.jse.co.za/services/ market-data/indices/socially-responsible-investment-index (last accessed 27 April 2021).

JSE (Johannesburg Stock Exchange). 2015b. JSE FTSE/JSE Responsible Investment Index. https://www.jse.co.za/services/market-data/indices/ftse-jse-africa-index-series/responsible-investment-index (last accessed 27 April 2021).

KPMG. 2017. The road ahead: Sweden. https://assets.kpmg/content/dam/kpmg/xx/ pdf/2017/10/kpmg-survey-of-corporate-responsibility-reporting-2017.pdf (last accessed 27 April 2021).

Lampinen, J. and Prahl, A. 2018. The transition from G$ to GRI Standards: A case study of Löfbergs AB. Unpublished Master's thesis, Karlstad Business School.

Maubane, P., Prinsloo, A. and Van Rooyen, N. 2014. Sustainability reporting patterns of companies listed on the Johannesburg Securities Exchange. *Public Relations Review*, 40, 153–60.

McElroy, M. 2013. Has the GRI consigned itself to irrelevance? GreenBiz, 22 May. https:// www.greenbiz.com/blog/2013/05/22/has-gri-consigned-itself-irrelevance (last accessed 27 April 2021).

McElroy, M. 2017. Is it possible that GRI has never been about sustainability reporting at all? https://www.sustainablebrands.com/news_and_views/new_metrics/mark_mcelroy/it_possible_gri_has_never_really_been_about_sustainability_r last accessed 27 April 2021).

Miller, K. C., Fink, L. and Proctor, T. Y. 2017. Current trends and future expectations in external assurance for integrated corporate sustainability reporting. *Journal of Legal, Ethical and Regulatory Issues*, 20(1), 1–17.

Morros, J. 2016. The integrated reporting: A presentation of the current state of art and aspects of integrated reporting that need further development. *Intangible Capital*, 12(1), 336–56.

Munoz, E., Zhao, L. and Yang, D. C. 2017. Issues in sustainable accounting reporting. *Accounting and Finance Research*, 6(3), 64–71.

Sesele, K., Marais, L., Van Rooyen, D. and Cloete, J. 2021. Mine decline and women: reflections from the Free State Goldfields. *The Extractive Industries and Society*. doi: 10.1016/j. exis.2020.11.006.

Torrence, M. 2017. New Global Reporting Initiative (GRI) Standards released. *Canadian Mining Journal*, 1 January, pp. 31–32.

WWF (World Wide Fund for Nature). 2011. *Coal and Water Futures in South Africa: A Case for Protecting Headwaters in the Enkangala Grasslands*. Cape Town: WWF.

CHAPTER 10

Residents' Perceptions of Coal Mining and Energy Generation

Anmar Pretorius and Derick Blaauw

Introduction

The Witbank Power Station started generating electricity from coal in 1925. Situated in the heart of the coalfields, it was able to provide electrical power very cheaply (Eskom, 2018). The combination of coal mining and energy generation brought employment opportunities and economic prosperity, but along with these came pollution and health problems. No analysis of a mining town can be complete without taking into account the long-term negative consequences of mining for the local communities (Mayes, 2014; Gamua, Le Billon and Spiegel, 2015).

Emalahleni suffers from long-term environmental problems in the form of air and water pollution. Acid water draining from deserted coal mines contaminates soil and groundwater. The levels of sulphate in the Witbank dam regularly exceed the level suitable for human consumption (McCarthy, 2011). Even some local industries find the water too polluted for industrial use. Eskom chooses not to use local water in its Emalahleni power stations and rather imports water from the eastern escarpment. The South African government has acknowledged the high levels of air pollution in and around Emalahleni. In 2007 the Minister of Environmental Affairs and Tourism proclaimed the region of eastern Gauteng and western Mpumalanga a national air pollution hotspot and the national government undertook to assess the levels of pollution continuously and implement emission reduction plans (Lourens et al., 2011). On 25 April 2013 *City Press* reported on a research project run by a team from the European Union. The team found that the levels of poisonous gases in Emalahleni's air were so high that their instruments could not measure them accurately. The levels of heavy metals in the air were the highest the team knew of in the world.

This raises the question: how do Emalahleni residents perceive coal mining and coal-generated energy? We link this chapter to the book's theme of a just transition by considering people's attitudes and the question of the sustainability of coal mining. The chapter presents residents' opinions of coal mining and pollution, coal mining and benefits for the local community, and the use of renewable energy sources rather than coal.

A just transition depends on people's acceptance of a shift away from coal. The survey results (see Chapter 1) show that the more people are embedded in coal (for example mine workers), the less likely they are to believe that coal has negative local consequences. This relationship is vital for the concept of a just transition. It emphasises how people's perceptions of the negative effects of coal depend on their economic dependence on coal. The results point to the fact that an alternative economic base is vital in the process of a just transition.

Literature on perceptions of mining and energy generation

Mining

Que, Awuah-Offei and Samaranayake (2015) provide a theoretical framework for analysing the determinants of community support for mining projects. They classify the mining project characteristics as social (population changes, improved infrastructure, impact on cultural sites, increased traffic and crime), economic (employment, higher income, effect on the housing market, local labour shortages), environmental (noise, air, water and land pollution; water shortages) and governance (how decisions are made, transparency of information, distance from mine, lifespan of the mine). They classify the community characteristics (demographic factors) as age, gender, income, education level, sector in which employed and number of children.

The factors that influence community acceptance of mining activity can be positive, such as employment and business opportunities, or negative, such as damage to the environment and health and safety concerns (Hilson, 2002; Petkova et al., 2009; Mutti et al., 2012). A study by Shi and He (2012) of how 454 residents of mining areas in China perceived pollution and the environment showed that these residents were most concerned about air pollution, followed by noise pollution and then water pollution. Certain demographic characteristics were found to influence these perceptions. Concern about the environmental impact of coal mining was expressed more strongly by the older respondents, the more educated, those who lived closer to the mines and those who had lived in the mining areas longer.

A Polish study (Badera and Kocoń, 2014) of 300 residents of a town where lignite (brown coal) excavation was already taking place and 302 residents of a town where such a mine was soon to be developed showed that 80% of the residents in both communities supported the mining activities. They felt that the benefits outweighed the negative effects. Young people, people of working age, women, and the more educated were the more supportive. The study found, however, that participants were reluctant to support mining if the mining activities were close to home.

Electricity in the Czech Republic is mostly generated from coal. After independence, the country put a restriction on new mining activities and tried to rehabilitate the environment in mining-affected areas. Recently, plans were announced to expand coal mining again. Frantál (2016) conducted a study of a hundred residents in each of two towns involved in this planned expansion. Coal mining was already in progress close to one of the towns. Overall, a third of the respondents were in favour of alternative energy sources rather than expanding coal mining. The strongest objections to coal mining came from people younger than 20 and older than 60. The study also found a strong place attachment. Residents who felt that the town was 'part of who they are' were more strongly opposed to coal mining expansion. Support for coal mining came from people working in the coal mining industry and those whose economic welfare depended on it.

In one of the few studies of how residents in fossil fuel reliant economies perceive renewable energy, Olson-Hazboun (2018) conducted interviews in two US communities whose economies depend on fossil fuels: coal mining in one case and oil and natural gas in the other. The study found that residents considered renewable energy a threat to the local economy. Furthermore, they perceived policies favouring renewables as punishment, because the shift from fossil fuels to clean energy could damage the local economy.

Energy generation

The literature on energy generation is largely concerned with people's views on fossil fuels versus renewable energy. Wüstenhagen, Wolsink and Bürer (2007) identify three dimensions of the social acceptance of renewable energy sources: socio-political acceptance, market acceptance and community acceptance. A just transition requires acceptance on all three dimensions. Socio-political acceptance means broad general acceptance by, among others, stakeholders in the energy industry and policymakers. Market acceptance means acceptance by consumers of energy, investors in the energy sector and energy producers. The extent of market acceptance can be gauged by how easy it is to convince consumers to buy renewable energy, how committed energy-generating firms are to using a specific technology, and how willing financial institutions are to finance the energy generating process. Community acceptance depends on the extent to which the community is involved during the decision-making process (procedural justice), shares in the financial and economic benefits of energy generation (distributional justice), and trusts the information provided by the developers and the intentions of the parties involved in the energy generation process.

Using these determinants of community acceptance listed by Wüstenhagen and colleagues (2007), Bronfman et al. (2012) conclude that an electricity generating source will generally be accepted by the local community if the associated risks are outweighed by the benefits and if they trust the risk management of regulatory agencies involved. However, their study of university students in Chile revealed that the trust–acceptability relationship holds for fossil fuels, nuclear and hydro, but not for renewable energy sources like wind and solar. The participants perceived renewable energy sources to be harmless, with no consequences for future generations. Consequently, risks, benefits or trust in regulatory authorities had no influence on their acceptance of renewables. The participants perceived energy generation through fossil fuels as having more benefits than risks. Community acceptance in this case therefore depended mostly on perceived benefits.

Study design

This chapter is based on data from a household questionnaire survey conducted in Emalahleni at the end of 2017. We analysed a total of 927 questionnaires. In a section on well-being and social cohesion, respondents were asked to indicate their perceptions (strongly disagree, disagree, neither disagree nor agree, agree, strongly agree) of nine statements, of which four were about coal mining, two about fossil fuels (coal-generated energy) and three about renewable energy:

- Coal mining benefits the local community.
- Coal mining activities lead to health problems.
- Coal mining activities lead to water pollution.
- Coal mining activities lead to air pollution.
- South Africa should use coal to generate electricity.
- Electricity generation using coal is harmful for the environment.
- South Africa should focus on using renewable energy sources (like wind and solar).
- Renewable energy is harmful for the environment.
- I would like to install solar panels at home if I could afford it.

Some of the demographic questions were related to the household in general, and some to the specific individual who completed the questionnaire on behalf of the household. In analysing the results we linked the responses to the nine statements to the details (country of origin, gender, age, place of residence, education) of the specific individual whose views were captured, as well as to the characteristics of the household (whether someone in the household has the title deed for the dwelling, whether members of the household are employed in mining). Table 10.1 summarises the characteristics of the respondents and their households.

Although we would expect that a major mining town would attract migrants from beyond the borders of the country, almost all of the household representatives were born in South Africa. Male and female respondents were equally represented. The average age was 34.8, with the youngest respondent being 14 and the eldest 87. The age categories in Table 10.1 show that mostly younger residents completed the questionnaire.

As would be expected in a mining town, in 46% of the households all the employed members were mine employees. However, a surprising 39% of households included no mine employees. The distribution of respondents born in Emalahleni and those from outside was very close to equal. Most of the newcomers had relocated to Emalahleni during the past five years. The median was seven

Table 10.1 Characteristics of respondents and their households (n = 927)		
Characteristic		**% of respondents**
Country of origin	South Africa	98.0
	Other country	2.0
Gender	Male	52.0
	Female	48.0
Age	15–19	2.5
	20–29	33.2
	30–39	38.3
	40–49	15.7
	50–59	6.9
	60 +	3.5
Occupations of respondent's household	All employed in mining	46.3
	Employed in mining and non-mining	15.0
	None employed in mining	38.8
Place of residence	Always lived in Emalahleni	50.3
	Moved to Emalahleni	49.7
	Years in Emalahleni (if not always)	
	0–5	39.3
	6–10	26.6
	11–15	14.0
	16–20	9.2
	20 +	10.9
Education	No schooling	1.4
	Some secondary schooling	29.7
	Secondary schooling	65.6
	Bachelor's degree	2.7
	Postgraduate qualification	0.5
Title deed	Someone in household has title deed for this dwelling	
	Yes	30.2
	No	6.4
	Refused to answer	63.4

years, which suggests a fairly recent influx to the town. Only 31% of respondents had not completed secondary school.

A common phenomenon in survey research is that questions on income are often not answered, and if they are answered the income level is underreported. Approximately 75% of the respondents did report the household's combined monthly income – with an average of R15,190 and a median of R12,600. However, only 13 of the respondents reported their own income level. The lack of reporting on individual income raised concerns about the reliability of the reported household incomes. Household income levels were also not found to be statistically significant in the empirical analysis. Consequently none of the income data is reported in Table 10.1. Table 10.1 reports on only one of the questions about household assets: whether someone in the household owned the title deed of the dwelling they were currently living in. This was reported to be the case in 30% of the households. An alarming 60% of respondents did not answer this question. It is therefore likely that the 30% could be an understatement of the actual situation.

Perception analysis

General picture

Table 10.2 summarises the responses to the nine statements. As the literature cautions against merely comparing averages when measuring perceptions on a scale from 1 to 5 (Sullivan and Artino, 2013), we also considered the median and the percentage of support at each level of agreement or disagreement. Following Shi and He (2012), we also classified the mean values for the responses on pollution and risk factors into three categories, with 1 to 2.4 meaning 'light perception intensity', 2.5 to 3.4 meaning 'general intensity' and 3.5 to 5 meaning 'very serious intensity'.

None of the statements scored a neutral mean value of 3. The highest median value (5), and the only median observed at one of the extreme points, is reported for respondents strongly agreeing that they would like to install solar panels, if they could afford to do so. These results show strong support for renewable energy. However, given the recent power outages in South Africa, this response could indicate a desire to be self-reliant and gain some independence from the national electricity supplier, Eskom. The Emalahleni Local Municipality's 2011–16 Local Economic Development Strategy publication (2012) makes four mentions of the problems related to Eskom power outages. It refers to the impact on infrastructure in general, breakdowns of mining machinery leading to lost production, and the severe difficulties Eskom's load shedding causes to small, medium and micro enterprises. The lowest median value in the table, 2, for the statement about renewable energy being harmful, can be interpreted as disagreement that renewable energy is harmful to the environment.

Except for the two statements about renewable energy already mentioned, all the other statements received a median score of 4. If we interpret the scores against the discussed perception intensities they also do not indicate many variations. The only two responses not indicating 'very serious intensity' are the one about potential harm done by renewable energy ('light intensity') and the one about coal mining benefiting the local community ('general intensity').

The picture of not much variation painted by the seven median scores of 4 changes when we look at the combined responses at the upper or lower end of the scale. An overwhelming 97.5% of respondents either agreed or strongly agreed that coal mining leads to air pollution, 94.7% that coal mining leads to

Table 10.2 Responses to nine statements

	Observations	Mean	Median	% strongly disagree	% disagree	% neither disagree nor agree	% agree	% strongly agree
Coal mining								
Coal mining activities lead to air pollution	930	4.32	4	0.22	0.32	1.94	62.8	34.73
Coal mining activities lead to water pollution	897	3.86	4	0.45	10.7	12.49	55.63	20.74
Coal mining activities lead to health problems	929	4.21	4	0.32	2.26	2.69	65.88	28.85
Coal mining benefits the local community	916	3.34	4	9.39	13.86	20.41	46.18	10.15
Fossil fuels/energy from coal								
Electricity generation using coal is harmful for the environment	921	3.99	4	1.19	9.88	6.3	54.4	28.23
South Africa should use coal to generate electricity	925	3.52	4	6.16	16.11	10.59	53.95	13.19
Renewables								
Renewable energy is harmful for the environment	862	2.3	2	18.91	54.99	8.93	11.83	5.34
South Africa should focus on using renewable energy sources (like wind and solar)	910	3.99	4	3.3	9.67	6.59	45.27	35.16
I would like to install solar panels at home if I could afford it	920	4.44	5	1.73	1.41	2.49	39.89	54.49

health problems, 82.6% that energy generation using coal is harmful to the environment and 76.4% that coal mining leads to water pollution. Three statements, not linked to negative implications of coal, received lower combined support: 80.4% agreed or strongly agreed that South Africa should focus on renewable energy, 67.1% that South Africa should use coal to generate electricity and only 56.3% that coal mining benefits the local community.

The above analysis points to overwhelming support for renewable energy. This observed support for renewables, however, is not accompanied by a total condemnation of coal-generated electricity, although there were some strongly negative perceptions of coal-generated electricity, and the perceptions of coal mining were even more strongly negative. Residents of this 'place of coal' were neutral in their response about the benefits of coal mining to the community, but they felt strongly that coal mining leads to air pollution, health problems and to a lesser extent water pollution.

Comparing respondents' ranking of the nine statements reveals interesting associations. As the data consist of scores between 1 and 5 (ranked data and categorical data), normal correlation is not an appropriate measure of association, so we used Kendall's tau and Spearman rank-order correlations instead. The strongest correlation (Kendall's tau of 0.59 and Spearman rank-order correlation of 0.60) was observed between residents who felt that coal mining leads to air pollution and those who felt it leads to health problems. The second highest correlation is between 'coal mining leads to health problems' and 'electricity generation using coal is harmful to the environment' (Kendall's tau of 0.59 and Spearman rank-order correlation of 0.52). The supporters of renewable energy ('South Africa should focus on renewable energy sources') wanted to install solar panels (Kendall's tau of 0.59 and Spearman rank-order correlation of 0.52), felt that coal-generated electricity is harmful to the environment (Kendall's tau of 0.32 and Spearman rank-order correlation of 0.35), and had a negative perception of coal-generated electricity (Kendall's tau of -0.26 and Spearman rank-order correlation of -0.28 for the statement 'South Africa should use coal to generate electricity').

Perception differences between groups
Table 10.2 reflects general perceptions of coal mining and energy generation in Emalahleni. We wanted to see whether the picture would become more nuanced if we delved a bit further below the surface. Would we find that perceptions differed between different groups within the community? The international literature suggests that this is likely to be the case – see Shi and He (2012), Badera and Kocoń (2014) and Frantál (2016). To test the situation in Emalahleni, we used analysis of variance and Kruskal-Wallis as tests for equality of means when dealing with categorical data (such as gender and occupation) and Kendall's tau correlation and Spearman rank-order correlation when dealing with nominal values (such as age and income).

We found that attitudes towards energy generation differed according to gender, mining occupation or not and years of residence. Women were less supportive of coal-generated energy than men (1% level of significance; $\alpha = 1\%$), and more supportive of renewable energy ($\alpha = 5\%$). Households where all the members were employed at the mines were more positive about coal-generated energy ($\alpha = 1\%$) than households with different employers, and less supportive of renewable energy ($\alpha = 1\%$). We observed a low but significant ($\alpha = 2\%$) positive correlation between the number of years respondents had been living in Emalahleni and their attitude to renewable energy.

The attitudes to the electricity generating method were mirrored in, and possibly based upon, the respondents' responses to the notion that electricity generation using coal is harmful to the environment. Women felt more strongly about the harmful effects than men ($\alpha = 5\%$) and so did respondents from households where not all members were employed at the mines ($\alpha = 1\%$). Those born in Emalahleni were less concerned about the harmful effects than those born elsewhere ($\alpha = 1\%$), and for those born elsewhere the perception of harmfulness increased with their length of stay ($\alpha = 2\%$).

The statement about the benefits of coal mining to the local community was agreed to and strongly agreed to by only 56% of the respondents. Women were less inclined to agree ($\alpha = 1\%$), while households consisting of only mine employees tended to agree more ($\alpha = 1\%$). The economic benefit of mining employment is a possible reason for the observed positive correlation between the log of household income and those respondents agreeing that the community does benefit ($\alpha = 1\%$).

Most respondents were of the opinion that coal mining leads to air pollution. There was, however, an indication that those who had lived in Emalahleni for their whole life feel more strongly about the effect of air pollution ($\alpha = 2\%$). Those who were not born in the town were inclined to be more concerned about air pollution the longer they had lived there (positive correlation, $\alpha = 1\%$). The same effect could be seen for water pollution – a positive correlation between awareness of water pollution and the number of years of residence ($\alpha = 1\%$). This awareness of water pollution also increased with the age of the respondents ($\alpha = 1\%$). The literature shows that poorer and more vulnerable people in the community are more affected by the environmental cost of mining (Rawashdeh, Campbell and Titi, 2016). The low response rate to the income questions in the survey makes it difficult to test for such a relationship. Table 10.1 shows that 30.2% of the respondents confirmed that someone in the household had the title deed for the dwelling. We used this indicator to distinguish between homeowners (possibly wealthier residents) and those who did not say they had a title deed for the dwelling. The belief that coal mining leads to water pollution was supported more by those who did not say that someone in the household had the title deed ($\alpha = 1\%$). This may suggest that the more affluent residents of Emalahleni (homeowners) were less concerned about water pollution, as they, for example, can afford their own systems to purify municipal water or buy bottled water.

The statement that coal mining leads to health problems was supported more by respondents holding a degree ($\alpha = 1\%$), by older people ($\alpha = 1\%$), and by those born elsewhere, the longer they live in Emalahleni ($\alpha = 1\%$). Households completely reliant on the mines for employment showed a positive attitude to coal mining. Respondents from such households were less convinced there was a possible link with health problems ($\alpha = 1\%$). (See Chapter 8 for a more detailed discussion on health.)

Regression analysis

To conclude our analysis, we used multiple regressions to explain the possible determinants of the reported perceptions. In a case where the dependent variable included in the regressions ranges between values of 1 to 5, there has been some criticism of the use of normal (least squares) regression analysis (Lu, 1999). Ordered probit models are preferred under these circumstances even though these two estimation methods usually produce the same results. Table 10.3 shows the results of the maximum likelihood estimations of the ordered probit models that could be obtained. For certain specifications only the least squares method provided results and these specifications are therefore not discussed. Only the sign of the estimated coefficients is reported in each column – with the level of significance below. Note that two specifications are reported in two instances. This provides for the inclusion of age squared in the regression for coal-generated energy and the alternation of the dummy variable 'Always lived in Emalahleni' with 'Years lived in Emalahleni' for the sample of respondents who were not born in the town.

The regression results confirm the trends we observed in the analysis of differences between groups. Older respondents were more concerned about the pollution created by coal mining. Regression analysis allows for the inclusion of age squared as an explanatory variable – which was not possible with the grouping analysis. The second specification in support of coal-generated electricity confirms a quadratic relationship with age. Support increases with the age of the respondents, but then starts to decline at a certain age. One possible explanation for this observation is that workers in this mining town benefit from the economic opportunities. Salaries increase as they age and gain more experience, but then at a certain age the economic benefits start to decline and the negative consequences of pollution dominate – leading to a more negative perception of coal-generated electricity. This trend has been reported in international studies as well – see for instance Badera and Kocoń (2014) and Frantál (2016).

Female respondents were less supportive of coal-generated electricity and coal mining. This observation requires further investigation. The current survey did not provide enough information to do so. However, various studies have shed some light on the plight of women living in mining towns (Sesele et al., 2021). Investigating the social and economic status of women in coal mining towns of Australia, Sharma (2010) found they were economically disadvantaged, excluded from employment opportunities in the mining sector, dependent on their male partners and confined to 'traditional' female roles in the household. Similar factors may underlie the negative attitude of female respondents to coal mining and coal-generated electricity in Emalahleni.

For respondents from households where all the members are employed at mines, the economic benefit of mines dominated. They were less supportive of renewable energy, more supportive of coal-generated electricity and more

Table 10.3 Regression results

	Observations	Age	Age²	Female	All mine employees	Always lived in Emalahleni	Years in Emalahleni	Degree	Title deed
Energy generation									
South Africa should focus on using renewable energy sources	901				- 0.00	+ 0.03			- 0.00
South Africa should use coal to generate electricity	916			- 0.00	+ 0.06				
	916	+ 0.06	- 0.05	- 0.00	+ 0.07				
Coal mining									
Coal mining benefits the local community	907			- 0.12	+ 0.00				
	453				+ 0.00		- 0.01		
Coal mining activities lead to water pollution	888	+ 0.00						+ 0.08	- 0.01
Coal mining activities lead to air pollution	921	+ 0.01				+ 0.02			

Notes:
Age = age of respondent in years
Age² = squared value of age
Female = dummy variable with value = 1 if respondent is female
All mine employees = dummy variable with value = 1 if all members of the household are employed by mines
Always lived E =   dummy variable with value = 1 if respondent has always lived in Emalahleni
Years in E = number of years respondent has lived in Emalahleni – if not born there
Degree = dummy variable with value = 1 if respondent has one or more degrees
Title deed = dummy variable with value = 1 if household member holds the title deed of their dwelling

supportive of coal mining. As a logical consequence, this variable is not significant in supporting concerns about pollution.

Respondents who had lived in Emalahleni all their lives were more concerned about air pollution and more supportive of renewable energy. Those born elsewhere became less convinced about the benefits of coal mining for the community the longer they lived in Emalahleni.

The literature has found that higher education levels correspond with a higher degree of concern about pollution and the environment – see for instance Shi and He (2012). Table 10.3 shows that holders of degrees were more concerned about water pollution. The last column of Table 10.3 reports on the possible explanatory power of ownership of the title deed of the dwelling. Deed holders were less supportive of renewable energy, possibly because renewable energy threatens the economic basis of the town where their property is located and could lower the value of this asset. They were also less concerned about water pollution than non-deed holders. Respondents not living on a property they owned (less wealthy residents) were more concerned about water pollution, possibly because they were less able to afford alternative water sources than the more affluent deed holders.

Conclusion

Responses to the general theme of energy generation converged into overwhelming support for renewables and the installation of solar panels. Regardless of the specific measure considered, support for renewables exceeded support for coal-generated electricity, even though a shift to renewable energy could threaten the town's economic base (see discussion in Terrados and Hontoria, 2007). The support for renewables should, however, be interpreted with caution (Simelane and Abdel-Rahman, 2011). It should not be interpreted as a complete rejection of coal-generated electricity – particularly against the background of regular episodes of load shedding (scheduled power cuts) in South Africa. The respondents may view renewables as an additional source of electricity, or an alternative during power outages when the national supplier Eskom fails to supply.

The survey showed that the respondents perceived the risks of coal mining to outweigh the benefits in Emalahleni. Serious concerns were evident regarding air pollution, health effects, damage to the environment, and water pollution (in that order). International experience in China has also shown that residents regard air pollution as more worrying than water pollution (Shi and He, 2012). All of the risk statements were more strongly agreed to than the benefit statements. This finding is in contrast to findings in Chile (Bronfman et al., 2012) and Poland (Badera and Kocoń, 2014), where the gains from mining were considered to be higher than the risks. A possible contributing factor may be a lack of trust in the South African regulatory authorities who have to deal with the negative consequences of mining and mitigate the risk factors, particularly those linked to pollution.

Tests for perception differences between groups and regression analysis indicated that a few factors contribute significantly to the observed perceptions. As has been found in international studies, characteristics such as age, gender, mining employment, length of stay, education and wealth all proved to be determinants of perceptions. Characteristics of those who thought coal mining and electricity generation from coal lead to pollution corresponded with characteristics of those who thought they cause health problems.

What do the results mean for a just transition? Older respondents were more concerned about the pollution effects and their support for coal-generated electricity decreased with age. Female respondents' acceptance of coal-generated electricity was lower than that of male respondents. Responses from households where all members were mine employees reflected the economic benefit of employment opportunities. These respondents were more supportive of coal-generated electricity, less supportive of renewables and more likely to agree that coal mining benefits the local community. The evidence shows that the more dependent someone is on coal, the less likely they are to oppose coal. Any attempt at managing a transition should keep this in mind, as mineworkers are likely to be protective of their jobs. A study in the Czech Republic suggested that people with higher place attachment (sense of belonging) are more inclined to protest against coal mining (Frantál, 2016). Some traces of place attachment were evident in our analysis. Lifelong residents of Emalahleni tended to be more supportive of renewable energy than those born elsewhere. But the opposite is also true and essential for managing a just transition. Less affluent residents were more concerned about water pollution and more supportive of renewable energy. A just transition needs to find a way between helping those dependent on coal and those vulnerable to its adverse effects. This implication also has racial consequences. Although a substantial portion of mineworkers (about 80%) are black, of our survey sample, 100% of those vulnerable households are black.

Finally, the support for renewables is essential. Although, there are discussions about declaring the area a focus area for renewables, most renewable projects have been located in other provinces across the country. A just transition needs to look at how workers who might lose their coal jobs could benefit from local employment in renewables.

References

Badera, J. and Kocoń, P. 2014. Local community opinions regarding the socio-environmental aspects of lignite surface mining: experiences from central Poland. *Energy Policy*, 66, 507–16.

Bronfman, N. C., Jiménez, R. B., Arévalo, P. C. and Cifuentes, L. A. 2012. Understanding social acceptance of electricity generation sources. *Energy Policy*, 46, 246–52.

City Press. 2013. Witbank air 'dirtiest in the world'. 25 April 2013. https://www.news24.com/news24/green/news/Witbank-air-dirtiest-in-the-world-20130425 (last accessed 28 April 2021).

Emalahleni Local Municipality. 2012. Local economic development strategy 2011–2016. https://cogta.mpg.gov.za/IDP/Nkangala2013-14/Emalahleni2013%2014.pdf (last accessed 7 May 2021).

Eskom. 2018. Witbank Power Station. www.eskom.co.za/sites/heritage/Pages/Witbank.aspx (last accessed 28 April 2021).

Frantál, B. 2016. Living on coal: Mined-out identity, community displacement and living of anti-coal resistance in the Most region, Czech Republic. *Resources Policy*, 49, 385–93.

Gamua, J., Le Billon, P. and Spiegel, S. 2015. Extractive industries and poverty: A review of recent findings and linkage mechanisms. *The Extractive Industries and Society*, 2(1), 162–76.

Hilson, G. 2002. An overview of land use conflicts in mining communities. *Land Use Policy*, 19, 65–73.

Lourens, A. S., Beukes, J. P., Van Zyl, P. G., Fourie, G. D., Burger, J. W., Pienaar, J. J., Read, C. E. and Jordaan, J. H. 2011. Spatial and temporal assessment of gaseous pollutants in the Highveld of South Africa. *South African Journal of Science*, 107(1–2), 1–85.

Lu, M. 1999. Determinants of residential satisfaction: Ordered logit vs regression models. *Growth and Change*, 30, 264–87.

Mayes, R. 2014. Mining and (sustainable) local communities: Transforming Ravensthorpe, Western Australia. In M. Bruekner, A. Durey, R. Mayes and C. Pforr (eds), *Resource Curse or Cure? On the Sustainability of Development in Western Australia*. Heidelberg: Springer, 223–38.

McCarthy, T. S. 2011. The impact of acid mine drainage in South Africa. *South African Journal of Science*, 107(5/6), Art 712. doi: 10.4102/sajs.v107i5/6.712.

Mutti, D. Yakovleva, N., Vazquez-Brust, D. and Marco, M. H. D. 2012. Corporate social responsibility in the mining industry: Perspectives from stakeholder groups in Argentina. *Resource Policy*, 37, 212–22.

Olson-Hazboun, S. K. 2018. 'Why are we being punished and they are being rewarded?' Views on renewable energy in fossil fuels-based communities in the U.S. west. *The Extractive Industries and Society*, 5, 366–74.

Petkova, V., Lockie, S., Rolfe, J. and Ivanova, G. 2009. Mining developments and social impacts on communities: Bowen Basin case studies. *Rural Sociology*, 19, 211–28.

Que, S., Awuah-Offei, K. and Samaranayake, V. A. 2015. Classifying critical factors that influence community acceptance of mining projects for discrete choice experiments in the United States. *Journal of Cleaner Production*, 87, 489–500.

Rawashdeh, R. A., Campbell, G. A. and Titi, A. 2016. The socio-economic impacts of mining on local communities: The case of Jordan. *The Extractive Industries and Society*, 3, 494–507.

Sesele, K., Marais, L., Van Rooyen, D. and Cloete, J. 2021. Mine decline and women: Reflections from the Free State Goldfields. *The Extractive Industries and Society*, doi: 10.1016/j.exis.2020.11.006.

Sharma, S. 2010. The impact of mining on women: Lessons from the coal mining Bowen Basin of Queensland, Australia. *Impact Assessment and Project Appraisal*, 28(3), 201–15.

Shi, X. and He, F. 2012. The environmental pollution perception of residents in coal mining areas: A case study in the Hancheng mine area, Shaanxi Province, China. *Environmental Management*, 50, 505–13. doi: 10.1007/s00267-012-9920-8.

Simelane, T. and Abdel-Rahman, M. (eds) 2011. *Energy Transition in Africa*. Pretoria: HSRC Press.

Sullivan, G. M. and Artino Jr., A. R. 2013. Analyzing and interpreting data from Likert-Type scales. *Journal of Graduate Medical Education*, 5(4), 541–2.

Terrados, J. A. and Hontoria, L. 2007. Regional energy planning through SWOT analysis and strategic planning tools: Impact on renewables development. *Renewable and Sustainable Energy Reviews*, 11, 1275–87.

Wüstenhagen, R., Wolsink, R. and Bürer, M. J. 2007. Social acceptance of renewable energy innovation: An introduction to the concept. *Energy Policy*, 35, 2683–91.

CHAPTER 11

Boom or Bust for Emalahleni Businesses?

Deidré van Rooyen and Johan van Zyl

Introduction

Dependence on a single resource like coal makes a town vulnerable to boom and bust cycles. Emalahleni's mineworkers are particularly vulnerable because they are directly dependent on the mines' growth or decline, but local businesses are also at risk, being indirectly dependent. Many local businesses do not directly benefit from mining, as the mines and the mineworkers tend to bypass the local value chains. The procurement systems of mines are often linked to large business elsewhere. But, do local businesses benefit from the mining industry, and the question is how these businesses plan for decline.

Natural abundance of a mineral resource can, counterintuitively, reduce local economic growth, stunt the development of non-mineral sectors, foster dependence on the mineral and make markets vulnerable (see for example Littlewood, 2014). To integrate mining economies with the local economy, the South African government has opted for open towns and the integration of mining activities into their local economies. The message from the South African mining policy is clear: mining must make a meaningful contribution to local economies. However, such integration creates dependence and might increase the risks associated with global resource price fluctuation and mine closure (Van Assche et al., 2017). Small business operators seldom see these risks.

This chapter investigates the responses from business owners in Emalahleni to the potential risks of mine closure. We ask whether the small business owners in Emlahleni understand the risk of an economic transition. This chapter's primary data source was a business survey with 275 responses and key informant interviews conducted with business people in Emalahleni (see Chapter 1). We found that small business owners are not considering mine closure or the implications for their businesses. Ensuring local value chains disguises the long-term problem of closure and could create a dependency that small business owners do not see. Of course, this long-term problem needs to be weighed against large mining firms often ignoring local value chains. A just transition will require a more diversified economy and reduce the dependence on a single sector such as mining.

Mining and local benefits

The link between mining and local economies has been central to mining town research for a long time. Robinson (1962: 118) noted more than 50 years ago that mining activities in Canada do not 'contribute to the development of, nor do they receive any flows from, their surrounding environments'. This observation elaborated on the development of the staples theory of economic growth (Watkins, 1963). In brief, the regions became overly dependent on the export of minerals but the exports did not contribute to the economic development of the remote mining areas in Canada. Beneficiation (the transformation of the raw mineral into a higher value product which can be consumed locally rather than just exported) was not a priority. Although the mines brought large-scale capital investment to mining areas in Canada, not much effort was made to link these developments to local investment. Drawing on the staples theory, studies also showed how mining prevented the development of more diverse economies and more specifically the development of manufacturing sectors (this later became known as the Dutch disease). Developing a diverse economy in mining areas has been an important goal (Elwerfelli and Benhin, 2018), but in reality it has been elusive. Governments might neglect economic diversification because of the rise in resource income, and the authorities might find local economic diversification difficult because of the dominant focus on resource extraction (Abubakar, 2015). Norway is an example of an open and very diverse economy. It has many minerals, like oil and gas, but also a wide range of other capabilities like ship-building, paper and textile manufacture and fishing. With a diverse economy that relies less on the mining industry, a country will be less affected by global price volatility (Cruz, 2011; Ville and Wicken, 2013).

Although the mining industry still receives criticism for bypassing local economies, the industry has over the years made a deliberate attempt to give local communities more autonomy. These attempts include corporate social responsibility programmes, programmes to ensure a social licence to operate, and reducing the industry's role in the management of local settlements and non-mining business operations (Marais et al., 2018). Nevertheless, some concerns remain. In many parts of Africa, mines still set up their towns, operate their worker camps or regulate who can benefit from their activities. In many cases, local communities cannot participate in the mining economy because they do not have the skills. Fly-in-fly-out arrangements also tend to bypass local economies, with employees' investments going to their areas of origin (Haslam McKenzie and Hoath, 2014).

Although links between mining and local economies have improved local people's participation in mining economies, they have also increased those people's dependence on the mines, making them vulnerable because mining remains a volatile industry dependent on global demand for resources (Randall and Ironside, 1996, Veiga, Scoble and McAllister, 2001; Wilson, 2004). Mines have little control over international prices and the boom and bust cycles negatively affect economic development. The booms can blind local government and businesses to the need for economic diversification and the need to hedge the risk of decline or closure.

Some service providers cannot afford to live in mining communities despite the demand for their service (Carrington, Hogg and McIntosh, 2011; Sincovich et al., 2018). Some non-mining businesses struggle to keep afloat because the mining industry inflates local salaries (Petkova et al., 2009). The dominance of mining in the local economy means that most people who live in a mining town are likely to be employed by a mining company or provide support services to the company. Economic diversification remains difficult. Auty and Evia (2001: 183) argue that 'the sustainable development of mineral economies lies in the successful diversification into competitive non-mining tradeables'. Governments should regard the mineral sector not as the backbone of the economy but rather as a bonus which can be used to accelerate economic growth and healthy structural change (Evans and Sawyer, 2009).

The abundance of revenue from a natural resource discourages long-term investment in infrastructure which could support a more diverse economy that could curb the sudden economic changes when the price of the resource drops (Abubakar, 2015). If communities use the opportunities created by the mining sector, they can invest the wealth they generate during a boom in infrastructure, education and job training to diversify forward and backward connections to other economic opportunities (Doukas, Cretney and Vadgama, 2008). But this requires good relationships between the mining sector, the business sector, the local authority and the community. Intensive planning is then necessary at the initial stages of mining development. However, many of these initial plans emphasise local buy-in and a local licence to operate but ignore long-term planning and economic diversification.

Business in Emalahleni

Background
The Emalahleni Municipality's integrated development plan (IDP) emphasises that the local economy depends on mining. The mining and energy sectors contribute almost 60% of Emalahleni's GVA. Approximately 33% of employed people in Emalahleni work in these two sectors. Over the past 20 years, the mines have actively dismantled company towns and reduced the industry's role in the public and urban development sphere (Van der Watt and Marais, 2019). The main aim of government policy was that such a move would allow the local economy and businesses to benefit more directly. Emalahleni is, therefore, an example of a town where local entrepreneurs could benefit indirectly from the mining industry. One of our business sector interviewees noted that Emalahleni is actually 'a great big town', which suggests that higher-order goods and services are available but those businesses do not have to deal with the problems typical of a city, like traffic congestion.

Despite an expansion of the regional service function, through the construction of malls and business opportunities, Emalahleni remains dependent on mining.

Earlier attempts to establish an industrial base had mixed results. Another problem was that the industries developed on the understanding that coal-fired energy would be available. In the mid-1969s Anglo American invested in the first private steel mill in the area (the other steel mills in South Africa belonged to the state-owned company, Iscor). However, in 2016 Highveld Steel (established initially by Anglo American) closed and Ferro Metals had to downscale because of pollution problems. These unexpected events had a major effect on the local population (see Chapter 16).

Profiling the business sample

The respondents in our business survey of 275 businesses in Emalahleni were a mix of business owners (27%), business managers (40%) and staff (33%). They were 48% male and 52% female and their average age was 36. Just over half (53%) had completed their high school education. A further 22% had obtained tertiary diplomas, degrees and higher education. Most of our sample (80%) were in the formal business sector, with 76% of the sample being VAT registered and 82% having a bank account. These businesses were well-established and had been in operation for nine years on average. The responses from the informal sector, which made up 20% of the sample, were not significantly different from those of the formal businesses. About half of the informal businesses were survivalists, moving around and selling goods that they could buy with the little money they had. Only 10% of our sample transacted directly with the mines, while 90% did business with the mine contractors and employees. The 275 businesses covered the sectors shown in Table 11.1, classified according to Toerien and Seaman's (2010) enterprise ecology.

Table 11.1 points to Emalahleni's regional service role and the proportion of the businesses in its economy. Large numbers of trade, tourism and personal services and the low number of manufacturing business provide evidence of this trend.

Table 11.1 Distribution of businesses in the survey per sector

Activity	N	%	Activity	N	%
Agriculture	2	0.7	Personal services	23	8.4
Construction	6	2.2	Processing	2	0.7
Engineering	4	1.5	Professional services	6	2.2
Factories	5	1.8	Telecommunications	11	4.0
Finance	7	2.5	Tourism	41	14.9
General services	32	11.6	Trade services	107	38.9
Health services	6	2.2	Transport	7	2.5
Mining	2	0.7	Vehicle services	13	4.7
News and advertisement	1	0.4	**TOTAL**	**275**	**100**

Evaluating the business environment

The respondents were asked to indicate the positive and negative aspects of doing business in Emalahleni, the events that had influenced the business positively or negatively in the past 10 years, what changes the business had made in the past two years, and the prospects of business in Emalahleni in future.

The most positive aspects were that there are many opportunities and customers (24%), customers are loyal and have a sense of community (18%) and there is a demand for the product (15%). Only about 10% of the responses directly related the positive business environment to the mines, while 9% said there had been positive economic growth. The mines also received credit for attracting people to sports and other events (probably through sponsorships). Respondents said the mines help to keep the town afloat, 'sponsoring sports events or school fundraisers, providing bursaries and skills training for matriculants'. It is interesting that only 10% of the respondents associated their good business environment with the presence of the mines, but other factors that they mentioned were closely associated with mining: customers, product demand and economic growth.

As regards the factors influencing business, there were slightly more negative (53%) than positive (47%). Among the negatives were the municipal services being 'awful' (15%), retrenchments when Highveld Steel closed (10%), retrenchments in the mining industry (7%) and strikes or protests (19%). One respondent mentioned two reasons for the strikes: the mines not providing enough employment opportunities for the locals, and the municipality not providing effective services.

Respondents also noted the social consequences of the closure of Highveld Steel. They said it caused not only unemployment but also related problems like drug and alcohol abuse and higher crime rates. Unemployment because of this closure or because of mine decline affected the schools too, because families who lost jobs were 'living from day to day' and more children had to be included in the feeding schemes. Other negative effects they said the mines had on businesses were to do with health (26%) and the environment (6%). A key informant said the smaller mines do not rehabilitate the environment after closing the mine and this causes even more air pollution and more children could suffer from respiratory illnesses. Although there is likely to be a decline in air pollution if power stations close down, pollutants can still come from mines that are not properly closed and continue to burn below the surface, emitting dust and smoke. This can happen when large mines sell to smaller firms that are unable to deal with the financial cost of closure (see Chapter 3). Positive factors in Emalahleni affecting business included sport, fashion and beauty events (20%), the opening of new malls and retail stores (10%), mines opening (8%) and some good municipal services (2%).

Table 11.2 sums up the positive and negative ways mining affects business in Emalahleni, according to our respondents. The negatives clearly outweighed the positives (61% vs 39%). Although mining affects business negatively through

Table 11.2 Positive and negative aspects of mining affecting business in Emalahleni				
	Positive		Negative	
	N	%	N	%
Economic	65	51.2	62	48.8 (57.4)
Social	4	30.8	9	69.2 (8.3)
Health	0	0	28	100 (25.9)
Environmental	1	14.3	6	85.7 (5.6)
Municipal services	0	0	3	100 (2.8)
TOTAL	70	39.3	108	60.7 (100)

Note: Pearson chi-square - 0.00

several aspects, like health (25%), environment (6%) and social (8%), the economic aspects (57%) outweigh all the others. Approximately 51% of the business respondents viewed the economic aspects of mining as affecting them positively. However, 49% of business respondents indicated that the mines also affect their businesses in negative ways. Mine closures and the potential of more closures were two of the main reasons provided by respondents. This means that the business sector is very dependent on the mines, either when there is a boom or when there is a bust in the mining sector. When there is a boom the business sector will benefit and grow and thrive, but in a bust cycle it will struggle to survive.

The respondents were asked what changes they had made in their business over the past two years. They said they intended to hire new full-time staff (48%), purchase or lease assets (27%), open a new branch (19%) and hold more stock in their business (20%). With regard to their future plans, they said they would continue in current mode (38%), plan a moderate business expansion (27%) or plan a large-scale business expansion (31%). Only 3% were considering closing their business. They had, however, encountered a few obstacles. These included registering for BBBEE (broad-based black economic empowerment) certificates, closure of mines, crime, and corruption affecting the municipal services.

The respondents were asked to rate the importance of services in the area for the operation of their business on a scale from 1 to 5, where one was 'not important' and five was 'very important', and to rate the quality of the services similarly.

Table 11.3 shows that the respondents regard the water (quality and availability), electricity (capacity and reliability), storm drainage, sanitation and refuse removal as very important services in Emalahleni. All these services were rated as very important by more than 60% of the respondents. Rated particularly important were electricity capacity (93%) electricity reliability (91%) and refuse

Table 11.3 Importance and quality of services in Emalahleni

Services	Importance			Quality		
	Not important	Importance depends	Very important	Very poor	Quality depends	Very good
1 Water quality	20.40	11.20	**68.40**	32.7	31	36.3
2 Water availability	14.70	10.60	**74.70**	28.7	27.2	44.1
3 Electricity availability (capacity constraints), lines and transformer capacity	4.10	2.60	**93.30**	**51.7**	23.8	24.5
4 Electricity availability (reliable supply), outages and poor maintenance	5.70	3.00	**91.30**	**50.2**	24	25.8
5 Storm water drainage	12.30	12.30	**75.40**	**72.8**	14.3	12.9
6 Sanitation services	5.90	6.80	**87.30**	**72.1**	16.8	11.1
7 Refuse removal	4.80	5.20	**90.10**	**74.3**	15.5	10.2
8 Traffic management	36.40	15.20	48.40	23.2	27.9	48.9
9 Local road conditions	37.40	6.40	56.20	**66.9**	12.7	20.4
10 Road condition to access markets	30.20	11.90	57.90	**51**	24.5	24.5
11 Railway services	**69.10**	12.70	18.20	**58.1**	24.2	17.7
12 Air services (flights)	**77.50**	6.90	15.60	**61.2**	22.4	16.4
13 Air freight	**71.30**	9.30	19.40	**51.9**	32.7	15.4
14 Internet services	13.40	12.20	**74.40**	12.5	17.6	**69.9**
15 Postal service	24.40	21.70	53.90	9.6	24.9	**66.4**
16 Courier service/ private postal	26.20	7.80	**66.00**	6	14.3	**79.7**
17 Telephone services	9.70	6.60	**83.70**	7.8	15.6	**76.6**
18 Police maintaining law and order	31.20	14.50	54.30	24.6	29.1	46.3
19 Effective detective and prosecution	40.00	12.50	47.50	29.6	41.1	29.3
20 Public sector health services	45.40	12.30	42.30	31.7	41.6	26.7
21 Private sector health services	45.60	12.80	41.60	16.7	30.4	52.9
22 Quality schooling	16.80	11.60	71.60	10.9	23.7	**65.4**
23 Communication between local business community and the local authority	10.00	15.10	74.90	42.9	29.9	27.2

removal (90%). But the quality of these services was rated very poor by between 51% and 74% of the respondents. The railway, air and freight services followed the same pattern. On the other hand, the respondents did not rate telephone landlines, Internet and courier services as important. This probably shows that the businesses are locally dependent. However, they rated the quality of these services 'very good' (77%, 70% and 80% respectively).

The poor municipal services affect the relationship between the private and public sectors. The municipality has lost the trust of the businesses due to 'constant denial' and 'not taking the blame for problems', and 'rather taking up crisis management'. This problem kept resurfacing during the key informant interviews with the business sector. One person said that 'the potholes in the roads do not help to attract people to the town'. Respondents said that the water and electricity supply was 'inconsistent' and that no town planning was taking place. A key informant said 'the city provides large parts of the country with electricity, but cannot keep the lights on in our own homes'.

Conclusion

The international literature suggests that mining areas often do not benefit from mining or do not diversify their economy because they are too reliant on mining. In response, the South African government has tried to ensure that local areas benefit more significantly. This has caused businesses in mining areas to depend on mining activities. Businesses in Emalahleni still depend on the mines and are growing because of the current boom. Although some of our respondents acknowledged their dependence on mining, many small businesses did not see the risks of decline or understand the consequences, and very few were actively planning for it. The reason for this is that Emalahleni is still in a boom period and has not reached the bust part of the cycle yet. A solution would be to think of sector diversification instead of the mining dependence.

We found the larger business sector was somewhat positive about Emalahleni's economy and had plans for moderate and large-scale business expansion, but was experiencing problems with municipal service delivery. In the past, the mines have assisted the local government, especially in terms of infrastructure development through their social and labour plans. But with mine decline in the area, the budget allocated to these plans has also declined, as has the mines' support for the local government. We argue in this book that a just transition requires good relationships between the mining sector, the business sector, the local authority and the community. Furthermore, a just transition would also have to make sure that enough information is available for the private sector entrepreneurs to make an informed decision about their current and future investments.

References

Abubakar, U. L. 2015. Resource curse and the need for economic diversification. In Proceedings of the Fourth International Conference on Global Business, Economic, Finance and Social Sciences, GBI5Kolkata Conference. Kolkata, India, 18–20 December 2015. Paper ID: KF578.

Auty, R. M. and Evia, J. L. 2001. A growth collapse with point resources: Bolivia. In R. M. Auty (ed.), *Resource Abundance and Economic Development*. Oxford: Oxford University Press.

Carrington, K., Hogg, R. and McIntosh, A. 2011. The resource boom's underbelly: Criminological impacts of mining development. *Australian and New Zealand Journal of Criminology*, 44(3), 335–54.

Cruz, S. 2011. The resource curse and Peru: A potential threat for the future? Master's thesis, University of San Francisco. https://repository.usfca.edu/thes/4.

Doukas, A., Cretney, A. and Vadgama, J. 2008. *Boom to Bust: Social and Cultural Impacts of the Mining Cycle*. Calgary: The Pembina Institute.

Elwerfelli, A. and Benhin, J. 2018. Oil a blessing or curse: A comparative assessment of Nigeria, Norway and the United Arab Emirates. *Theoretical Economics Letters*, 8, 1136–60. doi: 10.4236/tel.2018.85076.

Evans, N. and Sawyer, J. 2009. The mining boom: Challenges and opportunities for small business in regional South Australia. *Australian Journal of Regional Studies*, 15(3), 355–72.

Haslam McKenzie, F. and Hoath, F. 2014. Fly-in/fly-out, flexibility and the future: Does becoming a regional FIFO source represent opportunity or a burden? *Geographical Research*, 52(1), 430–41.

Littlewood, D. 2014. 'Cursed' communities? Corporate social responsibility (CSR), company towns and the mining industry in Namibia. *Journal of Business Ethics*, 120, 39–63.

Marais, L., McKenzie, F. H., Deacon, I., Nel, E., Van Rooyen, D. and Cloete, J. 2018. The changing nature of mining towns: Reflections from Australia, Canada and South Africa. *Land Use Policy*, 76, 779–88.

Petkova, V., Lockie, S., Rolfe, J. and Ivanova, G. 2009. Mining development and social impacts on communities: Bowen Basin case studies. *Rural Society*, 19(3), 211–28.

Randall, J. E. and Ironside, R. G. 1996. Communities on the edge: An economic geography of resource-dependent communities in Canada. *Canadian Geographer*, 40, 17–35.

Robinson, I. R. 1962. New industrial towns on Canada's resource frontier. Research Paper, Issue 73, Department of Geography, University of Chicago.

Sincovich, A., Gregory, T., Wilson, A. and Brinkman, S. 2018. The social impacts of mining on local communities in Australia. *Rural Society*, 27(1), 18–34.

Toerien, D. and Seaman, M. 2010. The enterprise ecology of towns in the Karoo, South Africa. *South African Journal of Science*, 106 (5/6). doi: 10.4102/sajs.v106i5/6.182.

Van Assche, K., Deacon, L., Gruezmacher, M., Summers, R., Lavoie, S., Jones, K., Granzow, M., Hallstrom, L. and Parkins, J. 2017. *Boom and Bust. Local Strategy for Big Events. A Community Survival Guide to Turbulent Times*. Groningen: Cooperative InPlanning UA.

Van der Watt, P. and Marais, L. 2019. Normalising mining company towns in Emalahleni, South Africa. *The Extractive Industries and Society*, 6, 1205–14.

Veiga, M. M., Scoble, M. and McAllister, M. L. 2001. Mining with communities. *Natural Resources Forum*, 25, 191–202.

Ville, S. and Wicken, O. 2013. The dynamics of resource-based economic development: Evidence from Australia and Norway. *Industrial and Corporate Change*, 22(5), 1341–71.

Watkins, M. H. 1963. A staple theory of economic growth. *The Canadian Journal of Economics and Political Science / Revue Canadienne d'Economique et de Science politique*, 29(2), 141–58.

Wilson, L. J. 2004. Riding the resource roller coaster: Understanding socio-economic differences between mining communities. *Rural Sociology*, 69(2), 261–81.

CHAPTER 12

Socio-economic Dynamics of the Informal Economy

Derick Blaauw, Anmar Pretorius and Rinie Schenck

Introduction

The lives of Emalahleni residents are inextricably bound up with the coal that gives the city its name. According to this municipality's 2017 Integrated Development Plan, in 2015 almost 60% of the local economy was dependent on mining and electricity generation from coal. The possible depletion of mineral resources and the closure of mines and related industries are foremost among the risks identified by the Emalahleni Municipality that confront the city and its inhabitants. Emalahleni and its socio-economic fortunes exist within a South African labour market characterised by extremely high rates of unemployment and relatively limited informal employment. According to the Emalahleni Municipality, the city's unemployment rate decreased from 27.3% in 2011 to 23.2% in 2015. Although this was the fifth lowest of all the municipal areas of Mpumalanga at the time, unemployment and the resultant hardships still feature prominently (Emalahleni Municipality, 2017). The possibility of mine closures is real.

To take the formal economy's employment statistics as a measure of the economic verve of any society is to ignore the existence of other forms of work (Leonard, 2000). This point was argued convincingly for the first time in a seminal study by Hart (1973), and since then the informal economy, of both developed and developing countries, has received ongoing attention in academic and policy circles.

In this chapter, following Hart (1973) and Chen (2008), we see the informal economy as a mirror that reflects the real-life struggles, ambitions and resilience of the people of Emalahleni, confronted by increasing levels of uncertainty forced on them by macroeconomic events and circumstances. As informal employment is not a homogeneous category, we use a broad definition that includes employment in informal enterprises and in casual work (Chen, 2008 – see the literature section).

The well-being of Emalahleni and its people is linked to boom and bust cycles in the mining industry. Events like the closure of Highveld Steel in 2016 have sent shockwaves through the local economy. Many people who lost their jobs as a result of that closure were forced to seek income earning opportunities in the informal economy. Day labour is one such strategy. This is a phenomenon that is on the increase in various developed and developing countries worldwide

(Theodore et al., 2015). In South Africa's towns and cities, day labourers congregate at informal hiring sites in public spaces. Here they stand waiting for jobs in construction, gardening and other forms of manual labour. Employment rates and the wages earned tend to be low. Day labourers have to cope with employment insecurity, workplace injuries that may prevent them from working, and a high risk of having their wages stolen – all of which means significant levels of physical and psychological hardship.

In countries like the United States, day labour offers temporary relief for people who have lost their jobs in the formal economy or acts as a stepping stone for new entrants into the labour market (Theodore et al., 2015). But in South Africa the case is different: here, day labour has long been a reservoir of workers who are surplus to the requirements of the formal economy (Blaauw, 2010; Theodore et al., 2015). Once in this informal labour market, opportunities to make the transition into the formal economy are limited – an informal labour trap that calls for further investigation. The study this chapter is based on investigated the dynamics of day labour in Emalahleni over a decade to show how the decline or closure of mines and businesses affects the local economy on a micro level. It also looks at theoretical models of the role of informal day labour markets in local economies. The chapter emphasises the day labour section of the informal economy for two main reasons. First, day labour as an activity is often the only feasible way to try to earn some income for many workers who lost their formal economy employment in the mines or related businesses (see for example the work of Blaauw, 2010 and Theodore et al., 2015). Second, the results of the main household survey are dealt with extensively on many levels in other chapters of this book, but little emphasis is placed on informal employment in these chapters. This leaves a gap in the overall picture of Emalahleni which this chapter attempts to address.

This chapter is based on the main household survey on which this book is based (see Chapter 1 for details of the survey methods), and also on two comparable surveys done in the city in 2008 and 2018 (see Blaauw, 2010, for details of the procedures and numbers involved in the 2008 study).

A reconnaissance phase preceded the 2008 survey. In 2005 and 2006 we contacted all municipalities, including the then Witbank local municipality, along with churches and NGOs, to gather information on the prevalence and extent of the day labour phenomenon. Our research team travelled throughout South Africa (including Emalahleni) to do in-person counts of day labourers at informal hiring sites. We identified more than a thousand places in South Africa where more than 45,000 day labourers came together, looking for temporary employment. From this research population, a sample of just over 9% was selected for the 2008 countrywide survey among day labourers. Cluster sampling was used to ensure proportionality of the day labourers sampled in rural and urban areas and at small and large hiring sites. The survey instrument was developed in a multi-stage process and fieldworkers were trained. The fieldwork across South Africa then took place from February 2007 to May 2008, during which period 3,840 day labourers were interviewed. As part of the countrywide proportional sample the fieldworkers interviewed 22 day labourers in Emalahleni in 2008. In 2018 we did a follow-up survey in Emalahleni using similar procedures, but changed the survey instrument (the same questionnaire of the 2008 South African Survey) to include further detailed questions about labour market outcomes. We interviewed all available and willing day labourers we could locate in Emalahleni. All the previously identified hiring sites were revisited and newly identified sites were included in our survey. We are therefore confident that the sample accurately reflects the day labour population in Emalahleni in 2018. As all surveys were completed anonymously, we do not know if we have interviewed some of the same day labourers as in 2008. In the 2018 survey, we interviewed a total of 58 day labourers, with a response rate of more than 90% (only three of the 61 day labourers we approached were unwilling to participate in the 2018 survey).

International and South African literature

The absence of a single, widely accepted definition or measure of the informal economy in the literature challenges all researchers in this field (Benjamin and Mbaye, 2014). A researcher's ideology and perspective often determine the definition chosen (Andrews, Sanchez and Johansson, 2011). This definition then generally informs the sampling method of the study and therefore also the conclusions and any policy recommendations (Benjamin and Mbaye, 2014). Chen, whose broad definition we chose to use for our study, defines the informal economy as people who are 'self-employed in informal enterprises (i.e. small and unregulated) as well as the wage employed in informal jobs (i.e. unregulated and unprotected) in both urban and rural areas', and informal labour markets as 'rural self-employment, both agricultural and non-agricultural; urban self-employment in manufacturing, trade and services; and various forms of informal wage employment (including day labourers in construction and agriculture, industrial outworkers, and more)' (Chen, 2008:19). According to this definition, therefore, a day labourer can be, for example, a person informally employed in a formal company.

Researchers have thus come to realise that more inclusive definitions of the concept are needed to capture the changing nature of labour markets and the continuous casualisation of employment that forms part of this change. The International Labour Organization has taken cognisance of this need and differentiates between employment in the informal economy and informal employment, that is, people employed in informal jobs (ILO, 2013). The ILO (2013) sees employment in the informal economy and informal employment as different

Table 12.1 Conceptual framework for informal employment								
	Jobs by status in employment							
Production units by type	Own account workers		Employers		Contributing family workers	Employees		Members of producers' cooperatives	
	Informal	Formal	Informal	Formal	Informal	Informal	Formal	Informal	Formal
Formal economy enterprises					1	2			
Informal economy enterprises	3		4		5	6	7	8	
Households	9					10			

Notes: Cells shaded in dark grey refer to jobs which by definition do not exist in the type of production unit in question. Cells shaded in light grey refer to formal jobs. Unshaded cells represent the various types of informal jobs (ILO, 2013: 367).

Source: ILO (2013: 37), from 17th International Conference of Labour Statisticians.

forms of the informalisation or casualisation of employment that is becoming more and more common in modern labour markets. This distinction is adopted in this chapter and summarised in Table 12.1.

A comprehensive discussion of the table can be found in ILO (2013: 36–7). The point of departure is that a person can simultaneously have two or even more formal and/or informal jobs at a particular point in time. Therefore, jobs rather than employed persons are considered as the observation unit for employment. The jobs held by an employed person can be described by various job-related characteristics, and these jobs are undertaken in production units (enterprises) that can be described by various enterprise-related characteristics (ILO, 2013: 36). With this in mind, the framework in Table 12.1 disaggregates total employment according to two dimensions: first, the type of production unit, and second, the type of job. The type of production unit (rows in the table) is defined in terms of legal organisation and other enterprise-related characteristics, while the type of job (columns) is defined in terms of status in employment and other job-related characteristics (ILO, 2013: 36).

Production units are divided into three groups: formal economy enterprises, informal economy enterprises, and households. Formal economy enterprises include, for example, corporations, non-profit institutions, enterprises owned by government units, and private enterprises producing goods or services for sale or barter (ILO, 2013: 37). Households as production units include, for example, subsistence farming. The category also includes households employing paid domestic workers, childcare workers, laundry workers, guards, gardeners, drivers and so on (ILO, 2013: 37).

Cells shaded in dark grey refer to jobs which by definition do not exist in the type of production unit listed in the table. The cells shaded in light grey refer to various formal jobs and the unshaded cells represent various types of informal jobs (ILO, 2013: 37).

In the framework shown in the table, informal employment (irrespective of whether it occurs in formal economy enterprises, informal economy businesses or households) covers cells 1 to 6 and 8 to 10. Cell 7 refers to a unique situation of somebody formally employed by a firm/enterprise in the informal economy. Employment (formally or informally) in informal economy enterprises covers cells 3 to 8. The framework also allows for an individual to be informally employed outside the informal economy either in the formal economy or in households (see cells 1, 2, 9 and 10). Day labourers in particular are informally employed either in the formal economy, informal economy or in households and can belong in either cell 2, 6 or 10 at any given time, depending on who informally employs him/her.

The various manifestations of the informal economy have been explained mainly by three theoretical models: dualist, structuralist (sometimes known as the neo-Marxist approach) and legalist (sometimes known as the neoliberal approach) (Chen, Vanek and Heintz, 2006; Wilson, 2011). The dualist model views the informal economy as a safety net for low-skilled, rural-to-urban migrants seeking to earn a living any way they can (Wilson, 2011). There is some indication in this literature that the informal economy can offer a viable alternative to formal employment (McKeever, 2007). The structuralist model emphasises that the informal economy is subsumed and exploited by the formal economy (Guha-Khasnobis and Kanbur, 2006; Wilson, 2011). The legalist model sees the emergence of the informal economy as a rational response to over-regulation in the formal economy (De Soto, 1989; Saunders, 2005). Each of these models has led to different research methods, results and policy conclusions.

The informal economy in South Africa has given rise to a body of literature that has revealed some of the key characteristics of this economy. While it offers people an alternative when faced with severe labour demand shortages in the formal economy, the South African sector's contribution to total employment is smaller than that of other comparable countries (Kingdon and Knight, 2004). Its contribution also appears to have been declining over the past two decades, from almost 20% in 2000 to roughly 16% in 2015 (Burger and Fourie, 2015). A further differentiating characteristic of South Africa's informal economy is that although it is relatively small, it is very much a long-term activity (Blaauw, 2010; Theodore at al., 2015). McKeever (2007) established that between 1951 and 1991 the average duration of an informal economy job was ten and a half years.

The long-term nature of South Africa's informal economy places a question mark on its theoretical ability to act as a shock absorber. We took this question into account in our analysis of the informal economy in Emalahleni.

Findings

The broader informal economy in Emalahleni

In the main household survey, 78 of the 937 respondents said they were self-employed. Their average age was 36, with a median of 33. The oldest respondent was 67 and the youngest 20. Their educational attainment was significantly higher than the national levels for informal economy workers in South Africa. It was impressive that 15 of them (19%) had a diploma or bachelor's degree, with one respondent even having a postgraduate qualification. This level of human capital allows some workers in Emalahleni's informal economy to engage in higher-tier informal economy activities, such being a consultant. There were, of course, also those who conformed to the norm of informal economy workers, having not completed secondary schooling. Another 10% had completed some primary schooling only, and 28% and 39% had completed some secondary schooling and matriculation, respectively. The respondents were involved in a diverse range of self-employed activities.

Of the 78 respondents, 31 (40%) were active in the retail sphere, selling food, clothes, perfumes and various other products. Around 45% were active in the service sector, providing services such as hairdressing, mechanical work, day care, tutoring and sales consultation. The remaining 15% (12) was made up of a diverse range of activities such as recycling, taxi ownership and other entrepreneurial endeavours.

As expected, we found that most of the informal economy respondents, 67 of the 78, did not receive a fixed wage for their labour but depended on the turnover generated by their activities. Respondents were asked how much money they take home monthly, after expenses. The average was R5,604 and the median R2,900. The reason for the much lower median was the R73,500 earned by one of the respondents, who was engaged in a very specific entrepreneurial activity which yielded this much higher income. If this outlier is not taken into account the (perhaps more representative) average is R4,722. At the other end of the scale, the minimum take-home amount was a mere R100. Around 67% of the respondents took home less than R10,000.

If we compare the economic outcome of these higher-tier informal economy activities with that of the lower-tier activities such as day labour (as discussed in the following section), we find that these informal economy workers fare much better. The median monthly income for day labourers in our 2018 sample in Emalahleni was only R300, scarcely 10% of the median of the 78 respondents in the higher-tier activities. Put differently, only four of the 78 people in this sample took home R300 per month or less. Clearly some informal economy activities in Emalahleni provide much higher monetary rewards than others. This supports the findings in the South African literature (see Saunders, 2005; Blaauw, 2010, for detailed discussions in this regard).

Socio-economic dynamics of informally employed day labourers in Emalahleni, 2008 and 2018

In this section we consider in more detail the dynamics of the lower tier of the informal economy, according to Chen's (2008) definition, by looking at the changing dynamics of informal day labour in Emalahleni over the last 10 years. Some of the demographic aspects have seen little or no change in the past decade. For example, it is still exclusively black men who engage in this activity. However, when other demographics are analysed the evolving nature of day labour in the city, and its links with its mining-dominated local economy, becomes clear. Table 12.2 acts as the departure point for this discussion by summarising the demographic characteristics and behaviour of our sample of day labourers in Emalahleni in 2008 and 2018. It must be noted that in 2008 and 2018 there were no women encountered as part of our samples.

Table 12.2 highlights changes in the demographics and behaviour of the informally employed day labourers in Emalahleni. The composition of the day labour force in the city appears to have changed dramatically in the past 10 years. Foreign migrants from various SADC (Southern African Development Community) countries now constitute almost 30% of the day labour population, with men from Mozambique accounting for the biggest proportion. This observation is not limited to Emalahleni. Recent research has reported growing ranks of foreign-born migrants within the day labour population who are attracted to South African cities by the prospect of a better chance of finding a job (Adepoju, 2004; Charman and Petersen, 2015; Theodore et al., 2017). Faced with few avenues for stable employment, many of these migrants have little option but to turn to the informal economy, such as day labour, for their livelihood (Crush, Chikanda and Skinner, 2015; Theodore et al., 2017). Here they compete in a curbside labour market with both local and internal migrants for limited temporary job opportunities. The day labour market in Emalahleni is therefore not unlike that of other reception cities such as Cape Town, Tshwane and Johannesburg. The local municipality is aware of the increased levels of migration and notes that many people migrate to Emalahleni in search of employment who may not have the right skills to work in the local economy (Emalahleni Municipality, 2017).

The education levels in the day labour market in the city seem to have declined in the past 10 years. The number of day labourers in our sample who had completed their secondary schooling decreased by 12 percentage points in the 10 years between the two surveys, while five day labourers (9%) of the sample in 2018 had not even completed primary schooling. This observation must be

Table 12.2 Demographics and behaviour of day labourers in Emalahleni, 2008 (n = 22) and 2018 (n = 58)

Characteristic	2008	2018
Country of origin	22 (100%) from South Africa	41 (71%) from South Africa 3 (5%) from Zimbabwe 1 (2%) from Swaziland 13 (22%) from Mozambique
Marital status	18 (82%) single	29 (50%) single 29 (50%) married or living with a partner
Age distribution	9 (41%) between 21 and 25 20 (90%) classified as youth*	7 (12%) between 21 and 25 33 (57%) classified as youth*
No. of dependants	Av. of 5	Av. of 5
Education levels completed	1 (5%) primary schooling 13 (59%) secondary schooling. 8 (36%) secondary schooling	5 (9%) some primary schooling 6 (10%) primary schooling 33 (57%) some secondary schooling 14 (24%) secondary schooling
Employment history before becoming a day labourer	6 (26%) previously had full-time job (below national av. of around 50%)	41 (71%) previously had full-time job (above national av.)
Length of time in full-time job and reason for losing it	Most had full-time job for less than a year (11 months on av., median 5 months) All who had lost jobs were retrenched when mine, factory or construction company closed	Most had full-time job for more than a year (24 months on av., median 13.5 months) 21 (37%) who had lost jobs were retrenched when mine, factory or construction company closed
No. of days per week seeking employment	6 to 7 days per week av. and median	6 to 7 days per week av., 7 days per week median
Does labourer negotiate wage before being hired?	Almost no negotiations for wages Never turns down a job	30 (52%) negotiated wages when hired 13 (22%) turned down a job because wage offer was too low

* In South Africa 'youth' is classified as 15 to 34 years of age by the National Youth Act of 1996

viewed against the fact that the day labourers in the 2018 survey were on average much older than their counterparts of 2008. In 2008 nine (41%) of the day labourers who were interviewed were between 21 and 25, with all but two of the twenty two day labourers in that sample being classified as youth (officially defined as people from the age of 15 to 34 in South Africa). This figure dropped to 57% (33 day labourers in the sample of 58) in 2018, with only seven (12%) of the respondents being between 21 and 25 years of age. This finding raises questions and suggests hypotheses. If, as our sample suggests, the unemployed youth in Emalahleni are not engaged in day labour work as before and not in other informal economy activities either, the question is why not? And what are the characteristics of those who do form part of this curbside labour market?

A possible answer to the first question may be found in the recent work of Zizzamia (2018). He found that among relatively unskilled black urban populations, 'younger workers, those with few dependants, those with alternative sources of support . . . appear to have stronger outside options and are consequently more likely to turn down "bad" jobs' (Zizzamia, 2018: i). Given the uncertainty, often precarious working conditions and low income levels, the day labour market certainly fits the 'bad' job description. The alternative sources of support may be family members who are working or perhaps older family members receiving some form of social grant. On the other hand, Zizzamia (2018: i) suggests, '[o]lder workers, those with dependants, those with less support in the household, and those with weaker social networks can be said to have weaker outside options, and are hence less empowered to turn down even the lowest paid, most degrading and precarious forms of work' such as day labour, waste picking (hunting through garbage bins in the hope of finding food or something to use or sell, or salvaging recyclables on landfill sites) and car guarding (offering to watch cars at places like shopping centres in the hope of tips from the driver). These hypotheses need to be empirically tested on a larger sample than ours.

To answer the second question would necessitate investigating the employment history of the day labourers in Emalahleni. Table 12.2 again shows an important change in our sample over the past decade. In 2008, only a quarter of the sample said they had had some form of formal job prior to becoming a day labourer. This was much lower than the South African average of around 50%. In 2008 the average length of these lost full-time jobs was 11 months (with a median of five months). During the next 10 years this labour market apparently changed to such a degree that three quarters of the day labourers in the 2018 survey reported that they had had some form of previous formal employment, and these jobs had lasted on average just over two years (with a median of 13 months). More than one in every three of the respondents in our sample in this predicament reported that they had had jobs either directly in mining or in related industries. Clearly, events in the mining sector influence every sphere of the local labour market, including that of informally employed day labourers.

Our sample suggests that mine decline, downscaling and closures have led to more men ending up on Emalahleni's street corners in an attempt to earn some money and provide for their families.

Day labour in Emalahleni seems, for the most part, to have become a catchment area for older, lower-skilled black men who have lost a formal job. More disturbing is the fact that their chances of re-entering the formal economy are minimal, with many of them having been day labourers now for many years. The average day labourer in our sample has been doing this kind of work now for almost five and a half years, with the median being three years. One respondent had been a day labourer for no less than 24 years. Long spells of unemployment diminish these men's human capital and skills, making a return to the formal economy unlikely. Our findings resonate strongly with those of Theodore et al. (2015) in their comparison of the South African day labour market with that of the United States.

For many day labourers in the United States (including undocumented immigrants), day labour can act as a stepping stone towards eventual integration into the formal economy (Theodore et al., 2015). But for most South African day labourers, as is the case in Emalahleni, inadequate labour demand and often low levels of education lead to a long-term presence in the informal economy. Working as a day labourer in South Africa is a survival strategy, which casts doubt on the notion of the informal economy being a stepping stone to employment in the formal economy (Valenzuela et al., 2006; Theodore et al., 2015). There is a clear and present danger that it may reinforce already existing income inequalities in the economy (Banerjee et al., 2007; Theodore et al., 2015). Like that of South Africa generally, Emalahleni's day labour market operates as a reservoir of underemployed workers. These markets in South Africa are attracting larger numbers and cannot provide sufficient employment opportunities or earnings (Theodore et al., 2015).

Day labour income and unemployment in Emalahleni
Table 12.3 shows various day labour income indicators for our sample, expressed in 2018 prices. The original 2008 nominal income values have been adjusted to 2018 prices using the appropriate consumer price index (CPI) obtained from the South African Reserve Bank (SARB, 2018).

The findings shown in Table 12.3 provide an indication of these labourers' difficult lives. Initial inspection of the results seems to suggest that day labourers are in fact slightly better off in real terms in 2018 than they were in 2008. The average and median of the lowest daily wage is consistently higher in 2018 than in 2008. The average highest daily wage is also higher, but the median is lower, at R200 per day, than the R216 (in 2018 prices) of 2008.[1] The pressures of the day labour market in Emalahleni are evident when we extend our analysis to the reservation wage (the lowest amount that the day labourers are willing to work for). The 2018

Income variable	Lowest daily wage received		Highest daily wage received		Reservation wage per day		Income in a 'good' week		Income in a 'bad' week	
	2008	2018	2008	2018	2008	2018	2008	2018	2008	2018
Average	114.72	124.54	212.05	228.85	279.90	165.48	353.27	564.42	119.16	163.03
Median	108.14	120	216.29	200	270.34	150	324.43	500	108.14	75
Min	90.12	0	90.12	100	180.24	30	72.10	37.50	90.12	0
Max	144.19	230	630.84	650	630.84	300	901.19	2250	144.19	1000

Table 12.3 Day labour average income for Emalahleni 2008 (n = 22) and 2018 (n = 58), in 2018 (rand)

reservation wage is significantly lower in real terms than in 2008. The difference is statistically significant at the 99% confidence level.

The lower 2018 values suggest a day labour market that is severely depressed and offering limited employment opportunities. Previous studies showed that the reservation wage drops even further if a day labourer endured an extended period of not being hired (Blaauw, 2010; Theodore et al., 2018). This is also the case in Emalahleni, where day labourers often go for days without being hired. In 2018 almost two thirds (62%) of our sample reported that they had not been hired at all in the week preceding the interview. The median number of days hired was zero, as could be expected. Only two of the respondents had been hired every day of the preceding week. The unemployment rates among Emalahleni's day labourers therefore appear to be astonishingly high, on average 86%. This is reflected in the incomes they reported for what they would term a 'bad' week.

The median income in a bad week was reported as R75. This translates into about R300 per month. This is, of course, not enough for the day labourers to survive materially, let alone support their average of five dependants. Without other sources of income in the families, such as social grants or working family members, their very survival will be in jeopardy. The situation for foreign day labourers, who are expected to send remittances home, is even worse. As Blaauw (2010) pointed out, the rationale for continuing to come and stand at the street corner in spite of the low and uncertain return needs to be investigated from a purely economic point of view.

From a theoretical point of view, the field of social psychology could provide some insight into the choices made by the day labourers after losing a job on the mine or in a related industry. Omar (2017) recounts how Dr Mandisa Malinga of the University of Cape Town studied the behaviour of day labourers from the angle of what it means to be a father and a man and how this is connected with employment. Malinga suggests that 'it's really about how as a society we've constructed fatherhood in a way solely around the idea that fathers have to provide'. She notes that men are expected to have paid jobs, and today that is not possible for everyone. She says that because their families expect them to provide, since that is what men are supposed to do, they are reluctant to go back and say 'I didn't make any money so I can't provide for you'. She observed that 'to avoid the shame and humiliation, they would go live under a bridge instead'. Some would just stay away from their families.

Komlos (2018) also describes the psychological impact of not being employed. Unemployment and underemployment are degrading, especially given the expectations of men described above. Skill levels may deteriorate during long periods of unemployment, making it even more difficult for them to find a job and increasing social misery in the process. The result is that the worker feels unwanted (UNDP, 2014; Komlos, 2018). Day labourers may well consider themselves not to be useful members of society and suffer from low self-worth (Komlos, 2018). In the case of Emalahleni the misfortunes of the mining industry therefore may filter through the social fabric via informal economic activities like day labour.

The day labourers in Emalahleni themselves are more often than not adamant about what keeps them coming back and their responses are in line with Malinga's interpretation. One of our respondents said: 'I know I am not lazy when I come here', which illustrates this sense of responsibility and response to the expectation created by society. Another summed it up by saying: 'It's better to come and try your luck.' We observed that day labourers display a remarkable level of agency and resilience (Béné et al., 2014) in their continued daily struggle to find employment and provide for their children. Their hope and their refusal to give up are remarkable. As one of them put it: 'Maybe next week will be better.' Their 'agency', as defined by Sen (2000) in his capabilities approach, is also reflected in the fact that even with their meagre income, they told us that they plan ahead. One of them said: 'If I get 100 rand today, I will use 50 rand to buy bread and pay for transport and try to save 50 rand for school fees for my children.'

In line with the work of Theodore et al. (2017) we suggest that Emalahleni can play an important role in putting into practice the vision described in its own IDP. The provision of shelters and the possible establishment of a worker centre for the informally employed would go a long way towards improving the lives of this marginalised segment of the city's population. That type of intervention could help current and future day labourers and increase their already impressive resilience. The changes that are inevitable in a city dependent on mining will require resilience at all levels of society.

Conclusion

Emalahleni is facing the real possibility of a decrease in the demand for coal in the long run. The implications of possible closures of mines and related industries will affect both the formal and informal economy. People who lose their jobs in the formal economy often have no choice but to venture into the informal economy.

Our two surveys of day labourers over the past decade show the socio-economic effects of boom and bust commodity cycles playing themselves out in Emalahleni's informal economy. The number of day labourers on street corners in the city has increased and the composition and dynamics of this economy have changed. Foreign-born day labourers now constitute about a third of the day labour population in Emalahleni. Around three quarters of the day labourers in the 2018 sample had previously had formal jobs and lost them for various reasons such as retrenchments and business closures. These men chose to stay in Emalahleni in the hope of getting another job, for example if a new mine opened. Congregating at street corners, they wait for six or seven days a week in the hope of temporary employment as manual labourers. Once in the informal labour market, they are there for the long haul as it is almost impossible to return to formal employment.

The labour market outcomes are not favourable for Emalahleni's day labourers. They are often hired only once a week or not hired at all. In our 2018 survey the day labour unemployment rate was 86%. Incomes are low and uncertain, making it very difficult to plan ahead. The day labourers are vulnerable to workplace injuries that may prevent future earning and their poor pay leaves most of them in abject poverty. These findings support the conclusion of Theodore et al. (2015) that the South African day labour market cannot function as a shock absorber for workers who have lost their jobs in the formal labour market. Yet, every day these men chose to leave the place where they sleep in order to make themselves available for essentially any form of employment, because it is 'better than sitting at home'.

The case is, of course, different for those involved in higher-tier informal self-employment such as being a consultant, or owning one or more taxis. In cases like that, the informal economy can be a viable alternative to formal economy employment. But for most informal economy workers such as the day labourers in Emalahleni this is, sadly, not the case. The long-term nature of their involvement in the day labour market, the absence of mobility back to the formal economy, low levels of education and low and uncertain levels of income ensure that lower-tier informal economy activities are not the stepping stone to formal employment as envisaged in some segments of the literature. South Africa's day labour markets clearly function differently from those in the United States.

The increased supply in day labour markets with limited demand will undoubtedly influence the lives and livelihoods of the day labourers in Emalahleni in the years to come. Therefore, policy that advocates an unqualified expansion of the informal economy as the best way to increase employment levels may prove to be unsuccessful. From a policy perspective it is important to acknowledge the permanent nature of the South African informal economy. The Emalahleni Municipality can give practical meaning to this by taking a policy decision to embrace informality to enhance the economic and environmental sustainability of Emalahleni. This must be followed by a process to determine fit-for-purpose initiatives to accommodate the agency and resilience of workers in the informal economy.

Essential elements of such a process will be to build on existing informal services, use and leverage existing social connections and relationships and, equally important, alleviate the day-to-day struggles of informal economy workers. These conditions could help to make informal employment a safety net or a springboard for these workers. This investment in respecting informality could yield improved economic and social returns by giving meaning to the notion of social justice. If workers in the informal economy do not constantly have to struggle against an environment that does not recognise the worth of their endeavours, this will also improve social cohesion. Creating an encouraging environment for informal workers, with interventions to provide shelter and basic amenities and possibly day labour centres, are proven ways of improving the lives of the informally employed. As a practical example in Emalahleni, men who have their own lawnmowers with which they provide garden services could be given a sheltered place where these can be serviced. Providing assistance in real and tangible ways to people living on the margins of society is crucial if Emalahleni is to make a just transition in the long run.

References

Adepoju, A. 2004. Continuity and changing configurations of migration to and from the Republic of South Africa. *International Migration*, 41(1), 3–28.

Andrews, D., Sanchez, A. D. and Johansson, A. 2011. Towards a better understanding of the informal economy. Working Paper No. 873. OECD (Organisation for Economic Co-operation and Development), Paris.

Banerjee, A., Galiani, S., Levinsohn, J., Mclaren, Z. and Woolard, I. 2007. Why has unemployment risen in the new South Africa? Working Paper No. 13167, National Bureau of Economic Research, Cambridge, MA.

Béné, C., Newsham, A., Davies, M., Ulrichs, M. and Godfrey-Wood, R. 2014. Review article: Resilience, poverty and development. *Journal of International Development*, 26, 598–623.

Benjamin, N. and Mbaye, A. A. 2014. Informality, growth, and development in Africa. Working Paper No. 2014/052, WIDER (World Institute for Development Economics Research), Helsinki.

Blaauw, P. F. 2010. The socio-economic aspects of day labouring in South Africa. Unpublished doctoral thesis, University of Johannesburg.

Burger, P. and Fourie, F. C. v.N. 2015. High unemployment and labour market segmentation: A three-segment macroeconomic model. Paper presented at the Biennial Conference of the Economic Society of South Africa, Cape Town, 2–4 September 2015.

Charman, A. and Petersen, L. 2015. A transnational space of business: The informal economy of Ivory Park, Johannesburg. In J. Crush, A. Chikanda and C. Skinner (eds), *Mean Streets: Migration, Xenophobia and Informality in South Africa*. Cape Town: Southern African Migration Programme, 78–99.

Chen, M. 2008. Informality and social protection: Theories and realities. *Institute of Development Studies Bulletin*, 39(2), 18–27.

Chen, M., Vanek, J. and Heintz, J. 2006. Informality, gender, and poverty: A global picture. *Economic and Political Weekly*, 2131–39.

Crush, J., Chikanda, A. and Skinner, C. 2015. *Mean Streets: Migration, Xenophobia and Informality in South Africa*. Cape Town: Southern African Migration Programme.

De Soto, H. 1989. *The Other Path: The Invisible Revolution in the Third World*. New York: Harper & Row.

Emalahleni Municipality. 2017. *Intergrated [sic] Development Plan (IDP) 2017/18–2021/22*. https://cogta.mpg.gov.za/IDP/2017-22IDPs/Nkangala/Emalahleni2017-22.pdf (last accessed 28 April 2021).

Guha-Khasnobis, B. and Kanbur, R. 2006. Introduction: Informal markets and development. In B. Guha-Khasnobis and R. Kanbur (eds), *Informal Labour Markets and Development*. UNU-WIDER Studies in Development Economics and Policy, Helsinki: Palgrave Macmillan.

Hart, K. 1973. Informal income opportunities and urban employment in Ghana. *Journal of Modern African Studies*, 11(1), 61–89.

ILO (International Labour Organization). 2013. *Measuring Informality: A Statistical Manual on the Informal Sector and Informal Employment*. http://www.ilo.org/wcmsp5/groups/public/---dgreports/---dcomm/---publ/documents/publication/wcms_222979.pdf (last accessed 28 April 2021).

Kingdon, G. G. and Knight, J. B. 2004. Unemployment in South Africa: The nature of the beast. *World Development*, 32(3), 391–408.

Komlos, J. 2018. Employment in a just economy. *Real-world Economics Review*, 83, 87–98. http://www.paecon.net/PAEReview/issue83/Komlos83.pdf (last accessed 28 April 2021).

Leonard, M. 2000. Coping strategies in developed and developing societies: The workings of the informal economy. *Journal of International Development*, 12, 1069–85.

McKeever, M. 2007. Fall back or spring forward? Labor market transitions and the informal economy in South Africa. *Research in Social Stratification and Mobility*, 24, 73–87.

Omar, Y. 2017. A bakkie-load of dignity. University of Cape Town News, 26 July. https://www.news.uct.ac.za/article/-2017-07-26-a-bakkie-load-of-dignity (last accessed 28 April 2021).

SARB (South African Reserve Bank), 2018. Selected historical rates. https://www.resbank.co.za/Research/Rates/Pages/SelectedHistoricalExchangeAndInterestRates.aspx (last accessed 28 April 2021).

Saunders, S. G. 2005. Estimates of the informal economy in South Africa: Some macroeconomic policy implications. Unpublished doctoral thesis, University of Johannesburg.

Sen, A. 2000. *Development as Freedom*. New York: Anchor Books.

Theodore, N., Blaauw, D., Schenck, C., Valenzuela Jr, A., Schoeman, C. and Meléndez, E. J. 2015. Day labor, informality and vulnerability in the United States and South Africa. *International Journal of Manpower*, 36(6), 807–23.

Theodore, N., Blaauw, D., Pretorius, A. and Schenck, C. 2017. The socioeconomic incorporation of immigrant and native-born day labourers in Tshwane, South Africa. *International Migration*, 55(1), 142–56.

Theodore, N., Pretorius, A., Blaauw, D. and Schenck, C. 2018. Informality and the context of reception in South Africa's new immigrant destinations. *Population, Space and Place*, 24(3), e2119. doi: 10.1002/psp.2119.

UNDP (United Nations Development Programme). 2014. *Human Development Report 2014. Sustaining Human Progress: Reducing Vulnerabilities and Building Resilience.* http://hdr.undp.org/en/content/human-development-report-2014 (last accessed 28 April 2021).

Valenzuela Jr, A., Theodore, N., Meléndez, E. and Gonzalez, A. L. 2006. *On the Corner: Day Labor in the United States.* Los Angeles and Chicago: UCLA Center for the Study of Urban Poverty and UIC Center for Urban Economic Development.

Wilson, T. D. 2011. Introduction: Approaches to the informal economy. *Urban Anthropology*, 40(3–4), 205–21.

Zizzamia, R. 2018. Is employment a panacea for poverty in South Africa? A mixed-methods investigation. Working Paper No. 229. SALDRU (Southern Africa Labour and Development Research Unit), University of Cape Town.

Note

1. At the time of the fieldwork the ZAR–USD exchange rate was 12.48 ZAR to 1 USD (SARB, 2018).

CHAPTER 13

A More Resilient Policy Approach to Spatial Fragmentation

Mariske van Aswegen and Ernst Drewes

Spatial fragmentation

Fragmented cities are a global problem, as various policy documents highlight. Colonialism has been central to this spatial fragmentation and has contributed to urban inequalities and the stratification of these inequalities (Bryceson and Potts, 2006). Mining has contributed to further spatial fragmentation and planning cities around mining dumps while minimising air pollution is no easy task. The New Urban Agenda sees a better understanding of city structure as the beginning of a solution to the problem: if cities are well planned and managed, this can be a 'powerful tool for sustainable development for both developing and developed countries' (UN, 2016). On the local level, this translates into appropriate land use planning and management, as well as overcoming the historical legacies of apartheid. Land use planning faces both threats and opportunities. It must deliver sustainable development and liveable communities, but it must also cope with conflicts over these two visions (Godschalk, 2003). Dealing with urban fragmentation and the accompanying sprawl is the main challenge of land use management. Urban fragmentation leads to low-density development dispersed over large areas of land, geographical separation of resources such as work, homes, schools and shopping, heavy dependence on motorised transport, and expensive infrastructure and services.

South Africa's cities still show the effects of colonial and apartheid planning in the form of racially exclusive and unequal residential areas and health, education and recreation facilities. The apartheid city not only segregated the race groups; it also separated home and workplace for most residents. It proposed controlled outward growth towards the periphery, as can be seen in the spatial form of Emalahleni, where the fragmentation is exacerbated by the coal mining areas between the built-up areas (Figure 13.1). Increased urbanisation has added to the difficulties, which include unequal access to jobs, amenities and public services, inefficient infrastructure, long travel distances, low-quality spaces, disintegration and separation. The inefficient and unadaptable layout and design, non-integrated land uses and inadequate planning have made it hard for Emalahleni to cope with its changing population.

A further problem for this city is the impermanence of the mines and the fluctuating commodity prices. The uncertainty puts pressure on the supply and

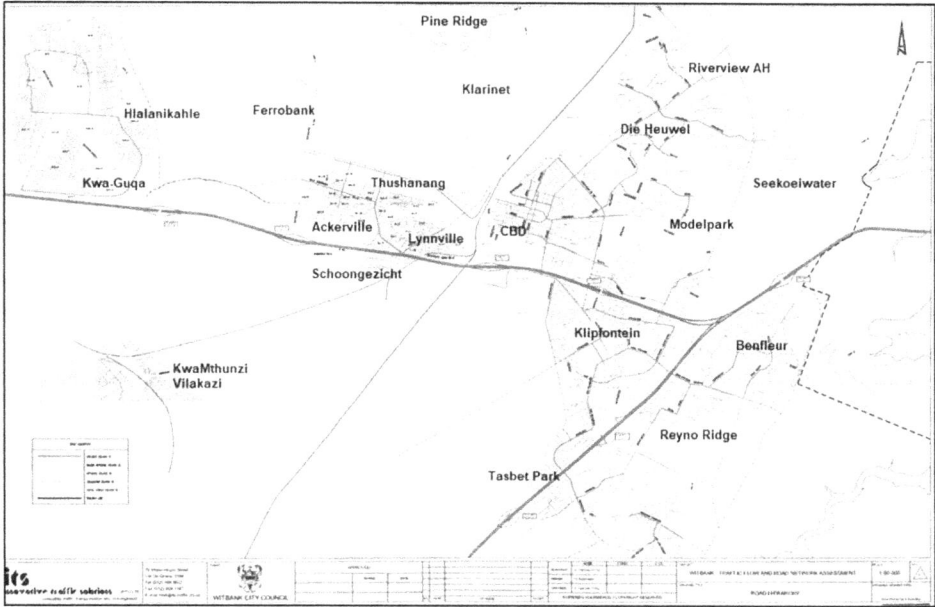

Figure 13.1 Spatial fragmentation of Emalahleni. Source: SDF, 2015.

upkeep of infrastructure, services and housing and makes the city's lifespan uncertain (Drewes and Van Aswegen, 2011). Planners will have to recognise that Emalahleni's economic structure is likely to change over time and that the mining workforce is likely to decline. A just transition will require careful consideration of current and future urban planning.

We ask specifically how mining has added to this fragmentation and what it would take to undo this. Appropriate municipal planning and local responses are crucial to addressing civil concerns (Matebesi, 2017). This chapter investigates the spatial impact of mining operations and the spatial legacy of segregation in Emalahleni. We show how mitigating the problems could increase the long-term sustainability and resilience of Emalahleni. In addition, we explore the spatial components that affect a city's capacity to respond to rapid changes. We propose a multifaceted approach, based on policy guidance, to increase the resilience and efficiency of urban areas. We hope that such a multifaceted approach can also deal with the structural and spatial problems associated with mining in general.

Resilience in spatial planning

'Resilience' means the ability of a system or person to recover equilibrium after a shock or disturbance. The concept is used in disciplines such as psychology, psychiatry, sociology, ecology, economics, engineering and more recently the spatial sciences (Kaplan, 1999; Adger, 2000; Vale and Campanella, 2005; Hill, Wial and Wolman, 2008). Neoclassical economic theory has influenced the study of how shocks affect cities and regions as 'complex systems' (Brugman, 2012; Lhomme et al., 2013). Systems theory explains the relationships and interactions in space and subcomponents. Hall and Fagen (1956: 19) describe a system as 'a set of objects together with relationships between the objects and between their attributes'. The literature identifies three pathways to resilience: persistence, transition and transformation.

The resilience literature across all disciplines focuses on what Meerow, Newell and Stults (2016: 46) refer to as the 'fundamental questions' or 'five Ws' of urban resilience (who, what, when, where, why). Urban resilience is formed by *who* sets the agenda, *whose* resilience is being prioritised, and *who* loses or benefits as a result. Resilience is recognised as a desirable state, but first it must be determined *what* is desirable and for whom, and *what* a city must be resilient to. Planners aiming for resilience are advised ask the question: 'Resilience for whom and of what to what?'. Resilience for '*when*' involves deciding whether the focus is on short-term disruptions or long-term stressors and applying the phrases 'quickly transform' or 'rapidly return' to a particular setting. Resilience for '*where*' means defining a city's spatial boundaries and global networks. And planners need to know *why* resilience is being promoted and what the motivations are for doing so. Answering the 'W' questions is considered central to approaching any state of resilience. (Further sources to consult on the topic of the 'W' questions are Brown, Dayal and Rumbaitis Del Rio, 2012; Raco and Street, 2012; Elmqvist, 2014; Vale, 2014; Chelleri et al., 2015.)

There is no single or correct answer to any of the questions, but dealing with them jointly and considering trade-offs between them should deliver an inclusive and open discourse to shape cities towards greater resilience. The trade-offs will help provide answers to the five Ws and suggest measures to improve Emalahleni's resilience. If a city is resilient it is prepared for any eventuality, whether growth and development or decline and stagnation. The trade-offs between the fundamental questions are managed by various role-players, such as institutions and leaders within the system, and in the case of Emalahleni the local government and the mining companies. Turok (2014: 752) points out that the concept of resilience requires contextualisation. He says that resilience should be 'locally specific and unique about the threats and opportunities facing every city', so policy needs to focus on the context-specific needs of a community or region, rather than a generic set of principles applicable across various spatial scales. Defining the settlement (for whom) and the shock (from what) makes the urban resilience concept more practical and concrete so it can be used to identify an approach and to prevent or absorb a shock within a specified space.

Desouza and Flanery (2013) have proposed a baseline model for more resilient cities, which links to systems theory (Hall and Fagen, 1956). This is shown

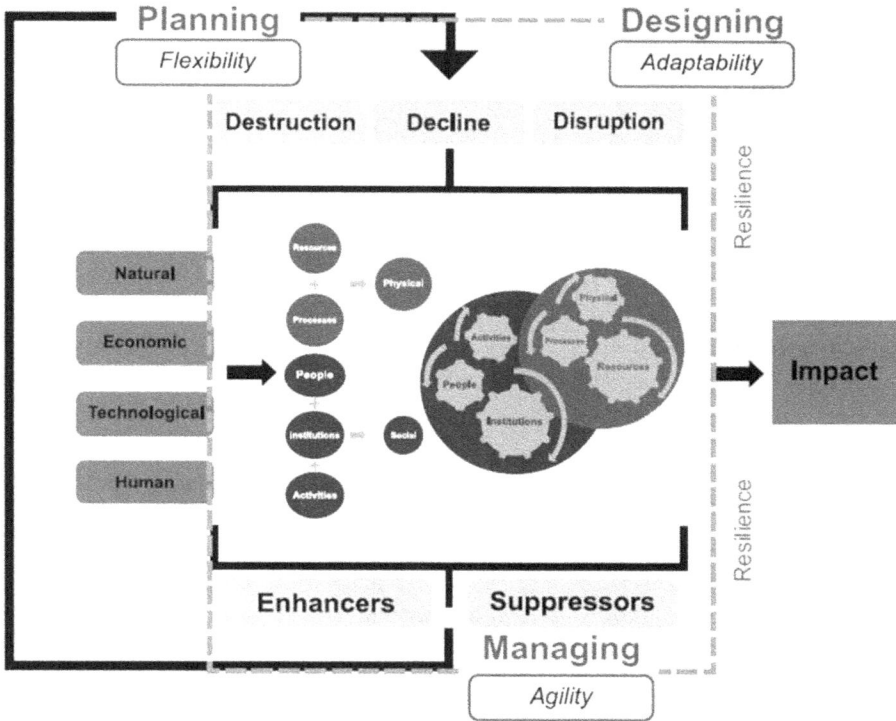

Figure 13.2 A model for resilient cities. Source: Desouza and Flanery (2013:95).

in Figure 13.2. It provides an overall perspective and does not take into account details or exact guidelines for making a city resilient. In this chapter we use this model as a basis for proposals for a more resilient Emalahleni.

The model includes the city's components, its stressors and outcomes, its enhancers and suppressors and their implications for the city, and sets of interventions for making the city resilient. The physical components are the city's natural resources (coal in the case of Emalahleni) and its manufacturers. The social components are the city's people, institutions and activities, including those that come and go as the city expands or contracts. The social and physical components interact with each other daily and either bring the city to life or lead to its decline or demise.

To measure the resilience of a system, we need to identify the stressors that the system should be resilient to, including components of destruction, decline and disruption. To be resilient, Emalahleni must manage the slow-burn processes associated with gradual decline, rather than destruction experienced as a single shock. It can influence the effect of its stressors by managing its components (i.e. coal resources, or infrastructure resources), plans (i.e. policy) and people (i.e. local government and mining companies). Enhancers and suppressors can mitigate the burden of stressors on a city. An enhancer is anything that increases the duration or intensity of a stressor; a suppressor is anything that reduces it. If a city has residents who are familiar with feedbacks from a particular kind of stressor, the impacts will possibly be lower with each successive occurrence as residents are more equipped and prepared. As the primary component of cities, people are essential in mediating the impact of stressors and other system disruptions on a city's governance by self-organising to facilitate appropriate action at appropriate scales.

Integrated land use planning is an essential management tool for land use decisions and zoning extensions. It has been argued that better land use management and particularly an integrated urban planning strategy are essential to improve the current and future resilience of cities and that they should involve all levels of governance and local communities (ICLEI, 2012; Paton, Mamula-Seadon and Selway, 2013; Saunders and Becker, 2015). Guidelines are very important for planning, designing and managing a city in order to build resilience.

Bearing in mind that 'urban resilience', 'sustainability' and 'smart city' are fairly new concepts, in Table 13.1 we summarise the main principles involved. We apply these principles to Emalahleni later in the chapter.

A policy approach to resilience

Resilience has become an objective in many policy documents and is often regarded as a politically neutral and common-sense objective, driven by a pragmatic attitude (Van Rijswick and Salet, 2012). The guidelines for the internationally recognised Sustainable Development Goals state that urban planning must aim to produce inclusive, safe, resilient and sustainable cities (UN, 2015).

Planners need to keep in mind that a city is a spatial system whose structuring elements are in constant interaction with one another (CSIR, 2000; CoGHSTA, 2012). The principles listed in Table 13.1 can be illustrated and applied through six spatial structuring elements (urban edge, mixed land use, densification, infill planning, activity networks, open space systems). These elements are practical policy tools to be used by all stakeholders to help create a resilient city, for scenarios of either growth or decline. The functions of the elements are to:

- contain urban sprawl, to avoid increasing the per capita cost of essential services and losing agricultural or natural land;
- promote urban and social integration by creating compact urban areas;
- promote acceptable higher densities, to achieve more efficient use of urban land, natural resources and service infrastructure;
- create good quality urban environments through urban renewal and landscaping;

Table 13.1 Principles for assessing a city's degree of efficiency, user-friendliness and resilience

Access and amenities	Ease of reaching other people, resources, services, places and information; and public transport, road networks and land use designed to aid access to amenities.
Choice	Circulation, utility systems and amenities designed to give people choice in housing consolidation, urban surroundings, service provision and movement modes.
Control	Use of, access to, modification and management of spaces and activities controlled by the people involved.
Convenience	Streets and highways purposefully constructed to be convenient to people.
Economy	Efficient land use, with public costs handled economically by the municipality.
Efficiency	Land and financial resources efficiently used in planning and maintaining the city.
Enclosure	Outdoor spaces, as defined by buildings, hills, trees and hedges, seldom entirely enclosed.
Fit	Form and capacity of the city's spaces, channels and equipment matched to the pattern and quantity of actions.
Health and safety	Regulations in place for health, sanitation, housing, building and so on, including control of density, hazardous areas and exposure to environmental damage.
Identity and change	Unique character of city areas maintained and care taken in site development to ensure that planners do not make changes that have unexpected chain effects.
Justice	Environmental benefits and costs distributed fairly.
Liveability	Physical city environment gives people a feeling of mental, physical and social well-being.
Opportunity	Promotion of economic opportunity and local economic development through appropriate planning of and investment in circulation, utility systems and amenities.
Placemaking	A 'sense of place' achieved not by standardised planning but by imaginative planning based on understanding the site and people's needs, function and culture.
Proportion and scale	Good proportion achieved by considering the internal relation between sites, and appropriate scale achieved by making elements proportional to the viewpoint of the observer.
Vitality	Vital functions supported by the form of the city.

Source: Adapted from Chapin and Kaiser (1979); Lynch and Hack (1984) and Behrens and Watson (1996).

- reduce the need for traffic movement and promote pedestrian and non-motorised movement;
- restore and maintain a defined sense of place;
- alleviate poverty and inequality;
- protect and enhance all inhabitants' properties and investments;
- improve and simplify decisions about development applications. (CoGHSTA, 2012)

Table 13.2 shows how the structuring elements are related. It shows that the principles listed in Table 13.1 and discussed in this chapter can be applied spatially through more concentrated, integrated and combined land use. This could lead to a more focused approach and improved implementation measures. The *State of South African Cities Report* (SACN, 2016) emphasises that spatial form, human settlement and public transport interventions are interdependent and will undermine each other if planned and implemented separately. The challenge

Table 13.2 Application of principles to six spatial structuring elements						
	Urban edge	Mixed land use	Densification	Infill planning	Activity networks	Open space systems
Access and amenities		X	X	X	X	
Choice		X	X	X	X	
Control						
Convenience		X	X		X	X
Economy	X	X	X	X	X	
Efficiency	X	X	X	X	X	
Enclosure	X	X				X
Fit		X	X		X	
Health and safety			X			X
Identity and change	X			X		X
Justice	X	X	X	X	X	
Liveability		X	X		X	X
Opportunity		X	X	X	X	X
Placemaking		X				X
Proportion and scale	X			X		X
Vitality					X	

for cities is to enhance their spatial form in a way that makes them increasingly economically efficient and resilient, as well as more inclusive, enabling people to access different economic opportunities across city space. Cities therefore need to use their spatial planning and land use management (zoning) instruments, and human settlement and public transport investments more effectively to concentrate and densify where people live and where they work along core public transport corridors and economic centres (SACN, 2016).

Contextualising resilience in Emalahleni

Table 13.3 suggests some answers to the five Ws for Emalahleni. Asking these questions establishes a baseline from which trade-offs can be translated into a policy response and can help planners to design and manage Emalahleni's land use to promote resilience. This section, based on Desouza and Flanery's model (Figure 13.2), analyses Emalahleni's situation with reference to the components, stressors and outcomes, enhancers, suppressors and influences, and sets of interventions for incorporating resilience. It must be noted that the resilience concept and planning for resilience do not favour a particular outcome (i.e. growth or decline); the aim is rather to make a city like Emalahleni 'safe to fail' in either case.

Table 13.3 Suggested answers to 'W' questions about Emalahleni's resilience	
Who?	The local community, daily users of the urban system, local government, mining companies
What?	Economic downturns, continued urbanisation, eventual decline, all land use components of the daily urban system, stressors caused by the fragmented urban form
When? *Trade-offs?*	Long-term The resilience of the present generation is critical, but the slow-burn process of long-term urbanisation means the effects may only be visible to future generations
Where?	Spatial boundaries of the daily urban system, i.e. the City of Emalahleni with its associated settlements No prioritisation of areas, rather a prioritisation of integration
Why?	To be prepared for a declining population

Figure 13.3 shows that Emalahleni's development pattern is severely fragmented, the result of separate development histories, but aggravated by the large areas within the municipality that cannot be developed for residential and business purposes because they have mining rights or are unsafe because of undermining (i.e. underground mines).

Emalahleni Local Municipality's western and north-western townships of Lynnville, Ackerville, Thushanang, Schoongezicht and Pine Ridge were established on the basis of historical racial separation (diamonds in Figure 13.3). Rapid urbanisation in the 1980s, along with the expanding mining operations, produced the townships of Kwa-Guqa and Hlalanikahle (triangles in Figure 13.3), which have grown enormously because of land invasion and the establishment of informal settlements. These townships are viewed as a duplicate of the original city, although smaller and with fewer amenities. This was typically due to apartheid racial segregation. The integration of these areas with the urban fabric is hampered mostly by areas of large-scale underground mining (black blocks in Figure 13.3) which cannot be developed without extensive geological and environmental studies being done first. The Emalahleni airfield, the prison and the regional refuse disposal site also

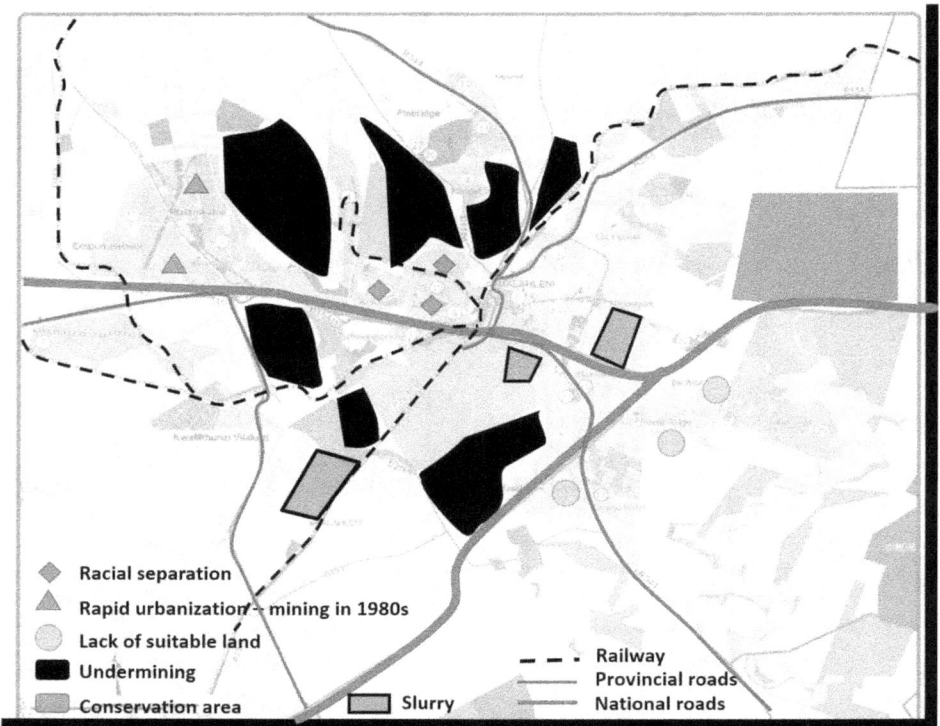

Figure 13.3 Stressors on Emalahleni's spatial structure.

hinder expansion to the north. Eskom's power lines (and the associated development restrictions) and natural barriers hamper development in Kwa-Guqa. The transport network reinforces separate development and hampers movement throughout the city. The original urban settlements of Emalahleni were to the north of the N4, but development pressure and lack of suitable land in the northern parts have produced settlements (Benfleur, Reyno Ridge and Tasbet Park) to the south of the N4 (circles in Figure 13.3). Future development is focused in a northerly and easterly direction. But the municipality notes that 'the rich coal deposits and associated coal mines and power stations throughout the southern extents of the municipal area are, undoubtedly, the most dominant structuring elements having a major influence on settlement development and expansion trends' (Emalahleni Local Municipality, 2015).

The city suffers from the inefficient planning that has produced these unintegrated separated and segregated areas, and from the lack of connectivity and unity. Public transport is not accessible to all. Continuous migration to the city puts pressure on space and housing and increases urban sprawl, which in turn increases travel distances to work and amenities, resulting in traffic jams, higher travel expenses and pollution. Urban sprawl further increases the cost of supplying basic services to residents, and increases segregation between residential and commercial uses. The municipal spatial development framework (SDF) (Emalahleni Local Municipality, 2015) calculates an increment of 251,289 people (12,564 per annum) up to 2030 (which is the long-term planning horizon for Emalahleni's SDF).[1] This translates to 76,148 additional housing units by 2030, which will add 3,807 ha to Emalahleni's current footprint.

Enhancers, suppressors and network implications for Emalahleni

Following the principle-based planning approach, we propose the six spatial structuring elements as policy tools or 'suppressors' to mitigate the slow burn of urbanisation and the imminent decline of resilience. The elements are urban edge, mixed land use, densification, infill planning, activity networks and open spaces (Table 13.2).

Planning the *urban edge* is a primary strategy to counter urban sprawl, encourage densification and protect natural resources. An urban edge policy facilitates efficient use of land and urban services within this boundary. It designates future spatial locations and developments. The urban edge should include and integrate the city and the townships. In Emalahleni, it is clear that this principle has played a relatively insignificant role in determining its expansion zones for the medium term (five years) spatial planning as per the SDF (2015). Most of the residential, commercial and industrial expansion zones clearly show sprawl patterns (see Figure 13.1). The urban edge as a planning instrument could increase the city's efficiency and resilience if it had a more extensive implementation framework with clearer guidelines for municipal officials to follow. This instrument could help to compact the city in the event of downscaling and allow for more effective use of land.

Mixed land use – that is, a mixture of business, industrial and residential development – directly contributes to urban resilience and improves efficiency, sustainability, liveability and sense of place by enhancing the area's unique identity and development potential. Areas will have continuous movement, which will decrease crime and prevent urban decay by enhancing revitalisation. Mixed land use encourages high-quality design by providing greater flexibility and more control. It increases opportunities and choices regarding housing, retail, public transport and recreation in a more compact form. It promotes pedestrian and bicycle movement and reduces dependence on cars, roadway congestion and air pollution by co-locating multiple destinations. Mixed land use nodes also promote efficient use of land and existing infrastructure and guide development towards established areas. The effective use of this instrument makes it possible to consolidate land use types, which will be more sustainable in the event of decline. Mixed-use areas should be planned adjacent to the main corridors and focus areas. This will ultimately accelerate the creation of liveable, resilient and efficient urban areas. Plans for mixed use are evident in Emalahleni in the latest SDF (2015) and will accordingly support urban resilience in principle. These two instruments (urban edge and mixed land use) must be used in support of each other. In practice, mixed land use often leads to urban sprawl. This defeats its purpose as a planning instrument in support of resilience.

If implemented appropriately, *densification* is arguably one of the most powerful tools for achieving a resilient, sustainable, competitive and liveable Emalahleni. Densification will provide more opportunity and choice for the residents of Emalahleni in terms of different densities and types of housing, leading to more affordable housing. Access to public facilities and other amenities will improve due to the proximity of services and amenities and the development of business and employment nodes closer to residences. This will improve the city's overall efficiency. The Emalahleni municipality should plan for densification along main corridors, within the CBD, and in secondary nodes such as Hlalanikahle, Lynnville, Reyno Ridge, and towards Pine Ridge and Klarinet. Densification will assist in creating more sustainable and affordable housing options and access to public facilities and other amenities, resulting in an overall efficient city which will be less affected in the case of decline. Emalahleni needs a densification focused policy. It should identify areas in need of densification as special use areas. The Seekoeiwater and Dixon agricultural holdings could help to compact the sprawling city by making available prime land for development, which will see the sprawling suburbs of Emalahleni merge together.

Infill planning can help to revive previously undermined areas and prevent urban decay through making available previously unused land for development. Infill planning encourages good affordable housing on vacant land, improving choice, opportunity and efficiency. These areas may include open or unplanned areas (note that this does not include open space or protected areas), and areas that are not being used effectively. The areas identified should have the potential to contribute to urban resilience, and could include agricultural holdings which are not intensively farmed, for example River View, Modelpark, Die Heuwel, Reyno Ridge and Tasbet Park. Using undermined land (after it has been determined safe) to the west of the CBD (the areas between Klarinet and Ferrobank and between Ferrobank and Hlalanikahle) would contribute to a more resilient urban form. Emalahleni's infill planning has been primarily the result of expansion of the urban edge in a reactive manner, rather than as a proactive approach towards densification, infill and integration. The SDF (2015) mentions the need for infill planning in the CBD, but it needed to focus on other areas as well. 'Brownfield' development (making use of unused sites that had previous development or buildings on them) barely features in the planning, although it could be a quick and easy way to achieve densification and mixed-use development and address the need for housing and social facilities. Similar infill developments in Gauteng include integrated development in pockets of the 'mining belt', such as Pennyville, which has provided almost 2,800 housing opportunities, and the renowned Fleurhof housing project which has provided 8,000 opportunities.

Activity networks in the form of street and movement networks could help to make Emalahleni resilient. They foster a sense of community by connecting people and giving them accessible public transport, taking into account their social or demographical status. Options for walking or cycling encourage a healthier lifestyle. Public transport also reduces the need for building car parks, leading to more efficient use of land and a less polluted natural environment. Important movement corridors and networks should be identified within the urban area, which specifically includes access routes to and from the various neighbourhoods to the N4 and into the main employment areas. Although the focus should be on the CBD of the city, it is essential that the Hlalanikahle and Reyno Ridge areas form part of this system, to eliminate the gap or zone of segregation. Public transport zones will give communities better access to social, economic and environmental facilities. With more alternatives, people will have better choices and access to workplaces and social amenities. Comparable policy initiatives in South Africa include the 'Corridors of Freedom' project in Gauteng, where a large-scale encompassing approach to transport-oriented development as a countermeasure to decades of segregation-based spatial development has been successfully implemented.

However, a regional perspective must be included as it forms the main link with other centres of development, which will strengthen the importance of

Emalahleni as a primary node in the area and help to diversify the economy. This interaction must be planned for and promoted to make the city resilient. The SDF (2015) takes into account the Maputo Corridor as an international development initiative between Mozambique and South Africa and supports these movement patterns. It pays less attention to the regional link with the Ekurhuleni Metropolitan area (the N12), and scarcely mentions the secondary corridor to Richards Bay, which has been identified by the national government as a critical focus for spatial targeting of development.

Open spaces are a vital part of any urban system, for people's physical and psychological health and to strengthen communities, which all contributes to resilience. Open spaces make cities and neighbourhoods attractive and liveable with fair proportion and scale. They encourage people to socialise and integrate irrespective of race or demographic status. The SDF (Emalahleni Local Municipality, 2015) has plans for open spaces with links to regional green corridors and biodiverse zones, but less focus on planning integrated open space systems in the built-up area. Although various 'regional open spaces' can be seen in the spatial plans, these are isolated pockets or even afterthoughts, and in many cases planned for sterilised mining land. The sterilised portions are unsafe for any sort of development at this stage and will require intensive rehabilitation before they can be used. If viable for development, these areas will greatly help to unify the segregated areas and could even be used for other purposes, such as small-scale farming.

Policy interventions: Towards increased urban resilience in Emalahleni

Figure 13.4 shows how these tools should be applied interdependently of one another and form part of a cohesive network of urban resilience and efficiency. Each of these tools contributes to a renewed urban form that is striving to be more resilient and more efficient. Resilient planning must be based on systems analysis. This will make it possible to pinpoint the vulnerability of urban systems and focus on key issues such as the gap or zone of inaccessibility between the city and the outlying eastern and western areas of Emalahleni and the areas to the north and south of the N4. It will provide opportunities in terms of access to workplaces, social amenities and other facilities, making the city more efficient. Public transport will reduce the dependence on oil and other fossil fuels and lead to an energy-efficient city. According to Ahern (2011) a centralised city function or service is vulnerable and likely to fail, whereas a decentralised system is more resistant to disturbance.

Densification and infill planning need to be accompanied by a mix of land uses, increased access to both social and physical infrastructure, better links to public transport, and integration with public and green spaces. This should

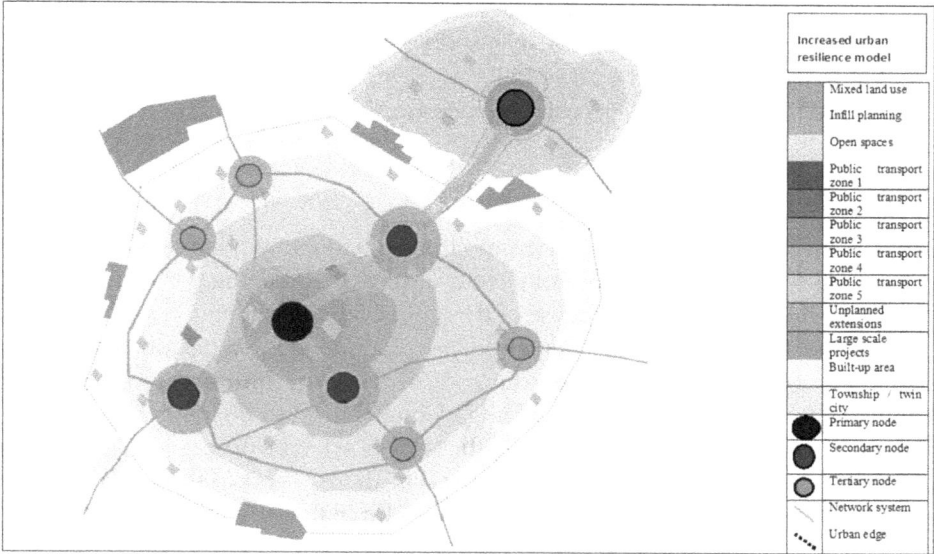

Increased urban resilience model
Mixed land use
Infill planning
Open spaces
Public transport zone 1
Public transport zone 2
Public transport zone 3
Public transport zone 4
Public transport zone 5
Unplanned extensions
Large scale projects
Built-up area
Township / twin city
Primary node
Secondary node
Tertiary node
Network system
Urban edge

Figure 13.4 Integrated land use policy as a tool for increasing urban resilience.

produce a more efficient, equitable, sustainable and resilient growth trajectory, capable of withstanding rapid growth. The urban edge will make the growth trajectory more resilient and efficient by combating urban sprawl and its associated detrimental impacts and further fragmentation through limiting the growth within the urban edge.

Land use management as a regulatory tool strongly influences the urban resilience of a city. How can Emalahleni become a 'safe to fail' diversified city, unlike some other ghost towns worldwide? One solution might be to mitigate the identified stressors (see Figure 13.3) within Emalahleni by the three action sets proposed: planning, designing and managing. This implies that during the planning phase of new development and infrastructure, all role-players should participate and that there should be an unremitting focus on the flexibility of the urban structure to allow for unforeseen shocks and slow-burn processes as currently being experienced in Emalahleni. Another possible solution is to ascertain a focus of adaptability (which is one of the cornerstones of resilience) in the placing and integration of land use types, for example by mixed land use development. Even though South Africa has sound principles supported by policies regarding land use and how to improve resilience and sustainability, Emalahleni has not always been successful in implementing them. We found there is a gap between the different levels of planning and policies (IDP and SDF, 2015) for Emalahleni, which leads to inefficiency and poor implementation. And another possible solution is to address the management component to bring all role-players to account, especially the Emalahleni municipality and the mining companies. Timely, proactive and responsive policymaking and implementation of policy, and the acceptance of inevitable change, could bring about the just transition Emalahleni urgently needs.

Conclusion

Emalahleni's coal has shaped the city and the region in an unplanned fashion. It is responsible for the very existence of the city and for maintaining the economy. But it could in the long run be the cause of the city's eventual stagnation and decline.

In its 2015 SDF, the municipality has planned for expansion and socio-economic development in the medium term. It is the interpretation that has scope for improvement. The structuring elements need to be integrated and the principles for increased resilience and efficiency need to be observed. The following policy approaches should be considered in the revision of the SDF to allow for novel approaches for a just transition of Emalahleni in the medium term based on the ever-changing economic and social environment. The existing SDF (Emalahleni Local Municipality, 2015) does not plan for a potential downscaling from the mines and only focuses on being responsive to a growing population and the growing need for services, housing and amenities.

- An urban edge policy for Emalahleni should be developed, stringently applied and proactively managed around the *existing* built-up area, focusing on combining densification, mixed use, integration and infill developments, rather than just pushing the edge outwards and encouraging further sprawl.
- Densification policies and incentives *within* the edge of Emalahleni would add significantly to a city focused on smart growth and urban resilience. Incentives must be used to help attract and retain businesses and encourage developers to focus on the identified areas for infill and densification.
- A redevelopment policy is needed that will focus on specific zones for brownfield redevelopment and support incentives, especially within the CBD and industrial areas of Emalahleni where decay is already visible. This will support the principles of densification and integration aimed at reducing urban sprawl. Brownfield redevelopment could further help to establish mixed use areas with the associated advantages of 'walkability', integrate public transport and renovate desirable locations that have fallen into disrepair.
- Activity corridors should be developed at local, urban and regional level to encourage the adherence to policy tools and structuring elements. The activities around these corridors should be focused on trade agglomeration, enhancing walkability and integrating previously segregated areas. The focus on productive land use and economic activities in areas where transport infrastructure, rail and road, is already present or being planned is key to the success of this proposal.

- Consideration should be given to converting undermined areas into open space or green networks. This will be a more inclusive approach to green spaces as part of a more extensive system and improve the quality of the environment.

There is potential for development of undermined areas for residential development using feasibility studies, as has been done in the City of Ekurhuleni. These policy responses, if applied effectively, will make Emalahleni 'safe to fail' and enable a just transition, whether the future brings growth or decline. Policy responses and all role-players in the municipality should focus on being proactive in the face of inevitable change. Through embracing the transition, and managing uncertainty, a new dynamic resilience could be on the cards for Emalahleni.

References

Adger, W. N. 2000. Social and ecological resilience: Are they related? *Progress in Human Geography*, 24, 347–64.

Ahern, J. 2011. From fail-safe to safe-to-fail: Sustainability and resilience in the new urban world. *Landscape and Urban Planning*, 100(4), 341–3.

Behrens, R. and Watson, V. 1996. *Making Urban Places*. Cape Town: Creda Press.

Brown, A., Dayal, A. and Rumbaitis Del Rio, C. 2012. From practice to theory: Emerging lessons from Asia for building urban climate change resilience. *Environment and Urbanization*, 24(2), 531–56.

Brugman, J. 2012. Financing the resilient city. *Environment and Urbanization*, 24(1), 215–32.

Bryceson, D. and Potts, D. (eds) 2006. *African Urban Economies: Viability, Vitality or Vitiation*. London: Palgrave Macmillan.

Chapin Jr., F. S. and Kaiser, E. J. 1979. *Urban Land Use Planning*. Urbana: University of Illinois Press.

Chelleri, L., Waters, J. J., Olazabal, M. and Minucci, G. 2015. Resilience trade-offs: Addressing multiple scales and temporal aspects of urban resilience. *Environment and Urbanization*, 27(1), 181–9.

CoGHSTA (Department of Cooperative Governance, Human Settlements and Traditional Affairs). 2012. Northern Cape Provincial Spatial Development Framework (PSDF). Kimberley: Office of the Premier of the Northern Cape.

CSIR (Council for Scientific and Industrial Research). 2000. *Guidelines for Human Settlement and Design*. Pretoria: Capture Press.

Desouza, K. C. and Flanery, T. H. 2013. Designing, planning, and managing resilient cities: A conceptual framework. *Cities*, 35, 89–99.

Drewes, J. E. and Van Aswegen, M. 2011. Determining the vitality of urban centres. In C. A. Brebbia (ed.), *The Sustainable World*. Southampton: WIT Press.

Elmqvist, T. 2014. Urban resilience thinking. *Solutions*, 5(5), 26–30.

Emalahleni Local Municipality. 2015. Spatial Development Framework. Emalahleni Local Municipality.

Godschalk, D. R. 2003. Urban hazard mitigation: Creating resilient cities. *Natural Hazards Review*, 4(3), 136–43.

Hall, A. D. and Fagen, R. E. 1956. Definition of system. *General Systems*, 1, 18–28.

Hill, E. W., Wial, H. and Wolman, H. 2008. Exploring regional resilience. Working Paper 2008-04. Berkeley: University of California.

ICLEI (Local Governments for Sustainability). 2012. Integrated land use planning for resilient urban communities. Proceedings of the Resilient Cities 2012 Congress, 12–15 May, Bonn, Germany. https://www.alnap.org/help-library/resilient-cities-2012-congress-report (last accessed 12 May 2021).

Kaplan, H. B. 1999. Toward an understanding of resilience: A critical review of definitions and models. In M. D. Glantz and J. L. Johnson (eds), *Resilience and Development: Positive Life Adaptations*. New York: Kluwer Academic, pp. 17–83.

Lhomme, S., Serre, D., Diab, Y. and Laganier, R. 2013. Urban technical networks resilience assessment. In D. Serre, B. Barroca and R. Laganier (eds), *Resilience and Urban Risk Management*. London: CRC Press, 109–17.

Lynch, K. and Hack, G. 1984. *Site Planning*, 3rd edn. Cambridge, MA: MIT Press.

Matebesi, S. 2017. Civil Strife Against Local Governance: Dynamics of Community Protests in Contemporary South Africa. Berlin: Barbara Budrich Publishers.

Meerow, S., Newell, J. P. and Stults, M. 2016. Defining urban resilience: A review. *Landscape and Urban Planning*, 147, 38–49.

Paton, D., Mamula-Seadon, L. and Selway, K. 2013. Community resilience in Christchurch: Adaptive responses and capacities during earthquake recovery. GNS *Science Report*, 37, 28–39.

Raco, M. and Street, E. 2012. Resilience planning, economic change and the politics of post-recession development in London and Hong Kong. *Urban Studies*, 49, 1065–87.

SACN (South African Cities Network). 2016. *State of South African Cities Report*. Johannesburg. SACN.

Saunders, W. and Becker, J. S. 2015. A discussion of resilience and sustainability: Land use planning recovery from the Canterbury earthquake sequence, New Zealand. *International Journal of Disaster Risk Reduction*, 14, 73–81.

Turok, I. 2014. The resilience of South African cities a decade after local democracy. *Environment and Planning*, 46, 749–69.

UN (United Nations). 2015. *Transforming our World: The 2030 Agenda for Sustainable Development*. https://sustainabledevelopment.un.org/post2015/transformingourworld (last accessed 29 April 2021).

UN (United Nations). 2016. The new urban agenda. United Nations Conference on Housing and Sustainable Urban Development (Habitat III), Quito, Ecuador, 20 October 2016. http://habitat3.org/the-new-urban-agenda/ (last accessed 29 April 2021).

Vale, L. 2014. The politics of resilient cities: Whose resilience and whose city? *Building Research and Information*, 42(2), 37–41.

Vale, L. and Campanella, T. 2005. *The Resilient City: How Modern Cities Recover from Disaster*. New York: Oxford University Press.

Van Rijswick, M. and Salet, W. G. 2012. Enabling the contextualization of legal rules in responsive strategies to climate change. *Ecology and Society*, 17(2), 18.

Note

1. An SDF is a document to guide the distribution of current and desirable land uses within a municipality in order to give effect to the vision, goals and objectives of the municipal integrated development plan (IDP), updated every five years. The SDF aims to promote sustainable functional and integrated human settlements, maximise resource efficiency and enhance the regional identity and unique character of a place.

CHAPTER 14

Planning in the Dark

Verna Nel and Mark Oranje

The planning conundrum

The survey on which this book is based revealed a large assortment of problems suffered by a mining town facing decline. Observing all the conflicting plans that are being put forward to solve Emalahleni's problems, we were reminded of this remark, attributed to H. L. Mencken: 'There is always a well-known solution to every human problem – neat, plausible, and wrong.'

Municipalities in South Africa are constitutionally mandated to undertake spatial governance and drive the economic development of their jurisdictions. This necessitates meticulous data-gathering and sense-making; well-informed planning to direct, regulate and facilitate spatial and economic development; targeted infrastructure investment, maintenance and upgrading; and wise land use management to ensure compliance with the municipality's plans. This is a big responsibility, fraught with divisive political demands, wide-ranging legal requirements, and contested claims to resources and services. Scott Campbell (1996) identifies three conflicts that arise when a city tries to plan for sustainable development: the 'property conflict', between economic growth and social justice; the 'development conflict', between achieving equity and protecting the environment; and the 'resource conflict', between protecting resources and exploiting them. These conflicts lead to the kind of intractable problem that Rittell and Webber (1973) labelled 'wicked'.

Wicked problems occur in societies where there are multiple perspectives and values, leading to disagreement about the nature and causes of problems, and hence about solutions. Besides the diversity of opinions, the uncertainties inherent to complex systems make it difficult to unravel problems. Friend and Hickling (2005) say the leading sources of uncertainty are shifting circumstances, differences in acceptable values and the effects of related decisions. Wicked problems tend to be 'slippery': they change with every attempt to deal with them, and shape-shift into new and often even more daunting problems (Camillus, 2008). A wicked problem can become even more wicked in a town facing potential decline, and in South Africa could threaten the chances of a just transition.

Uncertainty is particularly prevalent in a mining community where the various stakeholders have very different ideas about the spatial and economic development of the region. Take the three main groups of stakeholders discussed in this chapter: the community, the mines, and the municipality. The community members hope to make a decent living working on the mines or in mine-related employment and to enjoy efficient household services. The mines are driven largely by the need to ensure profits for shareholders. The municipality has to manage infrastructure and services cost-effectively and encourage development while planning for a post-mining future (Marais and De Lange, 2021). The aims of these three groups differ in their focus and time span and in the extent of their social, economic and ecological concern. Each group's activities affect the other groups and have ripple effects. For example, civil unrest erupting at a mine after a labour dispute can lead to the destruction of municipal buildings and infrastructure and a breakdown of service delivery for the municipality and loss of production and profits for the mines. Civil unrest can fuel the looting of shops, public violence, xenophobic attacks, injury and loss of life. Less dramatically, the disruption brings loss of incomes and loss of remittances to workers' families in remote rural areas and neighbouring countries.

The Municipal Systems Act (RSA, 2000) mandates municipalities to plan their town's socio-economic development, basic service provision, spatial development, transformation goals, budget and so on in an integrated development plan (IDP). Part of the IDP is a spatial development framework (SDF) that identifies what development should take place, where it should occur and how it should be phased. However, as mines seldom share their plans outside the organisation, or even beyond the head office (typically located in a world city far away from the mining region), municipalities in mining towns do not have the information they require to undertake their mandates effectively. Decisions taken in a remote head office are often the result of global political developments, economic trends, technological innovations and shareholder demands, and seldom entail any engagement with the municipalities in the mining areas. Mines have their own problems to deal with. The demand for a commodity can be affected by the uncertainty of international demand, which causes price fluctuations, or by concerns about the commodity's effect on health or the environment, coal being a particular cause of concern (Chamber of Mines, 2018). Planning for a city dependent on mining cannot ignore the commodity rollercoaster (Denoon-Stevens, Nel and Mphambukeli, 2017). But municipal councillors or officials may learn of a proposed expansion or reduction in production only when it appears in the media, which undermines their ability to plan for such events and the way they will affect the demand for housing, services and municipal revenue.

In South Africa, as in many other African countries, communities (and politicians) harbour high expectations of the employment that could be generated by mining, and the associated provision of infrastructure by mining companies, such as roads and water. But over and above the shareholders' expectations of dividends, the mining companies have to pay the government taxes and royalties, meet employment and ownership targets, create and implement social and labour plans (SLPs), and contribute to the social, spatial and economic development of the area where they operate and the labour-sending areas. In addition, the mining industry is very competitive, yet amenable to collusion, and fraught with uncertainties and risks. Production cuts or transgressions can have devastating consequences for a mining company and its managers (Oranje, 2013). These factors further discourage mining companies from sharing information with the municipality.

In this chapter we explore the relationship between the Emalahleni Local Municipality and the mines in the area. Collaborating with transnational corporations is difficult and requires flexibility (Matebesi, 2020). In contrast with the previous chapter's authors, we maintain that planning should be less rigid, accounting for uncertainty and the severe nature of problems, and that it should deal with community concerns (Matebesi, 2017). We look particularly at the way communication between them affects municipal planning and hence service delivery. We also discuss the extent to which municipal planning considers the long-term future of coal mining. Our findings are based on interviews with municipal officials, a presentation by the municipality's executive mayor at a business breakfast, interviews with mining companies' liaison officers and interviews with community members conducted between August 2017 and March 2018. Many problems in the municipality (see for example Campbell, Nel and Mphambukeli, 2017) are aggravated by poor communication between the role-players. This not only makes it difficult to plan for and implement socio-economic development; it turns this complex city's difficulties into wicked problems. And this is at a time when the city is experiencing a mining boom, so it is hard to imagine what it will be like when the boom is over.

Planning in the midst of wicked problems and social dilemmas

As communities have become more connected through social media and globalisation, the complexity of their relationship with each other and their environment has increased, bringing both benefits and problems. Some problems are easy to solve, but others, such as global warming, environmental degradation, urban degeneration and poverty, are more stubborn or 'wicked', with multiple causes and no simple answers. Unlike complicated problems that may be difficult to solve but do have a solution, there is seldom a single solution to a wicked problem and all that can be hoped for is some improvement (Rittell and Webber, 1973).

A solution to a problem can sometimes worsen the situation, causing further problems. For example, as a consequence of suburbs being built to de-densify the crowded cities of the industrial revolution we now have the problem of urban sprawl. Consequently, the search for solutions never stops, nor do the waves of long-term consequences of previous attempts that complicate future decision-making. As every wicked problem is unique, due to interdependencies across communities, space and time, no exact precedents can be found to guide decision-makers. Finally, power, group interests and politics shape the identification, delineation and description of wicked problems.

Although wicked problems lack simple solutions, some recommendations have been made for dealing with them, the most common being communication with stakeholders to obtain a range of insights, local knowledge and values. Others are collaborative planning (Innes and Booher, 2016), deliberative democracy and citizens' juries (Lundström et al., 2016), and constructive conflict and agonistic theory (Mouat, Legacy and March, 2013). A focus on communication, discussion and debate does not, however, preclude the use of other tools or heuristics (Norton, 2012; Stahl and Cimorelli, 2013; Huang and London, 2016).

Stakeholder participation is considered important. Hartmann (2012) and Ney and Verweij (2015) suggest using cultural theory to create 'clumsy solutions' to understand stakeholders' attitudes and create broadly acceptable plans. Cultural theory identifies four categories of 'rationality', according to the level of group cohesion and freedom to make decisions: egalitarian, individualistic, hierarchical and fatalist. *Egalitarians* seek environmental justice and collaborative planning, *individualists* seek competition and the opportunity to experiment, *hierarchists* emphasise expert knowledge and rules, and *fatalists* assume that one cannot influence events. Combining these rationalities in decision-making is preferable to adopting a single rationality. Alford and Head (2017) suggest that competitive strategies generate new ideas but may cause conflict. A sound strategy, useful in emergencies, may not produce the insights needed to deal with wicked problems. An 'expert' strategy can identify the questions that should be asked but may not include the range and breadth of knowledge needed.

Frame (2008) and Kwakkel, Walker and Haasnoot (2016) suggest the use of scenario planning, and Friend and Hickling (2005) include it in their strategic choice approach for managing complexity and uncertainty. Camillus (2008) recommends a 'feed-forward' orientation, where various futures are envisaged. Norton (2012) recommends combining critical systems theory with a general systems approach to identify the most appropriate scale for interventions. As these proposals all include an iterative approach to understanding and managing a situation, Zellner and Campbell (2015) advocate the use of complex systems tools including GIS (geographical information systems) based modelling – a practical recommendation amidst the welter of theories on planning for a large multicultural city today.

Expectations and responses

Many and varying demands are made on municipalities and the mines by communities, including small enterprises and emerging contractors. These communities tend not to be cohesive but comprise many groups splintered by age, race, ethnicity, class, level of formal education, income and citizenship. Different groups have different ideas and demands, and also a vastly different array of resources, power, and ability to influence those in power. In this section we explore the perceptions and expectations of Emalahleni's community, municipality and mining companies. First, we examine the municipal planning processes from a variety of stakeholders' perspectives. We then consider the demands made on the municipality by the community and the mines, and thereafter we look at what the municipality and the community expect the mines to contribute. Finally, we consider the mining companies' perspective and what they can contribute through their social responsibility programmes and SLPs.

Municipal planning processes

The IDP is the municipality's strategic instrument for building and maintaining infrastructure, delivering services, and communicating with the community and the mining companies. The executive mayor and senior officials in the municipality, however, said in interview that they believed the mines should be more involved in municipal planning. They said they had been trying to persuade the mining companies to align their corporate social responsibility plans with the IDP projects. They hoped their negotiations would encourage the biggest mining companies to build urgently needed infrastructure (sewers, roads and water infrastructure) rather than community halls, as the mines had been doing. One official suggested that the IDP and mining legislation should be linked in order to force mining companies to make a 'more impactful and better link to the IDP'.

Our respondents from the mining companies acknowledged the IDP and the request to align their SLPs with it. One said that high-level discussions about their plans for the following year are held annually with the municipality. However, most mines appear to view municipal planning as (as expressed by one mining company) 'plans that live only on paper'.

It also appears that the SDF does not inform new settlement development, expansion or densification, along with the implication for bulk services as intended. One municipal planner complained that it is ignored by some municipal departments, councillors, other agencies and the Department of Mineral Resources when approving prospecting rights.

Respondents' opinions varied as regards the future of coal mining in Emalahleni. Estimates of the remaining coal reserves varied from 10 years to 20–30 years. Although the senior planners agreed that economic diversification was essential for the 'post-coal scenario', no information about such plans was forthcoming, in the interviews or the SDF. Their focus was clearly on the immediate problems of a municipality in deep distress.

The SDF does not take a long-range view of the post-coal future, other than noting the influence of mine closure on specific, isolated settlements. For example, the SDF states that 'The long-term sustainability of resource-specific settlements, especially related to mining activity and power stations, is questionable, seeing that the mines and power stations have finite lifespans. Such isolated settlements are expensive to service and maintain, placing a high financial burden on the Municipality' (Emalahleni Local Municipality, 2015). Although the SDF quotes from the National Development Plan 2030, it does not mention the declining role of coal in the national energy mix and its possible subsequent replacement with renewable energy (NPC, 2012).

Expectations of the municipality: Infrastructure and housing

Emalahleni residents expect their municipality to provide potable water, sanitation, electricity and roads. However, it is failing to do so because infrastructure is ageing and obsolete and the population is growing rapidly. Plagued by this problem for several years (Campbell, Nel and Mphambukeli, 2016), the municipality has placed a moratorium on the approval of development applications. However, it acknowledges that it does not have the resources to upgrade the bulk or local distribution infrastructure, which could, according to one respondent, cost 'more than a hundred million rand'. This amount would be hard to find, given that the municipality owes Eskom (the state electricity utility) something in the order of R1.6 billion (Goldswain, 2018).

Our respondents had many complaints about services. Poor water quality obliges them to purchase bottled water. Boreholes are not viable, as the groundwater is contaminated. They complained of frequent interruptions of electricity and water and that the roads are in a poor condition, which they blame on the trucks serving the mines. They said the bad roads affect police response times, as well as those of other emergency services.

Improving the infrastructure and services in the municipal area is the highest priority of the IDP, but the municipality's dire financial situation is holding this back. Revenue collection is poor and credit control has been difficult. The municipality has found it impossible to evict defaulters. Its initiatives to recoup the cost of services have met with resistance and, at times, violent protests. There has been opposition to the installation of 'smart meters' and many residents have resorted to using illegal connections. Infrastructure is vandalised and cables and transformers are stolen (personal communication, Ms L. Ntshalintshali, Executive Mayor, 30 November 2017).

Expectations of the mining companies: Jobs and contracts

The mines in Emalahleni formerly owned and maintained small villages around their mines. The previously mine-owned houses have since either been sold to their residents or demolished as the mines extended their operations. The mines now provide living-out allowances instead, and have ceded responsibility for the provision of infrastructure to municipalities. But according to municipal officials, the memory of being 'looked after' by the mines has led residents to expect this should continue.

The municipality criticised the mining companies' living-out allowances, which they believe encourage the proliferation of informal settlements. When the mines do contribute to housing, they do it through the provincial government, not the municipality. One respondent suggested that rental housing, with the houses rented directly from a housing agency, would alleviate the pressure.

Nonetheless, municipal officials acknowledged that the mines have contributed to infrastructure and housing. South 32 has contributed to the construction of 250 houses through a land availability agreement, while Anglo American has assisted with the resettlement of 6,000 families in conjunction with the Department of Human Settlements. Glencore has constructed a bulk water supply system to treat effluent from mining operations at an estimated cost of R55 million, which also services several communities to the south of the town of Emalahleni (Nkuna, 2016). Water has also been supplied by Anglo American (at a cost) to the municipality, yet one municipal official complained that 'Anglo should provide the water that they are releasing for free to the municipality'.

Employment of local labour is one of the community's main demands. Closely associated with demands for direct employment are calls for the mines to support local businesses and to contract local companies to supply goods and services. A group called Pret SA (Practical Radical Economic Transformation South Africa) is demanding more jobs, the employment of local labour only, and greater community ownership of the mines. Their strategy is first to negotiate with the mines and then, if that fails, to shut down the mines. They are reputed to have instigated many of the recent protest actions in the area. Community protests are frequent and occasionally violent, aimed at the municipality, the government in general, and the mines. The main grievances are unemployment and poor provision of services.

We heard that blasting damages houses, even though the mines may be the legally required distance from the houses. A municipal official commented on complaints that the reopening of closed mines, made possible by improved technology, affects residential development and undermining makes land unstable. Illegal mines that operate for a few months contribute to residents' problems. Nonetheless, community members were aware of the mines' role in building and maintaining infrastructure, as in the case of a major water valve which had been repaired by one of the mines.

The mining companies' perspective

The mining companies' community liaison officials were well aware of the demands and expectations of the community and municipality. They have been willing to assist where it relates to their operations, for example by supplying purified water (Anglo and Glencore), upgrading roads (Sasol), and implementing their SLPs. They contribute to social infrastructure, such as clinics, social halls and recreation centres, but they do not maintain it once they have handed it over to the beneficiary. Respondents from the community and municipality viewed this approach as 'unsustainable'.

Employment is a thorny issue. With the global economic crisis, many mines had to downscale their operations and were unable to employ additional people. Furthermore, they require specialised skills that are not available locally. This mismatch between the skills needed and the absence of those skills in Emalahleni is at the root of many protests.

In response, mining companies make donations to registered non-profit organisations and support small business development through the SLPs. Training features strongly in all the mining companies' social responsibility programmes. Courses offered include driving (to obtain a driver's licence), welding, plumbing, plastering and bricklaying. The mines also support the Colliery Training College (for mine employees) and courses provided by the Tshwane University of Technology and the University of Johannesburg.

Several of the mining companies' social responsibility officials were concerned about the low skills and high poverty levels in the municipality (M3). In response to this problem and the effect it has on households, they suggested that SLPs should focus more on youth education, homeownership instruction and early childhood development. But the potential benefit of their SLPs was being held back by the lack of coordination between the mines in implementing them.

Community responses

The municipality is legally required to consult the community in its planning and operational activities (RSA, 1998, 2000). The frequent protests have forced the mining companies to engage with the community, possibly more often than they would otherwise have done. The companies have established several engagement forums, some of them very specific to an area and sector, such as the local farming community, or to a particular group, such as the youth or small businesses. The mines have also created 'zones of influence' with a radius of approximately 6 km around each mine and take responsibility for communicating with residents in the zone. Where two mines are close to each other, they have drawn boundaries to allocate their separate responsibilities. Mining companies also jointly engage with the youth or local businesses, using these platforms to inform the community about the SLPs and job and contract opportunities.

The community make some use of these platforms and the ward committee system, or approach the mines directly if they want a donation for a project. However, they frequently protest at the mines – moving from one mine to another and affecting production. The mines' community liaison officers lamented the recurrent protests. They also questioned the legitimacy of the protest leaders, claiming that the protests are caused mainly by criminals and drug addicts for their own nefarious purposes.

As part of their SLPs, the mining companies organise events on important days such as Youth Day or Nelson Mandela Day. However, communication between the mines, other than for community liaison matters, is limited. Collaboration between mines is viewed as risky, particularly where large projects are concerned (Van der Watt and Marais, 2021).

There are several formal engagement routes between the mining companies and the municipality. The respondents from the mines said they communicate directly with the municipality regarding their SLP projects through local economic development (LED) forums and IDP processes. Furthermore, there is a 'Future Forum' hosted by the municipality that seeks to ensure high-level engagement with the municipality and other stakeholders. But it would appear that the relationships are superficial. The respondents from the mines felt that there is still a lack of communication and trust.

Municipal respondents expressed mixed views about the quality of the relationship with the mining companies. Even though the mines often bypass the municipality and go straight to the community when implementing projects, there was a consensus that the IDP and LED forums were generally well attended by the mines. No mention was made of the 'Future Forum'. The focus was on aligning SLPs with the IDP and encouraging the mines to contribute more to the upgrading of infrastructure. No mention was made of collaborative spatial planning between the mines and the municipality.

The municipality holds community meetings and provides feedback on IDP projects and projects undertaken by government departments and mining companies. These are well attended. Ward committee meetings also provide community representatives with information about small contracts, or possible employment opportunities. However, the municipality's SDF makes no mention of community participation in compiling the SDF (Emalahleni Local Municipality, 2015).

Ships in the night

We found that communication does occur in the Emalahleni Local Municipality, but not much collaborative planning. Dialogue may occur during ward committees and meetings between mining companies and the senior management of the municipality. But much of the transfer of information appears to be unidirectional and takes one of three forms: informing, requesting and demanding (see Figure 14.1). The absence of genuine collaboration could reduce the likelihood of a just transition (Van der Watt and Marais, 2021). Right now, the three stakeholder groups we discussed in this chapter – the community, the municipality and the mines – seem very much at sea.

South African policy and legislation have entrenched participatory planning. In Emalahleni, it appears that the municipality attempts this, but primarily uses meetings to *inform* the community of its plans. Although community needs,

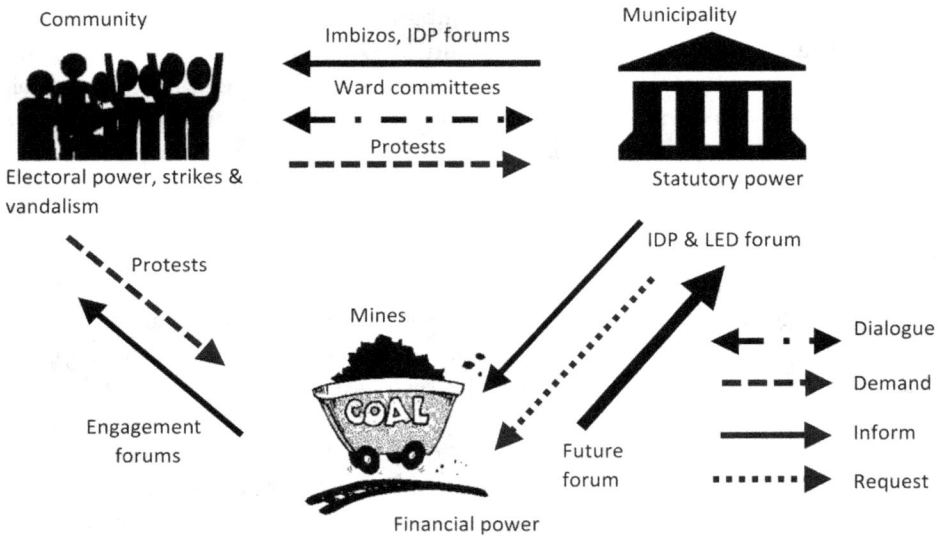

Figure 14.1 Communication between community, municipality and mines.

requests or comments may be noted at these meetings, they do not necessarily inform or alter municipal policy or programmes. Thus community participation seems to be little more than a 'talk shop' or a ritual that the municipality must undertake to *legitimise its planning* (Arnstein, 1969; Williams, 2006; Mautjana and Makombe, 2014). Although communities do approach the municipality or the mines with their problems and requests, they often voice their complaints through protests (Bond and Mottiar, 2013).

The relationship between the mines and municipality is polite and superficial. The mines are informed of the municipality's priorities and requested to align their SLPs with the IDP, and to contribute to the construction or repair of municipal infrastructure. The response by the mining companies is to focus on their core business (making a profit), undertake the corporate social responsibility required of them, and assist with infrastructure construction or maintenance in emergencies, or when it benefits them.

All in all, these are practices far removed from the communicative planning methods suggested to deal with wicked problems (Innes and Booher, 2016) and there is little to hope for in terms of change. While the mining companies steam ahead with their agendas and try to stay in operation for as long as a profit can be made, communities struggle to stay afloat and resort to protests when conditions become unbearable – and the municipality flounders. It is overwhelmed by the many interwoven wicked problems it faces and the many crises, all of which 'urgently need all available resources right now', leaving barely any energy for thinking about, deliberating or jointly planning a better future for all. With limited information available about mining companies' plans, the municipality tied up in attending to its multifarious problems, the communities caught up in their daily struggle for survival, and no sign of a joint, structured and constructive discussion about the future, including a post-coal future, Emalahleni is reduced to planning in the dark, looking ahead to the next morning and no further. What does this all mean for a just transition? It challenges the assumption that a just transition is simple and that effective planning will ensure such a transition. Mine closure might reinforce many of the social problems and the existing social stratification. Overall, it requires us to think about the limitations in planning a just transition.

References

Alford, J. and Head, B. W. 2017. Wicked and less wicked problems: A typology and a contingency framework. *Policy and Society*, 36(3), 397–413.

Arnstein, S. 1969. A ladder of public participation. *American Institute of Planners Journal*, 35(4), 216–24.

Bond, P. and Mottiar, S. 2013. Movements, protests and a massacre in South Africa. *Journal of Contemporary African Studies*, 31(2), 283–302.

Camillus, J. C. 2008. Strategy as a wicked problem. *Harvard Business Review*, 86(5), 98.

Campbell, M., Nel, V. and Mphambukeli, T. 2016. Emalahleni: Dirty but keeping South Africa's lights on. In *Beyond the Great and Mighty: Reflections on Secondary Cities in South Africa*. London: Routledge, 63–82.

Campbell, M., Nel, V. and Mphambukeli, T. 2017. A thriving coal mining city in crisis? The governance and spatial planning challenges at Witbank, South Africa. *Land Use Policy*, 62, 223–31.

Campbell, S. 1996. Green cities, growing cities, just cities? Urban planning and the contradictions of sustainable development. *Journal of the American Planning Association*, 62(3), 296–312. doi: 10.1080/01944369608975696.

Chamber of Mines. 2018. National coal strategy for South Africa. Chamber of Mines of South Africa. https://www.miningreview.com/strategising-future-coal-south-africa/ (last accessed 29 April 2021).

Denoon-Stevens, S., Nel, V. and Mphambukeli, T. 2017. Spatial planning for Postmasburg. In P. Burger, L. Marais and D. van Rooyen (eds), *Mining and Community in South Africa*. London: Routledge, 95–114.

Emalahleni Local Municipality. 2015. *Spatial Development Framework*. Emalahleni: Emalahleni Local Municipality.

Frame, B. 2008. 'Wicked', 'messy', and 'clumsy': Long-term frameworks for sustainability. *Environment and Planning C: Government and Policy*, 26(6), 1113–28.

Friend, J. and Hickling, A. 2005. *Planning Under Pressure*. London: Routledge.

Goldswain, Z. 2018. Breaking news: Executive Mayor of Emalahleni resigns. *Witbank News*, 13 March. https://witbanknews.co.za/107026/breaking-news-executive-mayor-emalahleni-resigns/?repeat=w3tc (last accessed 29 April 2021).

Hartmann, T. 2012. Wicked problems and clumsy solutions: Planning as expectation management. *Planning Theory*, 11(3), 242–56.

Huang, G. and London, J. K. 2016. Mapping in and out of 'messes': An adaptive, participatory, and transdisciplinary approach to assessing cumulative environmental justice impacts. *Landscape and Urban Planning*, 154, 57–67.

Innes, J. E. and Booher, D. E. 2016. Collaborative rationality as a strategy for working with wicked problems. *Landscape and Urban Planning*, 154, 8–10.

Kwakkel, J. H., Walker, W. E. and Haasnoot, M.N. 2016. Coping with the wickedness of public policy problems: Approaches for decision making under deep uncertainty. *Journal of Water Resources Planning and Management*, 142(3), 01816001.

Lundström, N., Raisio, H., Vartiainen, P. and Lindell, J. 2016. Wicked games changing the storyline of urban planning. *Landscape and Urban Planning*, 154, 20–28.

Marais, L. and De Lange, A. 2021. Anticipating and planning for mine closure in South Africa. *Futures*, 125, 102669.

Matebesi, S. 2017. Civil Strife Against Local Governance: Dynamics of Community Protests in Contemporary South Africa. Berlin: Barbara Budrich Publishers.

Matebesi, S., 2020. *Social Licensing and Mining in South Africa*. London: Routledge.

Mautjana, M. H. and Makombe, G. 2014. Community participation or malicious compliance? *Africa Insight*, 44(2), 51–67.

Mouat, C., Legacy, C. and March, A. 2013. The problem is the solution: Testing agonistic theory's potential to recast intractable planning disputes. *Urban Policy and Research*, 31(2), 150–66.

Ney, S. and Verweij, M. 2015. Messy institutions for wicked problems: How to generate clumsy solutions? *Environment and Planning C: Government and Policy*, 33(6), 1679–96.

Nkuna, F. 2016. Glencore serving as bulk water service provider. *Witbank News*, 3 November. https://witbanknews.co.za/80952/glencore-serving-as-bulk-water-service-provider/ (last accessed 29 April 2021).

Norton, B. G. 2012. The ways of wickedness: Analyzing messiness with messy tools. *Journal of Agricultural and Environmental Ethics*, 25(4), 447–65.

NPC (National Planning Commission). 2012. *National Development Plan 2030*. Pretoria: The Presidency. https://www.gov.za/sites/default/files/gcis_document/201409/ndp-2030-our-future-make-it-workr.pdf (last accessed 29 April 2021).

Oranje, M. 2013. The extractive industries and 'shared, inclusive and sustainable development' in South Africa. *Spatium International Review*, 29, 1–7.

Rittell, H. W. J. and Webber M. M. 1973. Dilemmas in a general theory of planning. *Policy Sciences*, 4, 155–69.

RSA (Republic of South Africa). 1998. Local Government: Municipal Structures Act, 117 of 1998. Pretoria: Government Printer.

RSA (Republic of South Africa). 2000. Local Government: Municipal Systems Act, 32 of 2000. Pretoria: Government Printer.

Stahl, C. and Cimorelli, A. 2013. A demonstration of the necessity and feasibility of using a clumsy decision analytic approach on wicked environmental problems. *Integrated Environmental Assessment and Management*, 9(1), 17–30.

Van der Watt, P. and Marais, L. 2021. Implementing social and labour plans in South Africa: Reflections on collaborative planning in the mining industry. *Resources Policy*, 71, 101984.

Williams, J. J. 2006. Community participation. *Policy Studies*, 27(3), 197–217.

Zellner, M. and Campbell, S. D. 2015. Planning for deep-rooted problems: What can we learn from aligning complex systems and wicked problems? *Planning Theory and Practice*, 16(4), 457–78.

CHAPTER 15

'The mines must fix the potholes': A Desperate Community

Phia van der Watt and Sethulego Matebesi

Mining and local government

Conversations with Emalahleni community members inevitably start with the terrible state of the streets and the size and prevalence of the potholes. The next topics are the influx of foreigners, the social decline and the escalating crime. In 2017 the crime statistics ranked Emalahleni first in the country for housebreaking. The conversation then moves on to the water and electricity cuts, uncollected garbage, sewage running in the streets – in short: the municipality. This local municipality has been under administration for years, regularly gets audit disclaimers and perennially stands accused of incompetence and corruption. The city is on the brink of bankruptcy.

Opening the local paper, the *Witbank News*, at any time between 2014 and 2018, we found a continuation of this conversation, with headlines like: 'No money to patch potholes', 'Two dead as roads are getting more dangerous', 'We want water', 'Eskom's dark humour: a company that supplies darkness and sometimes surprises with light', 'Big pool of pooh', 'Failed administrator now acting municipal manager', 'No electricity, no water and no sewerage, but billed' or 'Municipality loses R1.6 million due to fraud'. Yet, looking around, we saw ample reason to expect growth and prosperity, because of all the coal mines and power stations. Is it possible that the abundance of mineral resources has not led to economic growth, employment – and a contented community?

One would assume that an abundance of resources would generate wealth and boost economic and social development. However, it appears that resource booms globally are more often associated with poor economic growth, weak political and democratic institutions, high levels of corruption, dysfunctional state behaviour (for example, unsustainable budgetary policies and misallocations of public resources), inequality, conflict and social disruption (McFerson, 2010; John, 2011; Brueckner et al., 2014; Brower, 2016; Frynas, Wood and Hinks, 2017). The potential cure that the extraction industry could offer turns instead into a curse, which most mining communities in South Africa have not escaped (Marais, Van Rooyen et al., 2017). The literature has not yet sufficiently investigated how the curse affects local communities. This is a research gap that needs to be filled, as local governments throughout South Africa, and particularly in its mining towns, become increasingly dysfunctional – and even absent. Simultaneously, the development of the Transnational Corporation has also meant that these corporations take over public services. Simultaneously, the literature has pointed to the problems such an approach creates in mining towns (Matebesi, 2017, 2020). In this case, the communities see these corporations as institutions that will address their public services.

This chapter looks at how mining activities affect the Emalahleni community, through the eyes of a small but representative selection of community members and officials. They describe significant events and changes over the past three decades and reflect on the relationship between the community, the municipality and the mines. An intricate web is formed when an abundance of resources comes into contact with ordinary people's lives, local leaders' responses to changing demands, and industrialists' drive to generate profits for shareholders. Understanding this complexity on a local level can stimulate discourse on how to handle boom and bust cycles. What was rich and did not work will become poor and might still not work. The result is not likely to be a just transition.

The literature

Theory and international perspective

Natural resource industries seldom stimulate broader economic growth. Instead, capital, labour and entrepreneurial activity are drawn away from non-resource sectors (such as manufacturing and agriculture), resulting in single-industry economies. In such economies, revenue from resources is not reinvested into health, education, employment, services and diversification. Political bargaining is reduced and democracy undermined. In a mining town the mining company often takes on state-like power and responsibilities, while the state institutions shirk their responsibilities. In the process, the company becomes more accountable to local needs than the state, resulting in ambivalence and uncertainty about the nature of state power.

In the absence of an effective state, communities start to expect mining companies, rather than the state, to fulfil state-like responsibilities. The companies become a kind of local saviour, providing employment, development, education and infrastructure – which ultimately shapes how people imagine, experience and understand state power. When it comes to expectations for improved quality of life, mining town communities are trapped between the mining industry and the state. Many of these problems associated with mining have received attention in the global literature and South Africa. See for example McFerson (2010), John (2011), Besada and Martin (2013), Brueckner (2014), Brueckner et al. (2014), Roberts (2015), Aytaç, Mousseau and Örsün (2016), Brower (2016), Haslam (2016), Banks (2017), Frynas, Wood and Hinks (2017), Gardiner (2017), Marais, Van Rooyen et al. (2017), Marais, Wlokas et al. (2017), Ruddell (2017), Doro and Kufakurinani (2018), Marais, Cloete et al. (2018) and Marais, McKenzie et al. (2018).

The South African mining milieu experiences many problems like population influx, social ills, struggling local governance and limited economic diversification. On top of this, apartheid's legal disenfranchisement, spatial segregation and systemic exclusion have created a racially based mining industry. Since 1994, the mining landscape has changed, in line with political developments. Freedom of movement and the promotion of homeownership, for example, have escalated the population growth in mining areas, and the privatisation of housing by mining companies has shifted the responsibility for housing to municipalities (Marais, 2018). Ironically, this has resulted in exactly what the government tried to avoid: informal settlements around mining towns (BMF, 2014). With the current economic slump and downscaling of mining activities, communities risk becoming locked into shrinking mining towns (Marais, 2018). Remedies are few since economic diversification is often absent (Marais, Van Rooyen et al., 2017).

Local governments are unable to cope with the increased demands for service delivery and social amenities (Marais, McKenzie et al., 2018). They do not obtain significant revenue to benefit from the mines, because the government taxes mining at a national level and the mines usually do not purchase municipal services, although they share and put pressure on local infrastructure (BMF, 2014; Ledger, 2015). Ledger's research (2015) on the South African mining sector found a higher occurrence of poor audit outcomes in municipalities where mining contributes 30% or more of local GVA (gross value added). She found that mining municipalities are three times more likely to have dysfunctional administrations than non-mining municipalities. Of her sample of 24 mining municipalities, only one obtained a clean audit in the 2013–14 financial year.

Mining legislation requires mining companies to adhere to regulations for socially responsible mining by producing social and labour plans. These plans should facilitate collaborative planning and alignment with local governments' IDPs (integrated development plans). However, there is little evidence of such collaboration (Marais, Wlokas et al., 2017; Van der Watt and Marais, 2021). The regulations have limited impact since there are no consequences for mining companies when they contravene environmental, labour and social laws and norms (BMF, 2014).

The interviewees' thoughts

During November 2017 we conducted 25 semi-structured interviews with individuals and groups from various sectors, organisations and departments. This included leaders from non-profit organisations (NPOs), activist movements and the media. Interviews were also conducted with the community liaison official at a mining company, a local businessman and service provider to the mines, a medical intern at the state hospital, an estate agent, a school principal, a teacher, a community development worker and a ward councillor. We interviewed managerial-level officials from the local municipality, the Department of Social Development (DSD) and the South African Police Service (SAPS). Interviewees reflected on significant features, changes and events that affected life and relationships in Emalahleni. Out of the personal experiences, impressions and feelings they shared, the themes discussed in this section emerged.

The population influx

When asked to describe the community of Emalahleni, all interviewees had a lot to say about the massive population growth and gave their own interpretations of it. The newcomers are from other parts of South Africa (for example, from the former 'homelands' and more recently from surrounding small towns) or from Mozambique, Zimbabwe, Swaziland, Nigeria, Somalia, Pakistan, Bangladesh and China. Interviewees attributed the influx to three factors: more freedom of movement in the new South Africa since 1994, South Africa's hosting of the 2010 Soccer World Cup that drew attention to this economic hub, and the boom in mining activities between 2000 and 2008.

Interviewees pointed out that the mines do not 'invite' the masses to come to Emalahleni and they do not promise them jobs; the mines act as a magnet, drawing people into the area. The power stations are also magnets. There is a perception that the newcomers do not expect to find work at the mines: some migrants do not even go to the mines to search for work when they arrive in Emalahleni. They hope at least to benefit from the buying power of those who do have work at the mines. The opinion was also expressed that those who do not find work will never go back to where they have come from: they will stay in Emalahleni. The interviewees did not expect that the population would decrease again.

Statistics corroborate the interviewees' perception of an overwhelming population increase. Emalahleni and Rustenburg have been rated the fastest growing cities in South Africa. Emalahleni grew by 138% between 1995 and 2015, leaving its municipality hopelessly underprepared to deal with the increase (Steynberg, 2015).

Social realities

A grave picture of the social state of Emalahleni emerged. The community is battling with high levels of alcohol and drug abuse, prostitution, child neglect, illegal abortions and crime. In 2017 Emalahleni ranked highest for some crimes in the province and, as mentioned earlier, highest in the country for housebreaking (Shange and Gous, 2017). Interviewees believed that these social ills destroy the community. They drew a direct link between these 'foreign' problems (the scale of which they claimed were previously unknown in this community) and the influx of 'foreigners'. They believed it was especially the Nigerians, 'who are too naughty', who were responsible for the drug problem, the use of increasingly young children to trade drugs, and human trafficking. Interviewees were also concerned about the open practice of prostitution in the CBD. Some were disturbed that the sex workers, who wait along the roads for the truck drivers, have started to 'build tent-rooms', blankets strung between the bushes. In addition, the workers organised themselves into a 'forum' and these interviewees were especially irked by the name thereof: the Pleasure Executives Forum.

The escalating social problems have caused non-profit organisations (NPOs) to mushroom. According to a DSD manager, there are currently over 4,000 registered NPOs in Emalahleni. An interviewee claimed that though some of them may genuinely want to alleviate the social problems, others register as NPOs just to elicit funding for themselves. An interviewee, involved with community work, feared that 'starting an NPO is an easy way to access funding through government stipends and donations from the mines'. He perceived many of these to be fraudsters.

An economy based on mining

Emalahleni's economy depends on its coal mines and power stations. Most developments and businesses rely directly on mining or the buying power it creates. Interviewees noted the lack of substantial alternative industries. Significant industries, not related to coal-mining, had run into problems: Highveld Steel closed in 2016 and Ferrometals downscaled because of complaints about pollution. For the interviewees, the threat of downscaling or closure of mines brought back vivid memories of the suffering when Highveld Steel closed.

Employment thus remains directly linked to mining, through either direct employment or contract work. Interviewees believed that 'foreigners' found it easier to get jobs than locals. Skilled workers are mostly accessed from outside Emalahleni, through contracts with national and international companies (interviewees mentioned Italy and China), while low-skilled jobs go to people from Swaziland, Zimbabwe and Mozambique. Interviewees claimed that the foreigners did not have the minimum qualification of matriculation but got the jobs because they were more willing than the locals to accept lower wages. One interviewee claimed that the foreigners 'take things for granted – everything is fine for them – they do not complain when prices go up' and that 'we, the community of Emalahleni, are paying for the services and they are not'.

Contract workers mostly do not live with their families or spend their income in Emalahleni. Interviewees believed that skilled workers from Europe and Asia are earning huge salaries and so can afford to buy brand-name goods at the malls. They further believed that these highly paid workers find it easy to attract young women and an official was specifically concerned about the long-term social effect of casual relationships. The impact of contract work can also be seen in the housing market. The outside companies, doing contract work for the mines, pay high rentals for their workers' houses. One interviewee involved in the housing market said she alone rents out houses worth in total R200,000 a month to various companies. Another interviewee was concerned that the housing market is becoming skewed, apparently because 'rich people from outside' are buying property at inflated prices, which they rent out privately to the companies for up to R40,000 per month per house.

An official from the DSD expressed concern that where 'the richest of the rich and the poorest of the poor' live in such proximity, we can expect high levels of social ills and crime. An index of the average income of taxpayers in South African cities, based on data compiled from the 2011 census, confirms the high levels of inequality: Emalahleni ranked sixth (Grant, 2015). An interviewee stressed the level of despair that leads people to steal money to pay for 'bogus doctors' who promise luck and business success. The impression we received from interviewees was that the community is facing dire economic uncertainty.

A changing landscape

The influx of so many people has changed the shape of Emalahleni. Formal and informal settlements are sprawling in all directions. Interviewees emphasised that the problem is bigger and more complicated than can be seen at a casual glance. They mentioned families living in other people's backyards, shacks wherever a structure can be erected, houses built of plastic, and even houses on top of the Coronation mine that has been burning for decades. One interviewee said: 'I can't remember a year when you don't have a child who falls into an ash-hole, animals that get burned, and so on.'

The quest for housing involves the scramble for physical space, as well as for a position on the waiting lists for government houses. We heard many stories about nepotism and corruption by government officials. Interviewees were, for example, suspicious about how Nigerians get RDP (government subsidised) houses in Klarinet, a formal housing settlement towards the north-west of Emalahleni. We also heard about the opportunism of community members. One such story was about a few old women from the MNS informal settlement (adjacent to Klarinet), who received RDP houses in Klarinet. When they realised they had to pay rates and taxes, they simply moved back to their shelters in MNS, rented out their houses in Klarinet – and got their names back on the waiting lists. Housing appears to be the main reason for conflict and violent protests in Emalahleni. Interviewees felt that the newcomers 'take our space here'.

Another complaint was that mining activities in Emalahleni are constantly moving closer to human settlements. Interviewees said that the blasting damages their houses and the perennial dust causes inconvenience and illness (asthma, sinusitis, nose bleeds and eye problems). They were also quick to point out that the mines provide services only for their employees – while the whole community suffers from their activities.

Infrastructure and services

The influx of people has begun to put pressure on infrastructure and services in Emalahleni. An interviewee pointed out that the municipality budgets for people 'who are supposed to be here' and then has to cater for those not included in the budget. This puts a strain on the services. Interviewees mentioned problems in the public health services (patients lying on the floor in the state hospital), the education system (there are not enough schools), and social services such as youth drug rehabilitation. Interviewees from the SAPS raised the difficulty the police experience in responding to emergencies and fighting crime in a city with insufficient access roads, rising traffic volumes, the poor condition of the streets and the absence of police stations in newly established areas.

The mines and power stations aggravate the problem as they transport the region's wealth in their heavy vehicles – while damaging the roads that everybody else has to use. An interviewee poignantly said: 'Mines surround us, but there are potholes in Emalahleni, there are . . . Eish!'

Local governance

Local government problems were high on the agenda. A picture emerged of a municipality accused of incompetence, maladministration, corruption, poor financial management and inability to plan for or maintain infrastructure and services. The municipality was under administration between 2013 and 2015, failed to obtain clean audits for years, and some of its priorities and decisions are questionable. Interviewees wanted to know, for example, why R42,000 was being spent per month on security for the municipal manager, while the municipality was not paying off its debt to Eskom (the South African electricity provider).

Community members suffer the consequences of interrupted services. One of them said: 'When you move in here, you buy a Jojo tank [a rainwater tank] and a generator – it is very seldom that you will have water and electricity at the same time.' Neglected infrastructure was the cause of many complaints. An interviewee with a sense of humour said of Emalahleni's potholes, 'you can just put in water, swim there and enjoy it'.

Similarly, the community suffers from poor spatial and infrastructural planning. An example is the road linking the CBD with industries, mines and settlements north-west of Emalahleni. This busy road runs across the railway line and the waiting time for traffic can be up to 45 minutes. Emergency services often cannot get through. There is no police station on the other side of the railway line. Interviewees wondered why the government had not planned for a bridge.

It was unsurprising to find that interviewees were not very interested in talking about the mines: their immediate problem was the municipality. Some even called the municipality their 'enemy number one'. Perceptions of corruption included all government departments and officials with whom the community engages. Interviewees maintained that the police 'are friends with the crooks and much bribing is going on'. According to one interviewee, during a meeting about crime community members 'came out point-blank and said "but it is the police vans that bring the drugs in here, there's police participating"'.

Interviewees' accounts and perceptions of the municipality are to a large extent corroborated by reports and studies. The provincial government placed Emalahleni municipality under administration in 2013 (Mpumalanga Provincial Government, 2013). In 2015, the administrator was appointed as acting municipal manager and subsequently as municipal manager. There were calls for his suspension. The Council did not renew his contract and in September 2018 the position was still not permanently filled. Under the aegis of the previous administrator-cum-acting-manager-cum-manager, Emalahleni's Eskom account escalated from R204 million to R1.3 billion. During his tenure, Emalahleni received a fifth consecutive disclaimer from the Auditor General (Goldswain, 2017). This report showed that the municipality had been technically insolvent for years. It had spent only 50% of its capital budget, which refutes the claim that the municipality does not have the resources to deal with the population influx (Municipal Money, 2017). By 2018, the municipality had 'progressed' from disclaimers to a qualified audit report (Goldswain, 2018). By August 2018, its Eskom debt stood at R2 billion and Emalahleni was on a list of municipalities the provincial government considered placing under administration (again). In March 2018 the mayor was replaced by a previous incumbent (Mpumalanga Provincial Government, 2013; Goldswain, 2018). This recycling of municipal leaders does not help to build trust between the community and the municipality.

Preparation for downscaling and closure of mines
Despite the changes in the mining environment, coal mining remains the linchpin of Emalahleni's economy. Interviewees sketched a depressing picture of an Emalahleni without its mines. In this 'ghost town', they foresee that foreigners who came because of the mines will not go away again, the municipality will increasingly fail to provide services, the power stations will be redundant, small businesses will close because there is no buying power left, social problems will escalate and the crime rate will soar. An interviewee was able to give a first-hand description of potential social problems, because she had been involved with families touched by the closure of Highveld Steel in 2016. She described how, previously, the men used to work hard, drink hard and work hard the next day to sober up, but after the closure only the 'drink hard' part was left to them, and the next day they took it out on their families. Their wives blamed them for not finding new work, domestic violence increased and children began to exhibit behavioural problems.

Relationship between the community, the mines and the municipality

We received the impression that the community do not trust the mines and the mines do not communicate with them. The interviewees' perception was that the mines 'do not care' for the community. They found the mines inaccessible (for example, it is difficult to make contact with the person responsible for community development) and they said that NPOs do not get a response to their funding proposals. Conflicting messages about procedures often complicated matters. Interviewees from NPOs believed that they could approach the mines only through the municipality's Transversal Unit (a unit dealing with gender, women, AIDS, disability, the elderly and children). However, both the mine official we interviewed and municipal officials denied this, insisting that the community could approach the mines directly. This may have resulted from an assumption that, as the mines have to align their social and labour plans with the municipal IDP, their social contributions must also go through the municipality.

We invited interviewees to suggest the most appropriate structure or channel for the mines to make their social contribution to the community and to comment on how the municipality should be involved. All, including the municipal officials, agreed that contributions should not be channelled through the municipality, because 'the community will not see this money'. No clear suggestion of an alternative channel emerged. There was general scepticism about the idea of a community trust. It appeared they would prefer a direct link between the mines and the community.

A message to the mines

At the end of each interview we asked interviewees to 'send a message to the mines'. Apart from calls for the mines to 'give us jobs' and to support community-based organisations, the underlying message was, in one interviewee's words, that the mines 'must take care of Emalahleni – because the mines have got money'. The most common request was: 'The mines must fix the potholes.' One interviewee had this message for the mines:

> Why can't they provide the facilities which we need? For instance, for the removal of the refuse. Maybe they can take that tender to themselves, hire those people to work under them – since the municipality maybe can't manage everything? Maybe those mines combined could form a structure to take care of this area, Emalahleni, so that we can have a good life. For instance, the maintenance of the sewerage, and so on – to maintain order.

Who is responsible in the absence of the state?

This community faces grave social ills, a lack of economic diversification, a local government failing to carry out its mandate, and services and infrastructure under severe stress from rapid population growth and influx.

Underlying the problems is the close relationship between the community and the mines, which spanned many generations. The mines used to take care of the community, providing work, housing and a sense of economic security. Developments since 1994 have damaged the relationship between Emalahleni's community and the mines. Mining legislation decrees that the mines must interact with communities through social and labour plans, included in municipal IDPs, and no longer through a direct and personal relationship. Outsourced staff and contract workers have replaced much of the permanent workforce; private housing, made possible through housing allowances, has replaced mining villages and hostels; and medical aid contributions have replaced mine hospitals. The influx of people drawn to the area in the hope of a job on the mines is now the responsibility of the municipality. The Emalahleni community's way of life has changed irrevocably.

Despite these changes, the community continues to trust that the mines will rescue them in times of crisis, as it had done for generations. And this does still happen, as one interviewee's story showed. For almost three weeks in 2017, Emalahleni was without water because a valve in the main water supply system had broken. The interviewee told us: 'The municipality came with their contractors – and they tried, and it didn't work – and they came back and they tried and it didn't work – there was a smell hanging over us.' Then one of the mining companies approached the municipality with an offer to fix the valve at the company's expense so that the people could get water. The mine did repair the valve. For this interviewee, it proved that the mines with their expertise and resources can assist the municipality when things are not going well.

Incidents like these juxtapose the legislation regulating the mines' social and developmental responsibility with the reality of struggling local municipalities in a mining town. The mines are legally obliged to align their social and labour plans with municipal planning (IDPs). This assumes that the mines and the municipality are willing and able to cooperate closely in planning and implementation. But our interviewees were openly sceptical about the mines' willingness to engage with and make substantial contributions to the municipality. They felt that 'the mines don't care' and that it is their priority to 'make a profit for their shareholders'. What is not surfacing in this debate is that 'alignment' implies two functioning partners. It is technically challenging to engage with an 'absent' partner – in this case, a failing municipality. It is naive to assume that this legislation can be implemented without a communication structure between the community, the municipality and the mines. Such structure, according to our interviews with members of all three sectors, does not exist in Emalahleni. On the contrary, there seems to be a lot of misunderstanding and mistrust.

The community thus becomes trapped between a municipality unable to execute its mandate and mining companies that no longer have a custodial role. The companies may be taking advantage of loopholes in the legislation to avoid responsibility or they may genuinely be struggling to engage with a municipality perceived as incompetent and corrupt by its very constituency.

It is no wonder that in the psyche of this community the mines remain the pivot around which its economy and well-being turn. They expect or hope that the mines can save them, and believe that they should, especially now that their municipality does not seem willing or able to ensure their well-being. They thus rely on the mines' wealth and expertise to fix their potholes, build RDP houses, collect garbage, maintain parks and ensure sustainable access to water. They conflate the roles and duties of the mines with those of the municipality.

Many questions remain unanswered. The community expect the mines to take over the mandate of the municipality, but what purpose would that serve? It might yield an efficient service in the short term, but it would not be a long-term solution. It is the mandate of the municipality to serve the public. Can the mines take over such a public role? What guarantee is there that the mines will include the community in decisions about services? How will they be held accountable? But what alternatives are there? Should the mines fix the potholes, or should they be left to get bigger until the municipality becomes functional again? There is little indication that this will happen soon. If the mines start taking over local government, how will the municipality regain its rightful and allocated role? Is it at all possible that mines and municipalities can partner effectively to promote social, infrastructural and economic development, especially when the municipality is struggling? A just transition requires strong public institutions.

No solution in sight

The community's frustrations with their municipality, as expressed by our interviewees, and their expectation that the mines should step into the breach, raise the question of whether the government should allow the mines to take over municipal functions when the municipality is failing or absent. It is questionable whether this would be a long-term solution or how it could bring about a just transition if the mines themselves are not there in the long run. In the meantime, and amid the abundance of resources, the Emalahleni community continues to struggle with overstressed infrastructure and questionable long-term planning. They have taps without water, they wait in vain for emergency services to get to them through poorly planned and badly maintained roads, they go home and find their houses burgled. And they continue to read newspaper headlines blazoning more bad news about the decline and corruption around them: 'Mayor and mayoral committee suspended', 'No more roads left to repair', 'Sewerage problems for the whole year', '*Van Witbank tot Stinkbank*'. A just transition needs to consider this problem as mine closure is likely to exacerbate these problems and to contribute to less consideration being given to municipal services as a public good.

References

Aytaç, S. E., Mousseau, M. and Örsün, Ö. F. 2016. Why some countries are immune from the resource curse: The role of economic norms. *Democratization*, 23(1), 71–92.

Banks, E. 2017. We are Bruno: Citizens caught between an absentee state and a state-like corporation during water conflicts in La Guajira, Colombia. *Urban Anthropology and Studies of Cultural Systems and World Economic Development*, 46(1,2), 1–34.

Besada, H. and Martin, P. 2013. Mining codes in Africa: Emergence of a 'fourth' generation? North-South Institute research report. http://www.nsi-ins.ca/publications/mining-codes-in-africa-emergence-of-a-fourth-generation-2/ (last accessed 29 April 2021).

BMF (Bench Marks Foundation). 2014. South African coal mining: Corporate grievance mechanisms, community engagement concerns and mining impacts. Policy Gap 9. http://www.bench-marks.org.za/research/policy_gap_9.pdf (last accessed 29 April 2021).

Brower, T. 2016. Constitutions as counter-curses: Revenue allocation and the resource curse. *Journal of Law and Policy*, 24(2), 291–342.

Brueckner, M. 2014. On the social sustainability of development in Western Australia: A community perspective. In M. Brueckner, A. Durey, R. Mayes and C. Pforr (eds), *Resource Curse or Cure? On the Sustainability of Development in Western Australia.* Heidelberg: Springer, 239–55.

Brueckner, M., Durey, A., Mayes, R. and Pforr, C. 2014. Confronting the 'resource curse or cure' binary. In M. Brueckner, A. Durey, R. Mayes and C. Pforr (eds), *Resource Curse or Cure? On the Sustainability of Development in Western Australia.* Heidelberg: Springer, 3–23.

Doro, E. and Kufakurinani, U. 2018. Resource curse or governance deficit? The role of parliament in Uganda's oil and Zimbabwe's diamonds. *Journal of Southern African Studies*, 44(1), 43–57.

Frynas, J. G., Wood, G. and Hinks, T. 2017. The resource curse without natural resources: Expectations of resource booms and their impact. *African Affairs*, 116(462), 233–60.

Gardiner, A. D. M. 2017. The socio-economic wellbeing of small mining towns in the Northern Cape. MA dissertation, Stellenbosch University.

Goldswain, R. 2018. Positive news from the mayor's desk: Emalahleni Local Municipality has progressed from disclaimer to a qualified audit opinion. *Witbank News*, 5 February.

Goldswain, Z. 2017. Action plan aimed at getting a clean audit. *Witbank News*, 7 July.

Grant, L. 2015. SA's richest people live . . . where? *Mail & Guardian*, 12 March. https://mg.co.za/article/2015-03-12-sas-richest-people-live-where (last accessed 29 April 2021).

Haslam, P.A. 2016. Overcoming the resource curse: Reform and the rentier state in Chile and Argentina, 1973–2000. *Development and Change*, 47(5), 1146–70.

John, J. D. 2011. Is there really a resource curse? A critical survey of theory and evidence. *Global Governance*, 17, 167–84.

Ledger, T. 2015. The mining sector and local profiles and impact. http://forum.tips.org.za/images/forum%20papers/2016/58c2c3_79ffdb552b3d488691efdfb5911684b4.pdf (last accessed 29 April 2021).

Marais, L. 2018. Housing policy in mining towns: Issues of race and risk in South Africa. *International Journal of Housing Policy*, 18(2), 335–45.

Marais, L., Van Rooyen, D., Nel, E. and Lenka, M. 2017. Responses to mine downscaling: Evidence from secondary cities in the South African Goldfields. *The Extractive Industries and Society*, 4, 163–71.

Marais, L., Wlokas, H., De Groot, J., Dube, N. and Scheba, A. 2017. Renewable energy and local development: Seven lessons from the mining industry. *Development Southern Africa*, 1–15.

Marais, L., Cloete, J., Van Rooyen, D., Denoon-Stevens., S. and Nel, V. 2018. Place attachment and social disruption in Postmasburg, a rapidly growing South African mining town. *GeoJournal*. doi: 10.1007/s10708-018-9851-x.

Marais, L., McKenzie, F. H., Deacon, l., Nel, E., Van Rooyen, D. and Cloete, J. 2018. The changing nature of mining towns: Reflections from Australia, Canada and South Africa. *Land Use Policy*, 76, 779–88.

Matebesi, S. 2017. *Civil Strife Against Local Governance: Dynamics of Community Protests in Contemporary South Africa*. Berlin: Barbara Budrich Publishers.

Matebesi, S. 2020. *Social Licensing and Mining in South Africa*. London: Routledge.

McFerson, H. M. 2010. Extractive industries and African democracy: Can the 'resource curse' be exorcised? *International Studies Perspectives*, 11, 335–53.

Mpumalanga Provincial Government. 2013. Official website of the Mpumalanga Provincial Government, 23 April 2013. http://www.mpumalanga.gov.za/media/statements/cogta/23042013.htm (last accessed 29 April 2021).

Municipal Money. 2017. Emalahleni Local Municipality. https://municipalmoney.gov.za/profiles/municipality-MP312-emalahleni.pdf (last accessed 29 April 2021).

Roberts, C. W. J. 2015. The other resource curse: Extractives as development panacea. *Cambridge Review of International Affairs*, 28(2), 283–307.

Ruddell, R. 2017. *Oil, Gas and Crime*. New York: Palgrave Macmillan.

Shange, N. and Gous, N. 2017. Witbank becomes crime hotspot. *TimesLIVE*, 30 October. https://www.timeslive.co.za/news/south-africa/2017-10-30-witbank-becomes-crime-hotspot/ pdf (last accessed 29 April 2021).

Steynberg, D. A. 2015. Population explosion: South Africa's top growing cities hopelessly underprepared. *HomeTimes: Informing and Guiding Homeowners*, 23 October. http://home-times.co.za/2015/10/population-explosion-sas-top-growing-cities-hopelessly-underprepared/.

Van der Watt, P. and Marais, L. 2021. Implementing social and labour plans in South Africa: Reflections on collaborative planning in the mining industry. *Resources Policy*, 71, 101984.

CHAPTER 16

Municipal Finances

Chris Hendriks

Mining municipalities under pressure

Most of South Africa's mining towns are experiencing an influx of migrant workers searching for employment at the mines and in other related industries. The municipalities are under fire for their inadequate provision of decent housing, infrastructure and services. Often the available amenities do not meet the demands of the population, and mining municipalities are three times more likely than other municipalities to have dysfunctional administrations (Ledger, 2015). Many mining municipalities have large backlogs in service delivery because of the influx of new households.

Yet these municipalities often do not benefit sufficiently from the mines in their jurisdictions. Municipalities generate their income through levies and property rates, but mines pay rates only in proportion to the value of the surface land and not on their operations. This system of taxing mining companies means that municipalities do not receive benefits from them in the same way that they do from other businesses. A municipality will receive higher rates from a shopping mall, for example, than from a mine (Van Rensburg, 2016). Furthermore, in contrast to most other businesses, the mines generally obtain electricity and water directly from bulk suppliers. This mean they do not pay municipalities for these services, further limiting revenue for a mining town.

This chapter investigates the effect of mining activities on the financial health of Emalahleni Local Municipality. It assesses the current situation and concludes by outlining the threats to a just transition when the mines close. The chapter shows that local financial management improvement could help ensure a base for a just transition. Good financial management could help with the reinvestment of funds that support greener options.

International perspective on mining municipalities and the consequences of mining

Research in Australia shows it is mainly the service functions of local government that are resource-challenged in expanding mining communities (Barclay et al., 2012; Cheshire, Everingham and Lawrence, 2014). Local governments struggle to carry out these functions effectively when confronted by large-scale mining, which demands considerable financial resources to provide new infrastructure and expand services. Barclay et al. (2012) note that resource constraints make it difficult for local governments to respond to community and industry demands for better infrastructure and services in a context of rapidly expanding requirements. Collaboration between the mines and the municipalities is also difficult (Van der Watt and Marais, 2021).

In South Australia, O'Neil, Kaye and Trevithick (2013) found that a rapid increase in population caused by the growth of the mining industry presents a challenge for local governments. It places pressure on them to satisfy community expectations. Local governments can provide only what they can afford, and although an increase in population may bring in more rates revenue, community demand will usually exceed the local government's ability to deliver. In Zambia, Negi (2014) found that despite the relatively high rate of economic growth generated from mining, the local governments struggle to cope with thousands of new migrants moving into newly constructed, often unfinished, structures before utilities have been provided or even planned. The absence of adequately planned infrastructure results in a proliferation of slum-like compounds. In Latin America, Bacchetta (2003) found that although local governments in mining towns benefit from higher revenues because of the mines, they have proven incapable of using and managing the extra revenue efficiently and productively. Local governments in many countries suffer from a shortage of material, financial and human resources. These weaknesses jeopardise the potentially excellent use of funds generated in a mining municipality.

Ironically, rich deposits of natural resources can be detrimental to a country's development and good governance. The rapid economic growth produced by mining can bring problems. Among the possible adverse effects of mining are economic growth that is slower than expected, weak economic diversification, damage to social well-being, corruption, high levels of poverty and inequality, appalling environmental impacts at the local level, exceptionally poor governance and an increased frequency of conflicts and war. Policymakers need to understand mining and its implications at national, regional and local level and adopt preventive measures. For further on the resource curse, see Ross (1999), Egoávil (2011), Benghida (2017), Carvalho (2017) and Gardiner (2017). Planning for both mining and decline could be problematic (Marais and De Lange, 2021).

Peru is one country whose government reinvests mining proceeds creatively. Its central government transfers half of the taxes collected from the mining industry to the regions and municipalities where the minerals are extracted (Loayza and Rigolini, 2016). This sharing scheme, called the 'mining canon', makes Peru less centralised. The decentralisation aims to transfer power and administrative functions to local and provincial government. The scheme was put in place so that mining communities could benefit more from the resources generated by the industry. Far from being a curse, mining has been a blessing for Peru (De la Flor, 2014).

In contrast to Peru, South Africa makes mining companies pay taxes to the central government and the money becomes part of the national revenue fund, to be distributed again through the budget process, together with all other revenues collected. Mining-dependent local governments receive little or no compensation for the infrastructure and services they provide. This lack of response to mining-dependent municipalities flies in the face of the stipulation in the Constitution of the Republic of South Africa that local government 'is entitled to an equitable share of the revenue raised nationally to enable it to provide basic services and perform the functions allocated to it' (RSA, 1996: Section 227).

Financial health of mining municipalities

How a municipality manages its finances is usually a good indicator of the quality of its overall management. Ledger (2015) notes that mining municipalities' financial health is, in general, far worse than that of other municipalities. They have a much higher rate of 'red zone' audits – that is, a disclaimer or adverse opinion from the Auditor General. Ledger notes that, in the 2013/14 audit, 13 of the 21 municipalities where mining makes up 30% or more of local GVA (gross value added) received a disclaimer and one (Westonaria) failed to meet the audit deadline.

Malope (2017) notes that 19 mining municipalities were in financial distress in 2017 and struggling to provide services to their communities. Municipalities with mines that are downscaling, such as those with gold mines, are in sharp economic decline because of the decrease in economic activity and job opportunities; others, such as those with coal or platinum mines, are expanding and attracting an influx of migrant job seekers, increasing the need for infrastructure and basic services. Both types of problem put pressure on a municipality's fiscal base, and failure to deliver can lead to protests.

Financial health of Emalahleni Municipality

Emalahleni's economy is growing rapidly because of coal mining, power generation and the metal industry, which attract migrant jobseekers. Its population expanded by 3.6% per annum between 2001 and 2011, from 276,413 to 395,466, and the population estimate for 2017 was close to 500,000 (SACN, 2017). The result has been housing shortages, pressure on infrastructure, unreliable water and electrical supply, poor road maintenance, and potable and wastewater treatment plants operating beyond capacity. The difficulties are further compounded by the municipality's internal problems, such as alleged corruption and a financial crisis, and the high costs of doing business with external service providers (Campbell, Nel and Mphambukeli, 2017; SACN, 2017).

Audited financial statements from 2008 to 2017 were used in this study to assess the financial health of Emalahleni. The municipality received a disclaimer from the Auditor General for the fiscal years 2012/13, 2013/14 and 2015/16. On 23 April 2013, the Mpumalanga Provincial Executive Council put the Emalahleni Local Municipality under administration because it was not delivering in terms of the Constitutional mandate to provide basic services (SACN, 2017). The administrator assumed the executive powers of the municipal manager and the executive mayor, and an advisory committee was established to advise the administrator (Emalahleni Local Municipality, 2015).

In addition to the appointment of the administrator, during the 2015/16 financial year the National Treasury also stopped the transfer of the equitable share to Emalahleni for habitually defaulting on Eskom and Water Boards debts (FFC, 2015). At the time of writing, Emalahleni was receiving support from the government's Revitalisation of Distressed Mining Communities programme that was launched in 2012 and was still classified by the National Treasury (2017) as being in financial distress, mainly for the following reasons: overspending on the operational budget, underspending on the capital budget, increase in debtors, cash available to pay off current liabilities and total cash available in the bank accounts.

Assessment of Emalahleni Local Municipality's financial statements 2017/18

Local governments in South Africa provide basic services such as water, electricity, sanitation, refuse removal, municipal transport and roads. These are funded largely from their revenue bases, such as user charges and property rates. However, the South African Constitution (1996) entitles municipalities in South Africa to a share of the nationally collected revenue in the form of grants, collected through taxes such as personal income tax and value-added tax. In the 2017/18 fiscal year, municipalities received 9% of the nationally raised revenue. The government splits this allocation to municipalities into two parts: an equitable share and conditional grants. The equitable share subsidises the revenue that municipalities can raise themselves. It enables municipalities to deliver free basic services such as water, electricity and sanitation to indigent households and also subsidises the cost of other core services that municipalities cannot recover from their own revenue sources (National Treasury, 2016). The equitable share is an unconditional transfer as required by the Constitution, and it is up to elected municipal councils to determine how they use these funds in their budgets. Individual municipalities make different choices about their budget priorities. However, the 2018 Budget Review demonstrates that funds intended to support core functions and provide free basic services to poor households seldom comply with the original intent (National Treasury, 2018).

In addition to the equitable share, South Africa's intergovernmental fiscal relations system makes provision for the transfer of funds to municipalities for

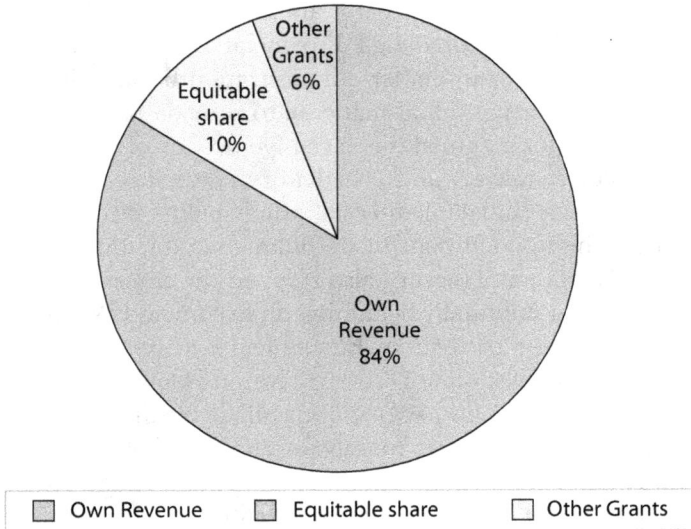

Figure 16.1 Share of municipal income per source, 2017.

infrastructure development and other purposes, which further boosts the flow of revenue to municipalities. Figure 16.1 compares the contribution of the national government's equitable share and other grants with Emalahleni's revenue in the 2016/17 financial year.

Revenue

South African municipalities collect their revenue mainly from the sale of water and electricity, property rates and taxes, and service charges for refuse removal and sanitation. In 2017, own revenue accounted for 84% of municipal income in Emalahleni. Although the percentage of own revenue may seem high compared with total revenue, Emalahleni has a much higher own revenue potential. The municipality fails to recoup large percentages of electricity and water revenue – amounting to more than R403 million in 2016/17. Figure 16.2 shows the percentages that various revenue sources contributed to Emalahleni's revenue in 2017, according to its financial statements for that year.

Figure 16.3 shows that between 2008 and 2017 Emalahleni's own revenue differed significantly from year to year, while the inflation rate stayed relatively constant. Own revenue grew by 17% in 2008, but in 2009 the growth was down to 3%, lower than the inflation rate of 6%. After that it grew faster than the inflation rate, by as much as 23% from 2010 to 2011. The growth rate thereafter decreased annually and 2014 saw a negative growth of -4.7%, mainly because less revenue was collected from the sale of water and electricity. Of significance is that Emalahleni has received several disclaimers (for the 2013/14, 2014/15

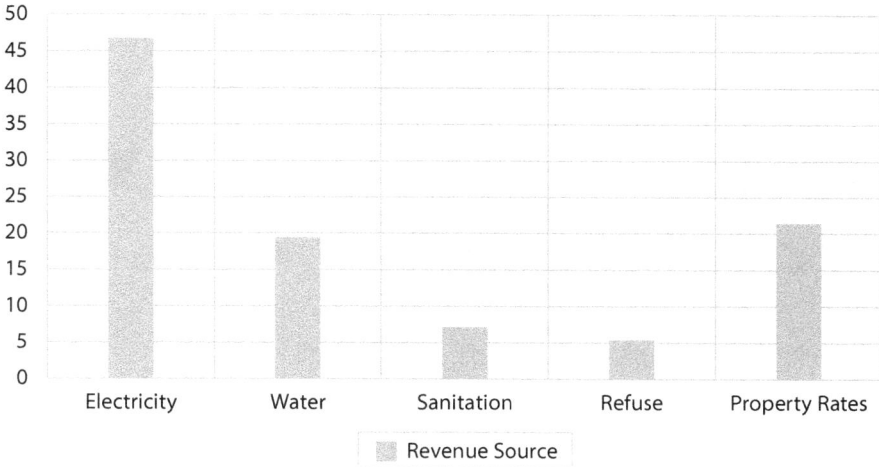

Figure 16.2 Contribution of own sources of revenue, 2017.

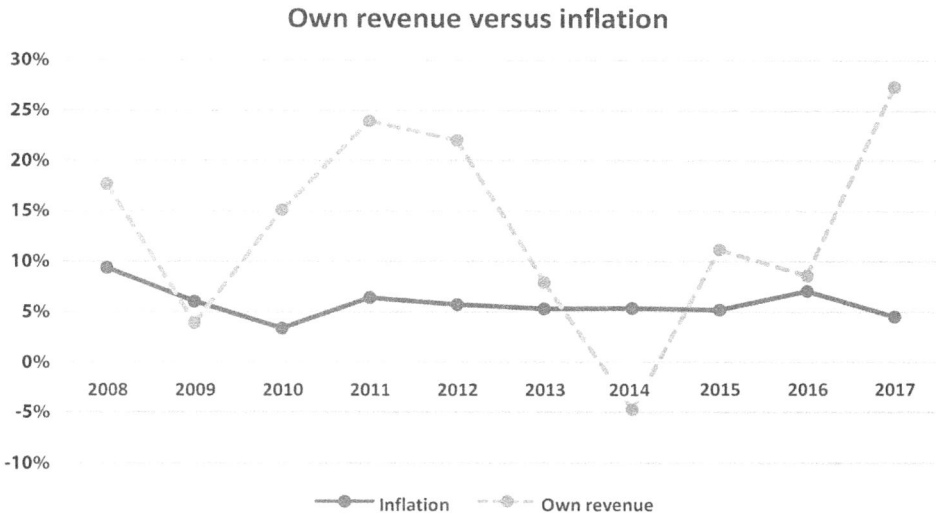

Figure 16.3 Own revenue compared to inflation 2008–17.

and 2015/16 financial years) from the Auditor General. In 2013/14 some of the reasons cited were that the municipality did not have adequate management, accounting and information systems to account for revenue, debtors and receipts of income, and it did not have an effective method of internal control for debtors and income (Auditor General, 2014). The increases experienced were mainly due to higher rates of revenue collection.

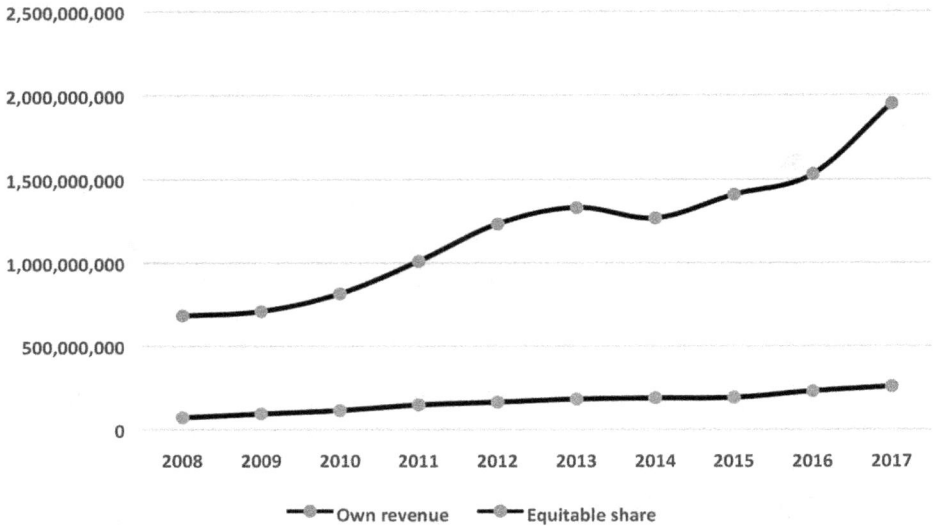

Figure 16.4 Own revenue compared with equitable share transfers, 2008–17 (rand).

Figure 16.4 shows that Emalahleni Municipality's own revenue was much higher than what it received from the national government. The population figure of 500,000 estimated for 2017 represents a growth of 27% since the 2011 census. To cope with this growth the municipality provided 5,300 houses, but there is still a demand for over 40,000 houses to accommodate households in informal settlements and backyard shacks. The population growth has brought more revenue from the sale of electricity and water, property rates and taxes, and charges for refuse removal, sewerage and sanitation. Figure 16.4 further shows that the equitable share did indeed react to the rapid population increase Emalahleni experienced from 2008 to 2017. Although the growth in the equitable share was slower than the growth in own revenue, it does suggest that the equitable share is a responsive grant and has probably helped to support services to poor households in Emalahleni.

Figure 16.5 shows the percentage increase in the annually collected revenue from 2011 to 2017. The calculated 58% increase in the inflation rate over the period is shown as a straight line. The significant gains in revenue from property rates, electricity and water reflect the contribution that new households made to the municipal finances.

A comparison of Emalahleni's revenues and equitable share revenues shows that the latter contributed approximately 10% of the total revenue and grew by 260% from 2007/08 to 2016/17. Own revenue grew by 186% over the same period (see Figure 16.4). However, from 2013 to 2017 the equitable share revenue

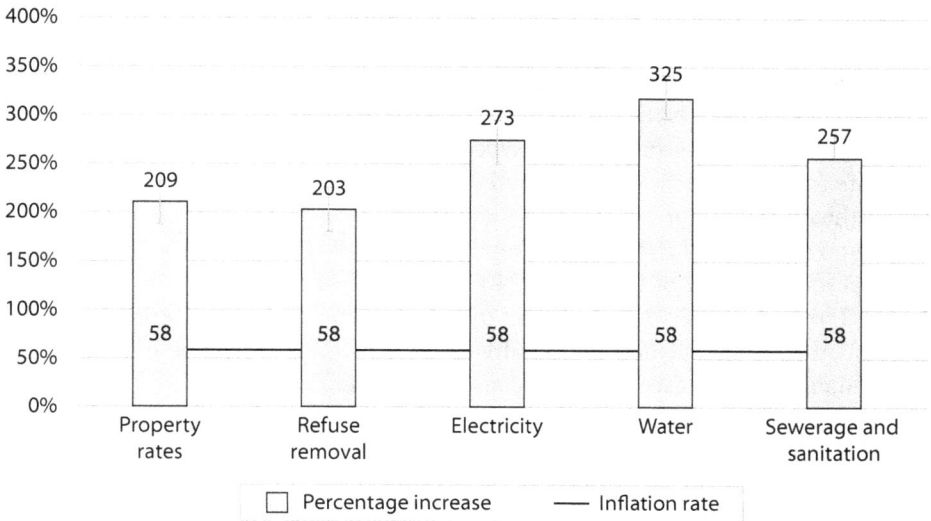

Figure 16.5 Increases in value of revenue resources, 2008–17 (rand).

grew by only 41%, while own revenue grew by 46%, largely because of increased collection of property rates and taxes and the sale of electricity and water.

Besides the equitable share, South African municipalities receive other grants that contribute to their total revenue, such as the Municipal Infrastructure Grant (MIG), the Expanded Public Works Programme Grant, the Financial Management Grant, the Energy Grant, the Human Settlement Grant, and the Capital Neighbourhood Development Grant. Of these grants, the MIG contributes most substantially, funding the infrastructure for basic services and roads and social infrastructure for poor households in all non-metropolitan municipalities. The MIG provides about 3% of Emalahleni's total revenue. In some financial years (2008/9, 2011/12, 2015/16 and 2016/17) the financial statements record having received grant income from Anglo American and BHP Billiton. However, these were minimal amounts contributing no more than 0.6% of Emalahleni's total revenue.

Expenditure
Emalahleni Municipality's main categories of expenditure for 2017 were bulk purchases of water and electricity (32%), personnel expenditure (25%), debt impairment (16%), depreciation of assets (10%) and general expenses (19%). In the financial years reviewed (2008–17), total expenditure exceeded total revenue, leaving the municipality with an operating deficit, an indication that it is struggling to cope financially, hence its classification by the National Treasury as being in financial distress.

One reason for the financial distress is that although the equitable share compensates municipalities for the free basic services they must provide to the needy, it does not cover increases in the bulk price of electricity approved after the budget has been tabled (National Treasury, 2016). Recent increases in the costs of bulk electricity and water have depleted the surpluses that municipalities usually generate from these services (National Treasury, 2016). However, the main reason is that Emalahleni experiences significant losses in purchases of electricity and water. In 2016/17 the losses amounted to 43% for electricity and 70% for water, a total amount of R403,350,243, or 20% of its revenue (Auditor General, 2017). The losses were due to ageing infrastructure, illegal connections, vandalism and theft. Furthermore, Emalahleni did not have a proper infrastructure maintenance and replacement programme in place, which should have formed part of the municipality's annual activities of the municipality (Goldswain, 2014).

Emalahleni's second-highest single expenditure item, personnel, includes all the current payments to municipal employees and councillors – not only salaries and wages but also social contributions such as for pensions and medical schemes. We found there was a slight decrease in the percentage of the total budget that was spent on employee compensation over 10 years (2008–17), from 27% in 2008 to 24% in 2017. The 24% is well within the national guidelines of 25% for personnel expenditure and implies that as the municipality's total revenues increased, the salary bill increased proportionally. This low percentage was probably the result of national guidelines regarding spending on personnel. Municipalities must guard against spending too much on staff, which could threaten the sustainability of the budget, while also making sure they have the people they need to deliver services effectively.

What should give Emalahleni most concern about its financial systems is the amount written off for bad debts. Bad debts rose from 4% of total expenditure (R35,537,649) in 2008 to 20% (R560,223,812) in 2016, and although this decreased to 16% (R455,592,437) in 2017, it is still unacceptably high. Many South African municipalities are failing to collect all their rates and taxes, resulting in the write-off of bad debts. They fail to collect all the money owed to them and their tariffs fail to cover the full costs of the services provided. The National Treasury (2016) believes municipalities can and should improve their revenue collection.

Figure 16.6 compares Emalahleni's total revenue with its total expenditure from 2008 to 2017. The rapid increase in spending experienced in 2014 is attributable to a restatement for bulk purchases of water and electricity of the previous years. In the previous years, the municipality accounted for expenses using the modified cash basis instead of the accrual basis of accounting. All expenditures were raised and captured only upon payment. An exercise was performed for the entire population, identifying invoices relating to the prior years. Journal entries were passed to correct the understatement in the previous years. During the

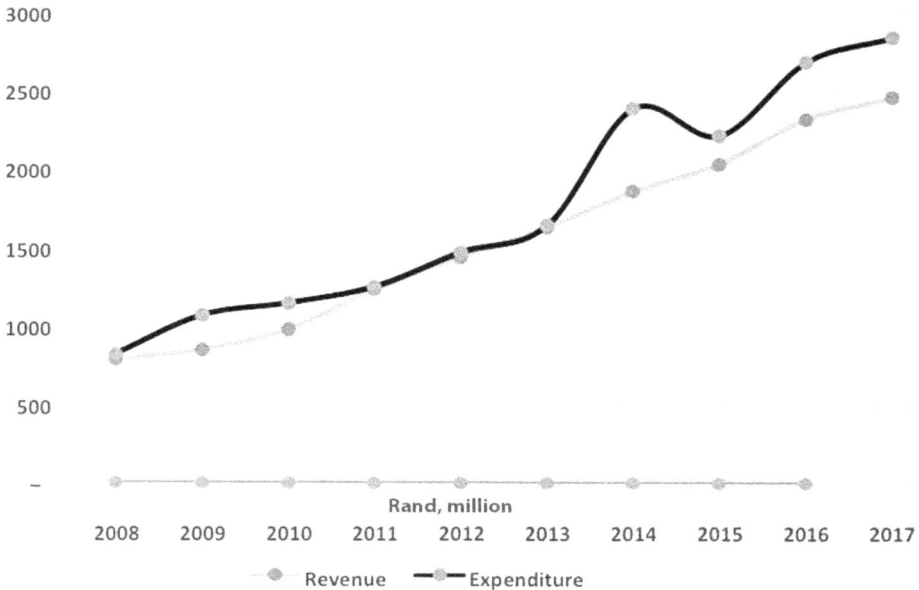

Figure 16.6 Revenue compared to expenditure, 2008–17 (rand).

whole period, expenditure exceeded revenue, implying that Emalahleni annually incurred a net loss. In the 2016/17 fiscal year, Emalahleni's liabilities exceeded its assets by R1,800 million, casting doubt on the municipality's ability to continue to provide services and meet its financial obligations (National Treasury, 2017).

The main reason for this worrying situation is the municipality's inability to collect money owed by its consumers. The resulting severe cash flow problems make it difficult for the municipality to settle its accounts in time. Another reason is the loss that Emalahleni suffered in water and electricity distribution during the 2016/17 financial year, as mentioned above. It is evident from Figure 16.6 that since 2014 there has been a sharp increase in Emalahleni's expenditure, mainly due to tariff increases in the bulk purchase of water and electricity and amounts written off to bad debt.

Conclusion

The study on which this chapter is based confirmed the effect of mining on Emalahleni Municipality's finances. Like other mining municipalities, Emalahleni is experiencing financial distress, which affects service delivery to its citizens. Although mining in the region increased Emalahleni's revenue by an average of 18% per annum from 2008 to 2017, expenditure increased even more. Emalahleni consistently spends more than it earns. The two main contributing factors are the huge loss of bulk purchased water and electricity in the distribution process and the under-collection of revenue, leading to large amounts of debt being written off. It is crucial for Emalahleni to curb the financial losses suffered in distribution and to increase its collection rate to provide its mandated services to the community.

The above picture portrays the reality of municipal finance in a period of large-scale economic growth in Emalahleni. If the mines decline, this might mean less water and electricity revenue for the municipality as people move out or cannot afford to pay for the services. Illegal connections might increase as decline sets in. More problematic could be large losses from property tax, as an increasing number of mine employees and people employed in mine-related industries will be unable to pay off their mortgages and will have to give up their properties. A just transition requires planning for this reality and probably requires the national and provincial government to support the municipality to avoid a total collapse. Furthermore, the current state of affairs will require substantial support from the national government to support the transition and to source funds to support renewables.

References

Auditor General. 2014. *Report of the Auditor General to the Mpumalanga Provincial Legislature and the Council on the Emalahleni Local Municipality.* Pretoria: Auditor General.

Auditor General. 2017. *Report of the Auditor General on the Financial Statements and Other Legal and Regulatory Requirements of Emalahleni Municipality for the Year Ended 30 June 2017.* Pretoria: Auditor General.

Bacchetta, V. L. 2003. *Mining Companies and Local Development. Latin America: Chile, Columbia and Peru.* Report, International Development Research Centre, Ottawa. https://idl-bnc-idrc. dspacedirect.org/bitstream/handle/10625/19481/119808.pdf (last accessed 30 April 2021).

Barclay, M. A., Everingham, J., Cheshire, L., Brereton, D., Pattenden, C. and Lawrence, G. 2012. *Local Government, Mining Companies and Resource Development in Regional Australia: Meeting the Governance Challenge.* Final report, Centre for Social Responsibility in Mining, Sustainable Minerals Institute and School of Social Science, University of Queensland. Brisbane: CSRM.

Benghida, S. 2017. Factors and challenges in developing countries under the resource curse. *International Journal of Civil Engineering and Technology,* 8(11), 901–10.

Campbell, M., Nel, V. and Mphambukeli, T. 2017. A thriving coal-mining city in crisis? The governance and spatial planning challenges at Witbank, South Africa. *Land Use Policy,* 62, 223–31.

Carvalho, P. 2017. Mining industry and sustainable development: Time for change. *Food and Energy Security,* 6(2), 61–77.

Cheshire, L., Everingham, J. and Lawrence, G. 2014. Governing the impacts of mining and the impacts of mining governance: Challenges for rural and regional local governments in Australia. *Journal of Rural Studies,* 36, 330–9.

De la Flor, P. 2014. Mining and economic development in Peru: A time for resurgence. https://archive.revista.drclas.harvard.edu/book/mining-and-economic-development-peru (last accessed 30 April 2021).

Egoávil, S. B. C. 2011. The resource curse and Peru: A potential threat for the future? Unpublished MA thesis, University of San Francisco.

Emalahleni Local Municipality. 2015. Draft Reviewed Integrated Development Plan 2015/2016. https://cogta.mpg.gov.za/IDP/2015-16%20IDPs/Nkangala/Emalahleni2015-16.pdf last accessed 14 May 2021).

FFC (Financial and Fiscal Commission). 2015. Financial and Fiscal Commission submission on stoppage of local government equitable share allocations. Midrand: FFC. https://static.pmg.org.za/150513FFC.pdf (last accessed 30 April 2021).

Gardiner, A. E. M. 2017. The socio-economic wellbeing of small mining towns in the Northern Cape. Unpublished MA thesis, University of Stellenbosch.

Goldswain, Z. 2014. Rain, electricity and water huge issues in eMalahleni. *Witbank News*, 19 November.

Ledger, T. 2015. *The Mining Sector: Local Profiles and Impact*. Pretoria: TIPS (Trade and Industrial Strategies).

Loayza, N. and Rigolini, J. 2016. The local impact of mining on poverty and inequality: Evidence from the commodity boom in Peru. http://pubdocs.worldbank.org/en/309641458726797039/Peru-Mining-Effects-January-2016.pdf (last accessed 30 April 2021).

Malope, L. 2017. Government says distressed mining areas climbs to 19. *City Press*, 11 July.

Marais, L. and De Lange, A. 2021. Anticipating and planning for mine closure in South Africa. *Futures*, 125, 102669.

National Treasury. 2016. *Budget Review*. www.treasury.gov.za/documents/national%20budget/2016/review/FullReview.pdf (last accessed 30 April 2021).

National Treasury. 2017. *The State of Local Government Finances and Financial Management as of 30 June 2017*. Pretoria: Government Printer

National Treasury. 2018. *Budget Rreview*. Pretoria: Government Printer.

Negi, R. 2014. 'Solwezi mabanga': Ambivalent developments on Zambia's new mining frontier. *Journal of Southern African Studies*, 40(5), 999–1013.

O'Neil, M., Kaye, L. and Trevithick, M. 2013. *Impact of Mining and Resource Development: A Case Study for Eyre Peninsula Councils*. Report, South Australian Centre for Economic Studies, Adelaide and Flinders Universities. https://www.adelaide.edu.au/saces/ua/media/74/impact-of-mining-on-local-government-eyre-peninsula.pdf (last accessed 30 April 2021).

Ross, M. L. 1999. The political economy of the resource curse. *World Politics*, 51(2), 297–322.

RSA (Republic of South Africa). 1996. *Constitution of the Republic of South Africa, 1996*. Pretoria: Government Printer.

SACN (South African Cities Network). 2017. *Emalahleni*. https://www.ufs.ac.za/docs/librariesprovider23/default-document-library/emalahleni.pdf?sfvrsn=0 (last accessed 30 April 2021).

Van der Watt, P. and Marais, L. 2021. Implementing social and labour plans in South Africa: Reflections on collaborative planning in the mining industry. *Resources Policy*, 71, 101984.

Van Rensburg, D. 2016. Mines in crisis: The supercycle is long gone. *City Press*, 22 June.

CHAPTER 17

Is a Just Transition Possible?

Lochner Marais, Philippe Burger, Maléne Campbell,
Stuart Paul Denoon-Stevens and Deidré van Rooyen

Introduction

Like death and taxes, mine closure is an eventual certainty. Mines can close for several reasons, but most often simply because of their inherently finite nature. In Emalahleni, coal mines are closing partly because of the phasing out of old and uncompetitive coal-driven power plants but particularly because of global pressure to use a cleaner energy source. The demand for South African export coal will fall away as countries move towards renewable energy (Simelane and Abdel-Rahman, 2011). But there is a dark side to the bright new energy story: workers in the doomed mines and power plants will lose their jobs. It is in this context that the notion of a just transition developed.

To avoid socio-economic damage when South African mines and power stations close, in 2017 the National Planning Commission embarked on a project titled 'Pathways to a Just Transition in South Africa', as a response to the National Development Plan's emphasis on a shift to a low-carbon economy. This is laudable, but there is always a danger that the focus will be predominantly on the plight of the workers, thus ignoring many of the broader consequences of mine decline and failing to deal with the interdependencies associated with mining. The transition will have implications not only for the workers but also for communities and institutions in the coal mining areas. Chapter 3 in this book made it clear that mine closure has complex implications that require a broad response. The slogan 'a just transition' is a good starting point, but our book warns that such a transition might be extremely difficult to achieve in practice if the narrow focus on workers persists.

The chapters in this book discussed these broader issues and the implications for a just transition when Emalahleni's mines close. The authors analysed the current situation and considered future scenarios. The evidence they have brought to light makes it clear that achieving a just transition will be difficult. A prominent theme running through the book is how to understand neoliberalism in the mining industry. The evidence presented by the authors leads us to argue that neoliberalism is a specific phase of economic development and is socially embedded in society (see Chapter 1). Policymakers need to take both these arguments into account.

The state versus company power: A phase of socially embedded neoliberalism

A prominent theme of this book has been the power of the mining companies. Companies often take the lead and implement policy to suit themselves. Chapter 1 outlined how the transnational and multinational corporations have become strong role-players since the mid-1980s. In the following, we offer three explanations as to how the South African state and the mining companies found common ground despite the mines' display of power in leading many of these processes.

First, socially embedded neoliberalism is evident in the way mineworker settlements and housing are managed. By the mid-1980s, mining companies had started to see the dangers of long-term commitment to peripheral activities like housing and the management of urban settlements. Such activities would be bad for their balance sheets and saddle them with liabilities beyond the life of the mine, so they started phasing them out (Van der Watt and Marais, 2019). Over the past two decades the mining industry has focused on core business. Getting rid of mine housing represents a specific period of thinking in the industry.

The mines found willing partners in the South African government and the labour unions. Government, unions and companies together agreed to reduce the role of the companies in managing public spaces. One might ask why the government and the unions bought into this. We think that the social embeddedness of neoliberalism lies at the heart of this reality.

The mining companies' primary motive was to cut expenditure to improve profitability. The government aimed primarily to promote open towns to encourage democracy, but also to reduce the power of the mining companies in managing public spaces like human settlements. The 1998 White Paper on Mining and Minerals emphasised the use of mining for local development and the creation of integrated communities. The hope was that the mining companies would continue to support planning but without the political control they had previously possessed. The White Paper's emphasis aligned well with the mining companies' thinking, although the two sides had different reasons for supporting the changes. The unions aimed primarily to improve the living conditions of their members. Rightly, they fought for the dismantling of the compound system and to secure living-out allowances (historically only available to white mineworkers). The mineworkers' salaries increased and they were able to find housing for themselves.

But what will be the long-term consequences of these changes when the mines close? Only the mining companies have been farsighted in formulating their policy. For them, transferring housing responsibilities to individuals and municipalities was a way to avoid the future liabilities of peripheral activities associated with their operations. The government, however, did not foresee the long-term consequences of dealing with rapid growth and it did not plan for decline.

The evidence from this book shows that local governments have been unable to cope. The mineworkers are faced with a strong possibility of job loss, with very little support through the process. They might need to relocate, or manage the long-term implications of housing finance if they are homeowners. The social embeddedness of the neoliberal norms and values means that the government and the mineworkers share in no small degree the risks of mine decline. A just transition should acknowledge these risks and find appropriate ways of dealing with them. What started as the mining companies' attempt to minimise their risks by transferring potentially long-term liabilities to their workers and the local government (evidence of mine company power) has ended up with the government and the unions agitating for the same outcomes as the mines.

Second, we see evidence that society has accepted changes in labour practices. Globally the mining industry has moved to shift work and outsourcing to remain competitive. Chapter 4 investigated current inequalities in the mining industry that have resulted from the changing labour regimes. The overall focus on a clean wage, shift work and contract work has not only come from the mining industry but has been actively pursued by the labour unions. The unions agreed to the regime changes because they brought parity between black and white mineworkers and had direct benefits for them. The evidence presented in Chapter 5 showed that mineworkers in Emalahleni reported mainly positive working experiences. This finding comes in the context of a long history of mine work being unsafe and shows how the mining industry has become socially acceptable. The coal mines have changed and are providing jobs in the industry with decent salaries and less arduous working conditions. But, the unions traded these changes for shift work, contract work and a clean wage. What started as the mining companies' way of dealing with the pressure of reporting to global shareholders became generally accepted by the unions and their mineworkers.

Third, the mining companies are likely to outplay the government during mine closure processes. They want to see closure as a short-term process and mining legislation provides for final closure. However, the 2002 Mineral and Petroleum Resources Development Act introduced an array of stringent environmental regulations to be followed when a mine closes. Many companies are trying to avoid them. Smaller companies are unlikely to comply with all the regulations. The evidence is already there that closure might mean 'care and maintenance' or selling the mine to a smaller role-player in the industry. In practice, this might mean mines where no operations take place, but which have not been formally closed and rehabilitated. The lack of rehabilitation might inhibit other economic activities. The authors of Chapter 7 argued that although one positive outcome is that there might be less air pollution in Emalahleni, the negative effects of mine decline will be felt for generations. The current focus on the mineworkers' immediate needs inhibits long-term thinking about how environmental degradation might affect communities. The real challenge for a just transition is how to manage the long-term implications for those affected by mine closure. We still do not know what the full implications will be, but a just transition should be able to anticipate some of them and it should be possible to plan to ensure appropriate mine closure.

The above three explanations show how mining companies often lead the change and government and unions follow. We see this as a specific phase of economic development in which multinational corporations have become the dominant force for change, but also as indicating the way these changes have been generally accepted by the mineworkers, the unions and the government, and by society as a whole. The outcomes described in this book are not only the result of changes in the mining industry; they reflect the complicated workings of the government and the unions (and their members) and the degree to which neoliberalism is socially embedded. This social embeddedness means that companies, government and unions find it difficult to think about mining in the long run. Consequently, the pressure for a just transition comes towards the end of a mine's lifecycle.

Because neoliberalism is socially embedded, the assumption is that local municipalities must plan for economic growth and population growth. Local institutions need to take long-term planning responsibility. In the mining context, this means planning for an influx of people and managing the settlements that the mining companies used to manage (Cloete and Marais, 2020). Mine decline and downscaling require a different mindset, or at least an understanding of the possibility that the population and the economy might grow or might decline. The call for a just transition mainly assumes growth or at least economic diversification by providing mineworkers with an alternative employment sector.

It does not seem to occur to planners that mine decline is not necessarily all bad but might have some value for mining towns. The immediate value of decline for Emalahleni would be a reduction in air pollution. It could also reduce water usage in this dry region. It could reconnect the citizens with the ecology of the area. Of course, this might not do much for the plight of mineworkers who lose their jobs, but we want to emphasise the importance of thinking beyond job losses. To take advantage of the value of decline would require a more flexible land management system in which land use could change quickly.

The front-end approach and a just transition

The authors of Chapter 3 distinguished between a front-end and a back-end approach to mining. They argued that mining requires a back-end approach to deal with decline; in other words, thinking about mine closure while the mine is still active. The concept of a just transition is an example of a back-end approach. However, it seldom receives attention when a mine is first opened. Concerns about closure only start to feature towards the end of the mine's life.

The predominant front-end approach to mining creates dependencies which go beyond the mineworkers' dependence on minework, such as the mine's dependence on financial and planning systems to secure its mining licence, and the interdependencies between the mining company and local institutions. Uneven power relations make it very difficult for local institutions to challenge these dependencies.

Local role-players seldom recognise these dependencies or see them as local benefits from mining. Some examples in Emalahleni include a large number of social projects implemented by the mines and the local municipality buying water from one of the mines. Ironically, the government's attempt to align local and mine planning through social and labour plans has probably increased these dependencies. There is even an expectation that the mines should fix potholes in the roads (Chapter 15). Mine closure means that these interdependencies will become liabilities or be discontinued. Thus, despite being a back-end approach, a just transition is likely to be difficult to implement as it seldom receives early attention. The development of a just transition requires long-term planning. The way the concept is currently being applied in South Africa does not spring from early planning and this will make success difficult to come by.

The planning and municipal finance conundrum

Four chapters in this book focused on planning and municipal finance problems. Ironically, despite its location in the coalfields and the energy-generating environment, Emalahleni owes vast sums of money to Eskom and Eskom has threatened on many occasions to cut the power to the municipality. The municipality has been under administration twice. Hendriks outlined the municipal finance problems in Chapter 16. The expansion of mining in the 2000s and a larger number of people falling directly under the municipality have created severe planning and municipal finance problems. Chapter 6 showed that mining expansion brings an influx of people and an increase in informal settlements. Chapter 13 outlined the planning problems in Emalahleni, while Campbell, Nel and Mpambukeli (2017) argued that corruption has damaged the municipal finance and planning system. The problem for a just transition is apparent: if the municipality has been unable to deal with growth, how will it deal with decline? In this context, Nel and Oranje in Chapter 14 (in contrast to Van Aswegen and Drewes in Chapter 13) argued that municipal planners should learn how to 'plan in the dark' by acknowledging uncertainties and not just assuming growth. Mining decline also requires a regional planning perspective. The evidence already shows that a decentralised government system alone cannot deal with the implications of mining. Closure and decline will simply increase the pressure. A regional planning approach requires a direct response from provincial and national governments.

Globally, a body of work has developed on the value of shrinking cities (e.g. Dubeaux and Cunningham Sabot, 2019; Ghosh, Byahut and Masilela, 2019; Long and Gao, 2019). However, the lessons from the shrinking cities literature have not received much attention in South Africa. Two of the main messages from this literature are that planners should understand the value of decline and that decline requires flexible land use systems. However, a planning system that pre-empts economic and population growth will find it difficult to consider the implications of decline.

The anticipated social consequences of closure for Emalahleni

Anticipating the future is difficult. It is easy to create the impression that antici-pating the future is simple or clear. We do not claim to be able to pin down the future. Instead, in this book we have aimed to identify possible consequences of mine closure to show the complexities associated with a just transition.

Mine closure will have several short-term implications for Emalahleni. Job losses will have a devastating effect on mineworkers' families. Those minework-ers who are near retrenchment age are likely to suffer less. But the average age of mineworkers in Emalahleni is 39, which means that for most mineworkers and their families closure would be disastrous. And although severance packages might soften the immediate effects, most mineworkers will have to find work again to sustain themselves and their families. The consequences of mine clo-sure for the workers and their families have been the primary (but not exclusive) focus of the just transition literature. The current planning focus on developing a renewable energy hub in the area is a good start.

However, mine closure planning should also consider job losses outside the mining industry. The non-mining households' dependence on mining activities means that many of them will be affected by mine closure. The evidence from this book shows that informal workers, such as casual workers, are the most at risk (see Chapter 12). The past few years have already seen an increase in the vulnerability of day workers. All of the above consequences are likely to affect the housing situation, with fewer people being able to afford their rent or mort-gage payments. The large rental housing market is likely to collapse. The already large percentage of informal settlements may continue to grow, despite some out-migration from the area.

Ironically, high levels of commitment to employers might mean that mine decline can catch employees off guard. Most mineworkers do not have the appro-priate skills to find jobs elsewhere in the economy. Their commitment might fur-ther limit their chance of developing skills outside the mining sector. Although the mines are supposed to attend to the reskilling of their employees through their social and labour plans, in practice this seldom happens.

Mine closure is most likely to reinforce the current inequalities and social stratification that mining has brought (Obeng-Odoom, 2020a). Contract workers will be the first to lose their jobs. Unskilled (mostly black) workers will soon follow. Although the intention behind a just transition is to mitigate these problems, finding an alternative will be difficult. It is unlikely that renewables will provide such an opportunity and it is more likely that they will reinforce historical inequalities and those created by mining. In the end, land degradation due to mining means that effective land reform in the area would have limited effects.

Mining has produced many dependencies between the mining companies, their employees and the municipality. The authors of Chapter 15 noted that these dependencies are evident in their respondents' expectation that the mines should fix the potholes. In many cases, these dependencies are the result of the front-end approach to mining (see Chapter 3). The need for a just transition perhaps indicates that these communities should have avoided these dependencies in the first place.

Mine closure will affect local government and the planning system. For example, the municipality depends heavily on mine employment that enables residents to pay property rates and services charges. Mine closure will seriously reduce municipal income. The Emalahleni Municipality's municipal finance is already in disarray and closure will exacerbate the current crises. The effects will go beyond municipal finance and include engineering services and the maintenance of existing public spaces. These are bound to come under pressure and require long-term planning. In Chapter 8 the authors argued that mine closure might affect the existing health system in adverse ways, despite the potential for cleaner air if many of the coal-fired power stations close.

Over the past two decades the mining industry has persistently emphasised its role in sustainable development. Pretorius and Blaauw (Chapter 10) found that the more their respondents depended on coal mining for an income, the less likely they were to support clean energy. At the company level, Crous (Chapter 9) found mining companies' sustainability reports disappointing. Rather than being transparent, the mines appear unwilling to make full disclosures on environmental consequences. It has become the norm to disclose in ways that do not damage the company's image. Crous argues in favour of stricter regulation. However, regulations might not be useful at all. Disclosure reports are used for impressing management rather than to report on critical concerns for local communities. Although some of the consequences require immediate attention, long-term and cumulative environmental impacts do not receive any attention.

Health is another sustainability issue that does not receive attention. In Chapter 8, Denoon-Stevens and Du Toit highlighted the contradiction between the area's wealth and its health profile. Part of the problem originates from dependence on mining companies that provided health services historically, and mostly to their employees only. Living in an area where the environmental health implications are dire and the health response poor does not constitute justice for the workers. Although mine decline will contribute to better air quality, many people will continue to suffer from poor environmental quality and will require continuous health services.

A just transition may bring immediate benefits, but the real cost of mining and the way mines are being closed may only be felt by generations to come. Water insecurity, as a result of acid mine water drainage, may have long-term negative consequences for the agricultural industry and in turn for Emalahleni's regional service function. The economic consequences for agriculture will be in addition to the other economic consequences of mine closure. Sustainability reporting ignores this potential reality and the government's response to the need to monitor and respond to these long-term implications has been inadequate (see Chapter 7). Appropriate closure could reduce the environmental damage. The international evidence shows that many mines opt for care and maintenance instead of applying for mine closure. This trend has two consequences: the much-needed environmental rehabilitation does not take place and the mine effectively stops operations (as with formal closure). The alternative to care and maintenance is that the larger mines sell their assets to smaller firms which do not have the financial means to address closure correctly.

A just transition has its limitations. It is too much focused on economic transition and does not consider broader debates about transitions. We have introduced the concepts of just sustainability and just ecology in this work (Obeng-Odoom 2020a, 2020b). Although these concepts require further development, they provide a broader framework and place sustainability issues at the core of these discussions. A focus on a just transition while ignoring the causes of inequality will undermine the likelihood of a just transition.

Finally, the danger of institutional collapse of the local municipality remains high. Dealing with decline is likely to increase the financial pressure on the municipality. It also requires good governance and competent managers. If the recent history is anything to go by, Emalahleni will find it difficult to deal with decline and effect a just transition.

So, is a just transition possible?

We think there are five preconditions for a just transition in Emalahleni. First, planning a just transition in Emalahleni will require a more realistic assessment of the effects of mine closure. For example, it will have to consider the multifaceted nature of a just transition, the short-term and long-term consequences, and the cumulative social and environmental effects that may develop over time. It may not be possible to predict these at the moment. Too quickly, the problem becomes only an employment problem for mineworkers. The debate should expand from a normative position to consider the broader realities.

Second, and as a consequence of the above point, the proponents of a just transition must consider the broader community implications of a just transition. The predominant focus on mineworkers only may skew the responses.

Third, managing mine closure and making a just transition will require competent governance and institutions. Emalahleni's recent history does not inspire confidence.

Fourth, the planning and governance system should learn from the global literature on shrinking cities and apply it appropriately to South Africa (Marais and De Lange, 2021). Planning and managing decline will be a crucial feature of bringing about a just transition.

Finally, a just transition depends primarily on finding an economic alternative for workers who will lose their jobs in coal mining and coal-generated power stations. At the time of writing this final chapter in July 2020, such an alternative remains elusive. Any belief that heavy industry can buffer the decline is probably misguided, as the area has already seen large-scale closures of heavy industries over the past 10 years. Some attempts are being made to redevelop the area as a renewable energy hub. *This makes sense, but only time will tell whether these two energy industries will survive close to one another. We doubt renewables will provide an alternative of sufficient scale, and as a result the inequalities brought by mining are likely to be perpetuated.*

References

Campbell, M., Nel, V. and Mpambukeli, T. 2017. A thriving coal mining city in crisis? The governance and spatial planning challenges at Witbank, South Africa. *Land Use Policy*, 62, 223–31.

Cloete, J. and Marais, L. 2020. Mine housing in the South African coalfields: The unforeseen consequences of post-apartheid policy. *Housing Studies*. doi: 10.1080/02673037.2020.1769038.

Dubeaux, S. and Cunningham Sabot, E. 2019. Maximising the potential of vacant spaces within shrinking cities, a German approach. *Cities*, 75, 6–11.

Ghosh, S., Byahut, S. and Masilela, C. 2019. Metropolitan regional scale smart city approaches in a Shrinking City in the American rust belt – case of Pittsburgh, Pennsylvania. In V. Kumar (ed.), *Smart Metropolitan Regional Development*. New York: Springer, 979–1021.

Long, Y. and Gao, S. 2019. Shrinking cities in China: The overall profile and paradox in planning. In Y. Long and S. Gao (eds), *Shrinking Cities in China*. New York: Springer, 3–21.

Marais, L. and De Lange, A. 2021. Anticipating and planning for mine closure in South Africa. *Futures*, 125, 102669.

Obeng-Odoom, F. 2020a. *Property, Institutions and Social Stratification in Africa*. Cambridge: Cambridge University Press.

Obeng-Odoom, F. 2020b. *The Commons in the Age of Uncertainty. Decolonising Nature, Economy and Society*. Toronto: University of Toronto Press.

Simelane, T. and Abdel-Rahman, M. (eds) 2011. *Energy Transition in Africa*. Pretoria: HSRC Press.

Van der Watt, P. and Marais, L. 2019. Normalising mining company towns in Emalahleni, South Africa. *The Extractive Industries and Society*, 6, 1205–14.

Index

Page references in **bold** indicate a table and references in *italics* are for figures.

EU representative:
Easy Access System Europe
Mustamäe tee 50, 10621 Tallinn, Estonia
Gpsr.requests@easproject.com

www.ingramcontent.com/pod-product-compliance
Lightning Source LLC
Chambersburg PA
CBHW051958270326
41929CB00015B/2700